AN INQUIRY CONCERNING
HUMAN UNDERSTANDING

The Library of Liberal Arts
OSKAR PIEST, FOUNDER

The Library of Liberal Arts

AN INQUIRY CONCERNING HUMAN UNDERSTANDING

with a supplement

An Abstract of A Treatise of Human Nature

DAVID HUME

Edited, with an introduction, by

CHARLES W. HENDEL

*Clark Professor Emeritus of Moral Philosophy
and Metaphysics, Yale University*

The Library of Liberal Arts

published by

THE **BOBBS-MERRILL** COMPANY, INC.
A SUBSIDIARY OF HOWARD W. SAMS & CO., INC.
Publishers • INDIANAPOLIS • NEW YORK

David Hume: 1711-1776

AN INQUIRY CONCERNING HUMAN UNDERSTANDING was
originally published in 1748

. . . .

CONTENTS
. . . .

AN INQUIRY CONCERNING HUMAN UNDERSTANDING

INTRODUCTION

The *Inquiry Concerning Human Understanding* is a "first reader" in the philosophy of Hume. It was so intended by the author. He hoped that this book would provide the right approach and introduction to the essentials of his philosophy.

I. THE IMPORTANT PLACE OF THE *INQUIRY* IN HUME'S LIFE

The reason for Hume's concern was that he had not had "the good fortune to meet with success" in his first book, the *Treatise of Human Nature*. His mortal disappointment is recorded in *My Own Life* and printed there in italics, saying that the *Treatise "fell deadborn from the press."* [1] This was the crowning event of his many years of study which began "when I was about eighteen years of age" and when "there seemed to be opened up to me a new scene of thought which transported me beyond measure and made me, with an ardour natural to young men, throw up every other pleasure or business to apply [myself] entirely to it." [2] He left Scotland for France in order to write there the great work which would expound his whole new "system" of human nature. He spent three years quietly at La Flèche, which, it will be remembered, is the place where the young Descartes had received his early education. Then Hume returned to London and secured a publisher. Two books of the *Treatise of Human Nature* were published anonymously in 1739. The "Advertisement" to these books which treated "of the Understanding"

[1] *My Own Life* is reprinted on pp. 3-11 of this edition.
[2] Letter to Dr. George Cheyne (March or April, 1734). *The Letters of David Hume*, ed. by J. Y. T. Greig (Oxford, 1932), Vol. I, No. 3, p. 13.

and "of the Passions" gave notice that they were intended "to try the taste of the public" and that if they received "the approbation of the public," a third would follow. They actually failed to elicit the appreciation Hume desired, but in spite of that he persisted in his purpose and published the very next year, 1740, his third volume, an "examination of morals, politics, and criticism." [3] That, however, likewise met with no success. The whole *Treatise* was a failure: a masterwork *manqué*.

Hume had his eye on the public and its approval. He frankly admitted to a "love of literary fame, my ruling passion." [4] Some since his time have criticized him for this last infirmity of a noble mind. But, as his most recent biographer has reminded us, "to be a philosopher is to be a man of letters: the proposition was received by Hume and the eighteenth century as axiomatic . . . . The primary requisite of a serious thinker, with original thoughts, . . . is to present his thoughts so that they may be understood by others." [5] But a philosopher who studies the "passions" as well as the "understanding" knows that if his philosophical thought is to be understood, the public taste and sentiment must be consulted. No harm from this need follow if it is true, in Hume's case, as E. C. Mossner rightly affirms, that "philosophy was always his dominant interest." [6]

In point of fact, Hume was not without a valuable intuition of the public taste. It turned out eventually that many of the "moral and political" topics of the third volume of the *Treatise* proved timely and very acceptable to the public, when presented in their later form. But it was the form that mattered, and here Hume adapted himself to the trend of taste in literature, which was not merely to be regarded as a passing fashion: ". . . Addison, perhaps, will be read with pleas-

[3] Advertisement to the *Treatise of Human Nature*, Green and Grose ed. (London, 1898), Vol. 1, p. 303.

[4] *My Own Life*, p. 10.

[5] E. C. Mossner, *The Life of David Hume* (Austin, Texas, 1954), p. 63.

[6] *Op. cit.*, p. 4.

ure when Locke shall be entirely forgotten." [7] So Hume started writing essays, in a style "elegant" and "easy." Only a year after the appearance of the third book of the *Treatise* he produced and published, again anonymously, a volume of *Essays, Moral and Political* (1741). The edition was sold out. A second and corrected edition was issued in 1742. Hume had now gained a success.[8] But it was not his ambition to be purely an essayist: the philosopher had to be satisfied as well as the man of letters. The "essays may prove like dung with marl, and bring forward the rest of my philosophy which is of a more durable, though of a harder and more stubborn nature." [9]

The philosopher had to bide his time. For several years Hume was engaged in affairs, "spectator to a rebellion," participant in "a military campaign" and "a military embassy." [10] He was continuing to write essays on moral, political, and economic subjects, as well as on criticism. A third and enlarged edition of the *Essays* came out in 1748 and it was the first time Hume published a work under his own name. And it was precisely then, too, that Hume brought out a distinctly different type of book, entitled *Philosophical Essays Concerning Human Understanding,* and stated on the title page "by the author of the *Essays, Moral and Political.*" With such shrewd art Hume introduced his "durable," "hard," and "stubborn" philosophy, companioned with a volume of the type of essays that had succeeded with the public. The "marl" was mixed with the "dung," and it was hoped that much good would come of it.

The book of *Philosophical Essays* was a rewriting of por-

---

[7] P. 17.

[8] On the role of the *Essays, Moral and Political* in making Hume's reputation in the eighteenth century see *Hume's Political Essays* (Liberal Arts Press, New York, 1953), Introduction, pp. viiff. and Section IV, pp. xli-lx. See also Mossner, Chap. 17, "Achievement of Ambition," pp. 228 ff.

[9] Letter to Henry Home, June 13, 1742. Greig, Vol. 1, No. 17, p. 43.

[10] Mossner, *op. cit.,* Chaps. 14, 15, 16, the titles of which are quoted above.

tions of the ill-fated first book of the *Treatise of Human Nature*. But the new form and style made little difference. Hume had only slight success with the work in 1748 and for the rest of his life. Instead, the essays and political discourses continued to attract readers and increase the reputation of their author, especially in France and on the Continent. The philosopher nonetheless persisted. Having had more luck with "moral subjects" in the essays he tried another reformulation of the *Treatise*, this time of the third book. Originally he had spoken of it, in the "Advertisement," as an "examination" into politics, morals, etc. Now he ventured to use the term "inquiry," which very appropriately indicated the nature of his mind and his philosophy. So he published in 1751 *An Inquiry Concerning the Principles of Morals*.

When the time came in 1758 to produce a collected edition of his works, including the essays and this *Inquiry Concerning the Principles of Morals*, for which Hume had a particular partiality, Hume changed the title of his *Philosophical Essays Concerning Human Understanding* to read, *An Inquiry Concerning Human Understanding*. And this is the work with which we are concerned here.

The *Inquiry* remained, despite the new name, a collection of philosophical essays, being sections of the *Treatise* restated in a more attractive form. There were, however, two novelties. They were enlightening applications of his philosophical thought to religious topics and calculated to pique the interest of the reader. At the same time Hume realized very well the possibility that the freedom of his thinking might arouse a theological odium and passion which would distract from the most significant meaning of his work. He had already written an essay on Miracles even at the time of the *Treatise*, but had withheld it from his book. Now he chose to publish it in its improved form, as "Section X: Of Miracles." The second novelty was "Section XI: Of a Particular Providence and of a Future State." This seems to have been a first attempt at a critical examination of the philosophical arguments for the existence of God, though there is abundant evidence of a very early concern, too, with this subject, antedating even the *Treatise*.[11] In this essay on "A Particular Providence," etc., Hume started writing in the dialogue form, a form which was more perfectly handled in his final work of philosophy, the *Dialogues Concerning Natural Religion,* published posthumously in 1779, over thirty years later.

The *Inquiry* contains this preview, as it were, of the *Dialogues* as well as being a very "artful" review of the essentials of his original *Treatise*. We can properly say, then, that it was truly Hume's own introduction to his philosophy. "The arguments have been laid before the world and by some philosophical minds have been attended to." [12]

II. LITTLE ATTENTION AND MUCH CRITICISM IN HUME'S LIFETIME

The *Inquiry* was not a success, and a sense of failure was present in Hume's mind, from time to time, to the very end of his life.[1] Indeed it had betrayed itself publicly quite early, as for example in the Essay "Of the Rise and Progress of the Arts and Sciences":

A man's genius is always, in the beginning of life, as much unknown to himself as to others, and it is only after frequent trials attended with success that he dares think himself equal to those undertakings in which those who have succeeded have fixed the admiration of mankind.[2]

1. FROM FRANCE: MONTESQUIEU'S APPRECIATION

"Success and failure side by side characterize the years following the publication of the *Philosophical Essays,*" writes

[11] See C. W. Hendel, *Studies in the Philosophy of David Hume* (Princeton, 1925), Chap. 1, "The Ambitions and Concerns of a Life Time"; Chap. 2, "The Youth's Discovery."

[12] To William Strahan, October 1775. Greig. Letter 509, Vol. I, p. 301.

[1] See the summary statement of Mossner, *op. cit.*, pp. 230-231.

[2] See *Hume's Political Essays*, p. 121.

Mossner.[3] But all was not dark-hued in 1748, the opening year of publication. Hume had the great satisfaction of receiving congratulations from Montesquieu in France, than whom none was more highly honored in the period of the Enlightenment. Montesquieu's *Spirit of the Laws* came out at the very same time as the *Philosophical Essays*. The two authors exchanged books as well as compliments. Montesquieu wrote, with a play on words which comes through the French better than in translation: "I read with very great pleasure your Essay on the Human Spirit [*sic*] which can only come from an extremely philosophical spirit [*esprit*]. All of it is full of fine ideas." [4] Here was proper attention from "a philosophical mind." Montesquieu and Hume had a little correspondence subsequently but the former died in February, 1775. Later, Hume was, of course, widely recognized in France as a great *philosophe*. Nevertheless, the chief point of his inquiry into understanding remained unattended to by the philosophers.

2. The Attack by James Beattie in Scotland

Why Hume remained so concerned about his philosophy to the very end of his life may be appreciated when we realize the sort of attention by philosophical minds his arguments had actually received. In 1770, Professor James Beattie, professor of Marischal College, Aberdeen, won acclaim for himself with a book, *An Essay on the Nature and Immutability of Truth: in Opposition to Sophistry and Scepticism*. This was a mean and satirical attack on Hume. It succeeded with the public beyond anything Hume had done—five editions from its first publication to the time of Hume's death. Beattie was immortalized in Sir Joshua Reynolds' painting, "The Triumph of Truth," robed and with his *Essay on Truth*

3 *Op. cit.*, p. 230.

4 Montesquieu to David Hume, Paris, 3 September 1749. *Oeuvres de Montesquieu*, edition Masson (Paris, 1954), Letter No. 506, t. III, 1255; see also Nos. 480, 486, pp. 1217, 1230 f.

under his arm, quietly enjoying the angel of Truth thrusting three demons—one of the demons being taken to be Hume—into "the bottomless pit." [5]

With the demon, of course it would be understood, went his books whose skepticism occasioned Beattie's pious postscript: "To read and criticise the modern systems of scepticism is so disagreeable a task that nothing but a regard to duty could ever have determined me to engage in it. . . ." [6] Beattie took great pleasure, indeed, in his virtuous task. The main target of his attack was the *Treatise,* but the *Philosophical Essays* were included: "The style of the *Treatise of Human Nature* is so exceedingly obscure and uninteresting that if the author had not in his *Essays* republished the capital doctrines of that work in a style more elegant and sprightly, a confutation of them would have been altogether unnecessary: their uncouth and gloomy aspect would have deterred most people from courting their acquaintance." [7] Mortified by Beattie's victory, Hume drew up a short advertisement "which I wish I had prefixed to the second volume of the Essays and Treatises in the last edition," and this, he told his publisher, "is a complete answer to Dr. Reid and to that bigoted silly fellow, Beattie." [8] The advertisement disavowed the unfortunate *Treatise* and asked all readers to attend only to the later pieces.

Thomas Reid was a philosopher of substance who hardly deserves the juxtaposition with Beattie. But there is a natural connection because both had had recourse to the authority of "common sense." Reid's own *Inquiry into the Human Mind* was a critique of the "ideal theory" of Locke and Berkeley, and it included Hume in the criticism. Reid no more than Beattie had perceived the essential significance of Hume's work.

---

[5] See the whole account in Mossner, *op. cit.,* Chap. 38.
[6] James Beattie: *Essay on Truth,* fifth edition corrected 1774, p. 485.
[7] *Ibid.,* pp. 470-471.
[8] To William Strahan, October 1775. Greig, Letter 509, Vol. 1, p. 301.

3. From America: The Interest of Benjamin Franklin

But America was a bright spot. Hume had several times met Benjamin Franklin, in London and Edinburgh, and corresponded with him. In one of his letters he wrote: "I fancy that I must have recourse to America for justice." Franklin was interested in promoting a new American edition of the *History of England* and Hume apparently was laboring under the misapprehension that it was to be of his collected writings which included the *Philosophical Essays*.[9] In any case, Franklin was a busy man in politics, and their correspondence was confined to that subject rather than to the "human understanding."

In the end we find Hume writing to his publisher and friend, William Strahan:

> But it will happen to me as to many other writers. Though I have reached a considerable age, I shall not live to see any justice done to me. It is not improbable, however, that my self-conceit and prepossessions may lead me into this way of thinking.[10]

III. RECOGNITION BY "POSTERITY"

1. By Immanuel Kant in the Eighteenth Century

Unknown to Hume was a philosopher in remote Königsberg in East Prussia, Immanuel Kant, who recognized his genius and eventually brought him to the attention of "philosophical minds" who were prepared to do justice to him. It is experiencing vicariously one of the ironies of history to read

---

[9] See *Letters*, Klibansky and Mossner (Oxford, 1952), p. 194. Mr. Klibansky has communicated to the editor a correction for the letter cited; it was not the collected writings but the *History of England*. See *Hume's Political Essays*, Introduction: "The Relevance of Hume's Political Writings to American Thought," pp. l-lx.

[10] To William Strahan, Bath, 8th June 1776. Greig, No. 521, Vol. II, p. 322. (Hume died August 25th of that year.)

the belated tribute in the *Prolegomena to Any Future Metaphysics* published in 1783, seven years after Hume's death. The words sound as if Kant had divined the very contents of those personal letters in which Hume had often expressed his disappointment, and they vindicate his stubborn belief in the originality of his work:

> But Hume suffered the usual misfortune of metaphysicians, of not being understood. It is positively painful to see how utterly his opponents, Reid, Oswald, Beattie, and lastly Priestley, missed the point of the problem; for while they were ever taking for granted that which he doubted, and demonstrating with zeal and often with impudence that which he never thought of doubting . . . I should think that Hume might fairly have laid as much claim to common sense as Beattie and, in addition, to a critical reason (such as the latter did not possess) . . .[1]

The historical irony is all the greater because the very passages from the *Treatise* which Beattie had quoted verbatim and held up to the judgment of "common sense" were also those that "really first revealed to Kant the scope and innermost meaning of Hume's analysis of the causal problem."[2] Thus Beattie had quoted Book I, *Treatise*, Part III, Sect. III:

> *Whatever begins to exist proceeds from some cause*—that maxim . . . is not intuitively certain . . . that the foregoing maxim is neither intuitively nor demonstrably certain, our author attempts to prove from this consideration that we cannot demonstrate the impossibility of the contrary. Nay, the contrary, he says, is not inconceivable: "for we can conceive an object nonexistent this moment and existent the next without joining it to the idea of a cause which is an idea altogether distinct and different."[3]

---

[1] *Prolegomena to Any Future Metaphysics*, ed. by Lewis W. Beck (The Liberal Arts Press, New York, 1950), pp. 6 and 7.

[2] Norman Kemp Smith: *A Commentary to Kant's Critique of Pure Reason* (Macmillan, London, 1918), pp. XXVIII-XXIX. See the section "Kant's Relation to Hume and Leibniz," pp. XXV-XXXII.

[3] James Beattie: *An Essay on the Nature and Immutability of Truth: in Opposition to Sophistry and Scepticism*. 5th edition corrected (London, 1774), pp. 104 and 107. (See also this edition, pp. 177 f.)

After some discussion Beattie concludes:

> We repeat, therefore, that this axiom is one of the principles of common sense which every rational mind does and must acknowledge to be true, not because it can be proved but because the law of nature determines us to believe it without proof and to look upon its contrary as perfectly absurd, impossible, and inconceivable.[4]

Norman Kemp Smith has shown that it was the Hume quoted in those statements who aroused Kant from his "dogmatic slumber." [5]

2. BY JOHN MAYNARD KEYNES IN THE TWENTIETH CENTURY

From the native British tradition comes another tribute of recognition in the work of John Maynard Keynes: *A Treatise on Probability*. Hume's skepticism, Keynes writes, was "fundamental and far-reaching." [6] And later, in the same work:

> Hume's sceptical criticisms are usually associated with causality; but arguments by induction—inference from past particulars to future generalizations—was the real object of his attack. Hume showed, not that inductive methods were false, but that their validity had never been established and that all possible lines of proof seemed equally unpromising. . . . Hume's statement of the case against induction has never been improved upon; and the successive attempts of philosophers, led by Kant, to discover a transcendental solution have prevented them from meeting the hostile arguments on their own ground and from finding a solution along lines which might, conceivably, have satisfied Hume himself . . . . Hitherto Hume has been master, only to be refuted in the manner of Diogenes or Dr. Johnson.[7]

---

4 *Ibid.*, pp. 111-112.

5 *Commentary*, pp. XXV ff. In the present volume the section from the *Treatise* is quoted entire, pp. 177-180, because of its historical and real importance. It was not repeated as a whole in the *Inquiry*.

6 J. M. Keynes: *A Treatise on Probability* (Macmillan, London, 1948), p. 82.

7 *Ibid.*, pp. 272-273.

There is an essential agreement, however, between Keynes and the philosophers who follow the lead of Kant. The disagreement is only in regard to the attempted *solution* of the problem which had been exposed by Hume's skeptical criticisms. The main question, Keynes asserts, is one of the *validity* of the method of reasoning in induction. This is the very same question as that on which Kant focused attention when he opened his argument to "answer" Hume with a "transcendental deduction" of the "pure concepts of the understanding" in his *Critique of Pure Reason:*

> Jurists, when speaking of rights and claims, distinguish in a legal action the question of right (*quid juris*) from the question of fact (*quid facti*); and they demand that both be proved. Proof of the former, which has to state the right or the legal claim, they entitle the deduction.[8]

Hume had not doubted either the fact or the usefulness of causal reasoning, as Beattie and others had supposed, but the validity of that way of reasoning, validity as judged by the very criterion of reason itself. "Among philosophers," Kant writes, "David Hume came nearest to envisaging this [critical] problem." [9]

IV. UNDERSTANDING HUME IN HUME'S OWN WAY: THE ABSTRACT OF THE TREATISE (1740)

Thanks to a few philosophers of "posterity," then, the essential originality and the significance of Hume's philosophy are now generally recognized. In the long run the *Inquiry Concerning Human Understanding* has borne fruit. It has served to educate "philosophical minds" away from the "arrogant" prejudices which first prevented Hume's contemporaries from appreciating his profound and far-reaching

---

[8] *Critique of Pure Reason*, tr. Norman Kemp Smith (Macmillan, 1950 ed.), p. 120.

[9] *Ibid.*, p. 55.

question concerning human understanding. However, it is also the fact historically that the light dawned on Kant when something from the *Treatise* was brought into conjunction with the *Philosophical Essays*. The latter work alone has hardly been a self-sufficient introduction to Hume. For the present-day reader, therefore, it is likely to be helpful, too, if the essentials of the *Treatise* are made part of an introduction to the *Inquiry*.

We shall do this in Hume's own way. For there is a remarkable biographical document which was originally meant to enlighten readers of the *Treatise*. It was a publication in the year 1740: *An Abstract of a book lately published entituled A Treatise of Human Nature, etc., wherein the Chief Argument of that Book is farther illustrated and explained.*[1] This *Abstract* has been usually attributed to Adam Smith, the friend and pupil of Hume. It is a great and important discovery of recent scholarship, however, that Hume himself had written the *Abstract* and published it anonymously so that it appeared as a favorable criticism of his own work. Nothing gives a better idea of the desperate disappointment of the young author than this strange performance of "boosting" his own book under the guise of anonymity. There he summoned all his powers to produce a brief of "the chief argument," adding illustrations and explaining it further. And Hume thus sketched an outline, as we shall see, of a version which he produced eight years later in the *Philosophical Essays*.

J. M. Keynes, who has had such a discerning eye for the originality of Hume's philosophical work, comments as follows upon the *Abstract*:

Hume has pointed with infallible finger to those passages which, in the eyes of posterity as well as those of the author,

[1] The *Abstract* is included in this edition, pp. 181-198. There is also a separate publication, published in Facsimile and with an Introduction by J. M. Keynes and P. Sraffa (Cambridge, 1938). In the following, page references to the Introduction are to the Cambridge edition; all references to the text of the *Abstract* are to pages in this edition.

"shake off the yoke of authority, accustom men to think for themselves, give new hints which men of genius may carry further and, by the very opposition, illustrate points where-in no one before suspected any difficulty." [2]

This *Abstract* written by Hume himself is our best introduction to the argument of the *Inquiry*.

There is something further to be said here in favor of this approach to the study of Hume. The very literary quality of the *Inquiry*, which may have been valuable enough in the age of essay-reading, is less effective in our time. Hume's biographer, E. G. Mossner, has made the very just observation:

In the *Philosophical Essays* Hume achieved a new plane of lucid philosophical exposition. Gone are the hesitations of the *Treatise*, the intricacies of detail, the tortured analysis —gone, too, inevitably, are some fine passages which had shown aspects of modern philosophy in the making, the autobiography, as it were, of a thinker in the act of thinking. The *Philosophical Essays* is a work of art, polished and impersonal.[3]

But this polish can be too smooth for the reader today, and the impersonality may leave us cold. The *Abstract*, on the other hand, gives us the points in sharp salience, with vivid imagery, and even with moving personal eloquence. These characteristics help us to see not only the real Hume but also the real argument.

V. THE "CHIEF ARGUMENT" OF HUME'S PHILOSOPHY

We shall proceed now to follow the "chief argument" of the *Abstract* and relate it to the respective sections of the *Inquiry*. The order of points made in the *Abstract* is almost identical with that in the later, more complete restatement:

[2] *An Abstract*, ed. Keynes and Sraffa, p. XXIX, and quotation from Hume's own Preface to the *Abstract*, p. 182. Read the whole account of the authorship of the *Abstract* in the excellent Introduction to that edition.
[3] *Op. cit.*, p. 175.

I have chosen one simple argument which I have carefully traced from the beginning to the end. This is the only point I have taken care to finish. The rest is only hints of particular passages which seemed to me curious and remarkable.[1]

1. "Reasoning from Cause and Effect": Fundamental for Life and Knowledge

We shall . . . chiefly confine ourselves to his explication of our reasonings from cause and effect . . . . of this nature are all our reasonings in the conduct of life; on this is founded all our belief in history, and from hence is derived all philosophy excepting only geometry and arithmetic.[2]

Reasoning from cause and effect is employed in the conduct of life. All belief in history is "founded" on this reasoning, that is, belief in regard to things of the past. And all philosophy, with two exceptions, "derives" from such reasoning. This reasoning, then, is fundamental to action, to belief, and to all philosophical thinking.

This statement is much too succinct for us, and indeed some of the very language itself must be interpreted before we can grasp the argument.

We wonder, in the first place, at the fact that science is not mentioned, excepting geometry and arithmetic which are at the same time excluded from "philosophy." This indicates, however, that the term "philosophy" had a very broad meaning in Hume's day. In fact, philosophy included all knowledge, with whatever degree of certainty, of that which is "matter of fact" or "existence." There were two sorts of philosophy of existence, "natural philosophy" and "moral philosophy." Newton's science of nature was designated a natural philosophy: his *Principia* was indeed translated as "The Principles of Natural Philosophy." By contrast, "moral philosophy" comprised the knowledge of all things relating to man, in contradistinction from nature, the things where man himself is implicated in the facts, where his opinions, taste, judgment,

---

[1] Conclusion of Hume's Preface to the *Abstract*, p. 182.
[2] *Abstract*, pp. 185 and 187.

reason, and action are in some way involved.[3] Hume's statement means, then, that this particular mode of "reasoning from cause and effect" is fundamental for conduct and for *all* beliefs as to fact or existence, whether they be in *history, science,* or *philosophy.* Even in philosophical "speculations" we employ this type of reasoning.[4]

Section I of the *Inquiry* is "Of the Different Species of Philosophy" and it forthwith identifies Hume's own philosophy with "moral philosophy or the science of human nature." A distinction is then made between man considered as "an active being" and man considered as "a reasonable" being. The moral philosophy of Hume has both aspects in view but it is concerned in this book chiefly with the reasoning aspect of man or human understanding.

2. The Problem is One of Logic

Another case of unfamiliar usage of language appears when Hume treats his whole work on the understanding as a logic. For moral philosophy comprises "logic," "morals," and "criticism" and "politics." And "the sole end of *logic* is to explain the principles and operations of our reasoning faculty, and the nature of our ideas."[5] Logic is thus a science of very wide compass. It includes what we call today the theory of knowledge.

The important thing to note here is the *distinction* which Hume is insisting upon within traditional logic.

> The celebrated M. Leibniz has observed it to be a defect in the common systems of logic that they are very copious when they explain the operations of the understanding in the forming of demonstrations, but are too concise when they treat of probabilities and those other measures of evidence

[3] See the more extensive definition of moral philosophy in *Hume's Political Essays,* Introduction, p. xi.

[4] *Abstract,* p. 185. This philosophical "speculation" is illustrated in the *Inquiry,* pp. 142-157.

[5] *Abstract,* p. 184.

on which life and action entirely depend, and which are our guides even in most of our philosophical speculations.[6]

Here is the locus of Hume's question—and it is a question, or a "difficulty," "which no one suspected before," a difficulty regarding *the logic* of the operations of the understanding in such reasoning.

3. A "First Proposition" concerning "Perception" [7]

Hume is not offering anything essentially new in regard to the nature of perception. Just as he has already indicated a sharpening of and greater emphasis upon a distinction which Leibniz had previously recognized between reasoning that is probable and that which is demonstrative, so he follows Locke in his theory of perception but insists that the distinction should be observed between "impressions" and "ideas" in the strict sense of the latter term. The impressions "arise immediately from nature"; they are "antecedently felt" and "take the precedence of" the ideas. "The first proposition" Hume "advances," then, is "that all our ideas, or weak perceptions, are derived from our impressions or strong perceptions." [8]

Much capital has been made by subsequent critics of this "first proposition." They see it as a principle which commits Hume inevitably to an "atomism" in epistemology, as well as to his avowed skepticism. The whole "system" of Hume follows deductively, they seem to say, from this initial concept of the original separate perceptions as the sole source of ideas. But whatever be the ultimate judgment of Hume's philosophy, the reader makes a poor start toward understanding it if he approaches his study prejudiced by this view. For it makes Hume a systematic metaphysician in spite of his own contrary intention. His "first proposition" is literally that,

---

[6] *Abstract*, p. 184.
[7] Relating to *Inquiry*, Section II, "Of the Origin of Ideas," pp. 26-30.
[8] *Abstract*, pp. 185 f.

namely, only a *proposal,* something to be tried out experimentally and with a view to learning or discovering something else which is *not* contained in the proposition. What Hume means can be seen clearly by the way he works. In accordance with his first proposition, "wherever any idea is ambiguous he has always recourse to the impression which must render it clear and precise . . . . and it were to be wished that this rigorous method were more practiced in all philosophical debates." [9]

That wish is being amply fulfilled in our time. Many are the "philosophical minds" now who practice this method of making ideas "clear and precise." It is above all the *method* that is important, not the particular designation we give to the things with which we are operating, be they called perceptions, impressions, ideas, terms.[10] We can see plainly that the "analytic philosophy" current today is in the Humian tradition. But a truer way of putting it is to say that Hume himself is British. For the fact is that Hume never pretended that *he* began the tradition—he was not the "inventor" of it.[11]

Corresponding to this part of the *Abstract* is Section II of the *Inquiry* on "the Origin of Ideas." This is more elaborate and, of course, more fully illustrated, and the case where Hume allows of a "contradictory phenomenon," viz., the shade of blue that might be appreciated in a gradation of colors prior to its being actually perceived, shows that his "proposition" claims only to be a "general maxim." Though we begin with perception, it is what we do afterwards that is the proper subject of the inquiry, the "reasonings concerning *matter of fact.*"

---

9 *Abstract,* p. 186.

10 Cf. John Dewey: *Experience and Nature,* Chap. 1, "Experience and Philosophic Method" (Chicago, Open Court Publishing Co., 1925), especially p. 10. " . . . experience for philosophy is method, not distinctive subject-matter."

11 In the final paragraph of the *Abstract,* p. 198, Hume reserves "so glorious a name as that of an "inventor," for his "discovery" about the "association of ideas."

4. The Problem is about Causal Relation and Inference [12]

Such reasonings are evidently "founded on the relation of cause and effect," and "we can never infer the existence of one object from another unless they be connected together, either mediately or immediately." The question is, then, of which sort is this connection or relation of cause and effect? A graphic case where we have the idea of cause is that in which one billiard ball in motion strikes another at rest and the second ball acquires a motion. At first sight one notes only these two "circumstances" in the case, the contiguity of cause and effect in time and place, and the priority in time of the cause. On experimenting with "other balls of the same kind in a like situation," however, we always find the same movement of the second ball occurring. Here is a third "circumstance," the "constant conjunction" between the cause and the effect. Beyond this nothing is known about the "relation." Yet if we afterward see one ball moving toward another we "immediately conclude" to the coming shock and the subsequent motion in the second. This is the inference in question —and the question of logic is how to explain this inference.[13]

Imagine "Adam created in the full vigor of understanding." He could not instantly infer the motion in the second ball without having had experience for—

It is not anything that reason sees in the cause which makes us *infer* the effect. Such an inference, were it possible, would amount to a demonstration, as being founded merely on the comparison of ideas. But no inference from cause to effect amounts to a demonstration. Of which there is this evident proof. The mind can always *conceive* any effect to follow from any cause, and indeed any event to follow upon another: whatever we *conceive* is possible, at least in a metaphysical sense; but wherever a demonstration takes place the contrary is impossible and implies a contradiction. There is no demonstration, therefore, for any conjunction of cause and effect.[14]

[12] Relating to *Inquiry*, Section IV, "Skeptical Doubt, etc.," pp. 40-53.
[13] *Abstract*, pp. 186 f.
[14] *Abstract*, pp. 187 f. So far the *Abstract* restates in part the argu-

Causal reasoning is therefore not *a priori* or demonstrative reasoning. It is only possible on condition that one has had experience of events or of causes and effects.

Suppose, then, Adam was an empiricist. Having seen a "sufficient number of instances" of the movements of such billiard balls, "his understanding would anticipate his sight and form a conclusion suitable to his past experience." [15] This is not only possible for an imaginary Adam; it is regularly done by all the sons of Adam—indeed they cannot do otherwise:

> . . . all reasonings from experience are founded on the supposition that the course of nature will continue uniformly the same. We conclude that like causes, in like circumstances, will always produce like effects. It may now be worth while to consider what determines us to form a conclusion of such infinite consequence.[16]

Now this "conclusion of such infinite consequence" is not the same thing as the inference from particular cause to particular effect illustrated in the case of the billiard balls. It is a *general proposition,* and it does not follow from any reasoning but, on the contrary, it is a *presupposition* of all inference or reasoning from experience. The presupposition is, however,

---

ment of Section III, Part III of the *Treatise,* "that the foregoing proposition [that whatever begins to exist must have a cause of existence] is neither intuitively nor demonstrably certain." *Treatise,* Vol. I, Green and Grose edition, pp. 380 f; p. 177 of this edition. In the very late *Dialogues Concerning Natural Religion,* Hume gives the consummate statement of his negative argument: "there is an evident absurdity in pretending to demonstrate a matter of fact or to prove it by any arguments *a priori.* Nothing is demonstrable unless the contrary implies a contradiction. Nothing that is distinctly conceivable implies a contradiction. Whatever we conceive as existent, we can also conceive as nonexistent. There is no being, therefore, whose nonexistence implies a contradiction. Consequently there is no being whose existence is demonstrable. I propose this argument as entirely decisive, and am willing to rest the whole controversy upon it." *Treatise,* Vol. II, *Dialogues,* etc. Green and Grose, p. 432. See also pp. 171-172 of this edition.

[15] *Abstract,* p. 188.

[16] *Abstract,* p. 188.

not an arbitrary act of the mind: we are "determined" to make it. The question is, therefore, what *determines* us to make this assumption.

From the very nature of the supposition, however, we can see that it is *not* reason that determines us:

> Adam . . . would never have been able to *demonstrate* that the course of nature must continue uniformly the same, and that the future must be conformable to the past. What is possible can never be demonstrated to be false; and it is possible the course of nature may change, since we can conceive such a change. Nay, I will go further and assert that he could not so much as prove by any *probable* arguments that the future must be conformable to the past. All probable arguments [themselves] are built on the supposition that there is this conformity betwixt the future and the past, and therefore [he] can never prove it. This conformity is a *matter of fact*, and if it must be proved will admit of no proof but from experience. But our experience in the past can be a proof of nothing for the future but upon a supposition that there is a resemblance betwixt them [past and future]. This, therefore, is a point which can admit of no proof at all, and which we take for granted without any proof.[17]

The argument concludes, negatively as before, that reason, in the strict sense, does not determine us to proceed as we actually do in "reasoning." Not only can no demonstration be given for the supposition, but also no argument from probability, because any such argument presupposes exactly what has to be proved. So far the negative result.

But new things have been brought to our attention as "new discoveries." We reason about matters of fact and existence on the strength of a supposition which seems to be something we are determined to make even without any warrant from reason. And secondly there is the view of nature which, it is shown, we are taking for granted, viz., that the course of nature is uniform or that the future will conform to the past. Here are things disclosed about both man and nature, about the operations of man's understanding and the supposedly uniform course of natural events in time.

17 *Abstract*, pp. 188 f.

The whole of the above argument is repeated, with all the art that Hume can muster, in the centrally important Section IV of the *Inquiry*, the title of which is "Skeptical Doubts Concerning the Operations of the [Human] Understanding." But not all of the "hints" Hume gave of "new discoveries" were followed out or elaborated there in the *Inquiry*. For Hume kept a close rein, in the later work, on that "restless imagination" to which he confessed in a letter to Sir Gilbert Elliot, when speaking about a draft of the *Dialogues* where the primary datum for all the different hypotheses discussed was the order of nature, its uniformity, and its regularity. Hume saved his restless thoughts along that line for the *Dialogues*.[18] In the *Inquiry*, therefore, he hewed strictly to his chief question, which was still unanswered, even by himself:

> Let the course of things be allowed hitherto ever so regular, that alone, without some new argument or inference, proves not that for the future it will continue so. . . . [change] happens sometimes, and with regard to some objects. Why may it not happen always, and with regard to all objects? *What logic, what process of argument* secures you against this supposition [of change]. . . . as a philosopher . . . I want to learn the foundation of this inference. . . . Can I do better than propose the difficulty to the public, even though, perhaps, I have small hopes of obtaining a solution? [19]

5. The "Skeptical" Solution: Some "Curious Discoveries"

But the *Inquiry* offers a solution nonetheless in Section V: it is called, however, a "Skeptical Solution of These Doubts." Leaving aside for later discussion the meaning of "skeptical," let us consider what it was in the "chief argument" stated in the *Abstract* that seemed worth calling a "solution."

---

[18] Hume began the *Dialogues* about 1751. See letter to Sir Gilbert Elliot, March 10, 1751. Greig, *op. cit.*, No. 72, Vol. I, pp. 153-157. For discussion of Hume's "restless imagination" see Hendel, *Studies*, Chaps. XI-XII.

[19] Pp. 51-52. Italics mine.

"Custom" [20]

The *Abstract* mentions "a very curious discovery" which follows from the preceding inquiry, and from which in turn other discoveries "still more curious" follow. The present discovery is that custom "alone determines the mind in all instances to suppose the future conformable to the past." [21]

As the *Inquiry* expresses it: "Custom, then, is the great guide of human life" (p. 58). Custom, and not reason.

"Belief" [22]

A "still more curious discovery," according to the *Abstract* in the case of the billiard balls, is that "I also *believe* that it [the second ball] will move." [23] Belief is something quite different from merely conceiving the effect. Hume finds it "impossible by words to describe this feeling, which everyone must be conscious of in his breast." One can call it "A *stronger* conception, . . . a more *lively*, a more *vivid*, a *firmer*, or a more *intense* conception." Belief "has a more forcible effect on the mind." [24] And these same difficulties about the characterization of belief are again expressed by Hume in Part II of the "Skeptical Solution" (pp. 61-63).

The situation of man is a curious one. He makes a supposition that the course of nature is uniform and that future events will follow the standard of the past. Acting on this supposition he finds objects constantly conjoined which he takes to be necessarily connected. His inference has a necessary character. He is determined to make it by the specific experience which he has had. In himself it is a habit, not reason, that is operative. But despite the lack of rational understanding, strangely enough, man *believes* his conclusion by causal inference in a way that would be thought appropriate only to the most cogent demonstration. Indeed, extensive and intri-

---

20 Relating to Part I of Section V, pp. 54-61.

21 *Abstract*, p. 189.

22 Relating to Part II of Section V, pp. 61-68.

23 *Abstract*, p. 189.

24 *Abstract*, p. 191.

cate abstract reasoning often lacks the quality of conviction that naturally attends any belief in matters of fact and existence arrived at by inference.

Hume concludes his "Skeptical Solution" (Sect. V of the *Inquiry*) with a reflection that there is a kind of correspondence between our thoughts and the course of nature. The "operation of the mind" is like an "instinct" given man by nature. The forecasts which man makes, on the supposition that nature is uniform, are actually borne out. Customs of thinking are formed and followed which prove to be in accord with the course of external objects. It is, if you please, a "pre-established harmony." [25]

But it *is* "skeptical," this solution. The meaning is that man as a reasonable being, the philosopher, is *not* satisfied. The solution only says that man has so far got along in the world with his peculiar habits and manner of thinking.

6. REVIEW AND SUMMARY

The further consequences and new discoveries we shall indicate more briefly, for when the reader has mastered these sections of the "chief argument" on skeptical doubt and skeptical solution, he is, so to speak, "over the hump" and needs only to keep his bearings to reach his destination. The main points "of the whole compass of the doctrine" have been these: On the ground of past experience we reason from cause and effect (this includes from cause to effect or from effect to cause), inferring the existence of an instance of a species of object not now present but which has been customarily observed to be constantly conjoined with some instance of another species of object. The operation of the mind is not one of demonstrative reasoning. We are not drawing conclusions from a relation of ideas as in geometry or arithmetic: the concept of one object in this case does not entail the *existence* of another object. We are operating in a region where time as well as experience is a factor to be reckoned with. Our experience is

[25] Pp. 67-68.

of the past, and it is an experience of certain particular conjunctions of objects or certain events. Our actual *procedure* in a causal inference is to transfer the order of such experienced conjunction to the future and make it the "standard" for future events and the appearance of objects in the future. But there is no rational ground discoverable for this mode of proceeding. No demonstration can be given that the future *must* resemble the past of which we have had experience. No proof from "probable reasoning" will suffice, because this proof would only consist in arguing from past experience of success with the procedure to its likely success in the future, which amounts to an assumption in the proof itself of the very point which is to be proved. The conclusion of Hume's scrutiny of our procedure in causal inference is that we make a "supposition" or "take for granted" a uniformity of nature, that is, that the course of nature in time remains the same. But this striking disclosure of what is involved in our thinking is only a first "discovery." The "whole operation of the mind" in such reasoning comprises, besides this supposition-making, the custom or habit of the mind formed through actual experience and the feeling of *belief* which the mind has with respect to the conclusions of such inferences. Hume has thus discovered a complex of phenomena of "human understanding" not previously realized. Since reason seems to be excluded from the affair, this "whole operation" of the mind may be attributed to a wonderful "instinct" bred in man by nature and enabling him to act and live.

7. New Light on "Probability" [26]

The life of man depends upon these beliefs that follow from his attitude of treating nature as uniform and regular, and relying upon the information of his experience. Now it happens, as the *Abstract* states, that "our past experience is not always uniform." [27] This exception or even contrariety in

[26] Relating to *Inquiry*, Section VI, "Of Probability," pp. 69-71.
[27] *Abstract*, p. 192.

our very experience does not shatter our faith, so to speak, for we still suppose, as before, that nature is generally uniform. We proportion our belief, not deliberately but yet very naturally, to the degree of difference in the case at hand from our customary experience. Hence the phenomenon of probability —on which Section VI of the *Inquiry* elaborates.

8. The Idea of "Necessity" or "Cause" [28]

Throughout this study the idea of cause has been in view, but never itself explained. The "reasoning from cause and effect" has been analyzed and disclosed in its threefold complexity of supposition, custom, and belief. This whole analysis with its resulting discoveries had to be made because no "relation" could be seen to be the *ground* for the inference. Only the attendant "circumstances" of contiguity, priority of the so-called cause, and constant conjunction were discernible. But actually a "necessary connection" is *thought* there in every case of inference. We are perfectly convinced, too, that we are "determined" to draw the conclusion by inference and are not doing so as a matter of fancy or arbitrary action. Necessity is somehow in the affair. It is an essential element in what we mean by "cause." The same idea of necessity is also referred to in such terms as "power" or "force" or "energy." Looking outward we cannot, however, perceive this necessity. Some philosophers, recognizing this much of the truth, have claimed that they could know it in God. But they can only know what God is by reflecting upon their own minds. Now in fact we always do experience necessity in our inferences— and it is nothing more than that "determination of the thought," the *Abstract* says, which is operative every time we conclude to some particular cause or effect.[29] The necessity then is a factor of *feeling*, and it belongs with belief as an ingredient of the "whole operation of the mind."

[28] Relating to *Inquiry*, Sect. VII, "Of the Idea of Necessary Connection," pp. 72-89.

[29] *Abstract*, p. 193.

Section VII of the *Inquiry* (pp. 87-88) concludes further with two alternative definitions of the term "cause" in accordance with this view of necessity as being felt in the mind, in the "whole operation" previously described.

9. "Hints" of Further Skepticism [30]

The *Abstract* at this juncture reads as if the author were now concluding his "chief argument":

> By all that has been said the reader will easily perceive that the philosophy contained in this book is very skeptical and tends to give us a notion of the imperfections and narrow limits of human understanding.[31]

One further new skeptical item is mentioned, however—our belief in the "external existence" of objects.[32] Still other "skeptical topics" are hinted at. But this philosophy is not a Pyrrhonism, an extreme, even dogmatic skepticism, as Hume understands the ancient doctrine: the moderate skepticism of Hume is expressed in this phrase that we "employ our reason only because we cannot help it." [33]

10. Two "Peculiar Opinions"

Regarding "Personal Identity"

"I shall conclude the logics [*sic*] of this author," the *Abstract* reads, "with an account of two opinions." [34] The fact that these two topics come after what was virtually a conclusion indicates, perhaps, that Hume was less sure of himself in these "opinions" yet that they were important enough to be brought to the attention of a wider public. The first topic is that of "personal identity." There had been an explanation, in the

---

30 Relating to *Inquiry*, Sect. XII, "Of the Academical or Skeptical Philosophy," pp. 158-173.

31 *Abstract*, p. 193.

32 Pp. 162 f.

33 Pp. 167 ff.

34 *Abstract*, p. 194.

Treatise, of the natural belief we have in the existence of ourselves. After the *Abstract* itself had been finished, Keynes has argued, Hume apparently wrote the *Appendix* to the third volume of the *Treatise* which appeared later that same year (1740), wherein he said:

> . . . I find myself involv'd in such a labyrinth, that, I must confess, I neither know how to correct my former opinions, nor how to render them consistent. If this be not a good *general* reason for scepticism, 'tis at least a sufficient one . . . [35]

And Hume has no section in the *Inquiry* devoted to this topic that so baffled him.

Geometry without Metaphysics [36]

The second "opinion" of the *Abstract* is about geometry, "denying geometry to be a science exact enough to admit of conclusions so subtile as those which regard infinite divisibility." [37] The question about "infinite divisibility" is taken up in the summarizing Section XII. Hume there restricts demonstrative science to quantity and number, and excludes the metaphysical notions of infinite divisibility.[38]

11. "IT MAY PERHAPS BE MORE ACCEPTABLE TO THE READER . . . WHAT OUR AUTHOR SAYS CONCERNING FREE WILL" [39]

This final topic of the *Abstract* seems to have been offered as a sort of alleviation of the skeptical result of the whole work.[40] Hume's preceding argument has established that we reason always the same way about all matters of fact, making the same presupposition, and being likewise guided always

---

[35] From the Appendix to the *Treatise of Human Nature,* Selby-Bigge ed., p. 633. See also Keynes' Introduction to the *Abstract,* pp. XXIV ff.

[36] Relating to *Inquiry,* Sect. XII, "Of the Academical or Skeptical Philosophy," Parts II and III, pp. 164-173.

[37] *Abstract,* p. 195.

[38] Pp. 164 ff.

[39] *Abstract,* pp. 196 f.

[40] Relating to *Inquiry,* Sect. VIII, "Of Liberty and Necessity," pp. 90-111.

by custom, and believing our inferences, and this applies no less to mind than to material objects. There is a uniformity and regularity in the behavior of men consequent upon their motives. There is no evading this fact.[41] Yet it does not exclude a meaning for "liberty," though this is indeed given only in the later *Inquiry*.[42] Still Hume has a way of expressing himself in the *Abstract* which gives the cue to his interpretation. "Our author pretends that this reasoning puts the whole controversy in a new light by giving *a new definition of necessity*." [43] The new definition removes from necessity its externally coercive character. Necessity is internal to the mind, the determination of the thought to pass from one object to the usually attendant object. But liberty, too, is internal, as the *Inquiry* declares, being "a power of acting or not acting, according to the determination of the will." Hume considers himself to be engaged in "a reconciling project" with regard to the question of freedom and necessity.[44]

12. Hume's Title to "Inventor": His Use of the Principle of Association of Ideas! [45]

The *Abstract* ends in an enthusiastic vein as the author contemplates his "great pretensions to new discoveries in philosophy," for he now introduces the one thing with respect to which he thinks himself entitled to the glorious name of "inventor." The invention is the "discovery" and the "use" of the "principles" of "association of ideas."

The principles are employed to explain "what we call the *apropos* of discourse; hence the connection of writing; and hence that thread or chain of thought which a man naturally supports even in the loosest *reverie*." [46] But these principles are not confined to thought and discourse, for they are of

[41] *Abstract*, pp. 192 f. and 197.
[42] P. 104.
[43] *Abstract*, p. 197. Italics mine.
[44] P. 104.
[45] Relating to *Inquiry*, Sect. III, "Of the Association of Ideas," pp. 31-39.
[46] *Abstract*, p. 198.

"vast consequence." The author writes here with an elated eloquence, "these are the only links that bind the parts of the universe together ... they are really *to us* the cement of the universe, and all the operations of the mind must, in a great measure, depend on them." [47]

That exaltation is gone in the *Inquiry*. The argument does not culminate in a presentation of the great invention. The role of the "principles of association of ideas" is more modest and restricted. No more talk about the universe, but only about operations of the mind. The illustrations are from the province of human art, not nature's order, though these purely human applications have great intrinsic interest, as when Hume speaks of the "kind of *unity*" effected in the different genres of writing, in poetry and history, in drama and epic poetry, "loose hints I have thrown together in order to excite the curiosity of philosophers. . . ." [48]

Above all, it should be noted by the reader that this Section III of the *Inquiry* (the last word of the *Abstract*) is placed there *immediately before* the Section which states the "Skeptical Doubts Concerning the Operations of the Understanding." The principles of association of ideas are thus not an adequate *solution* of those doubts. They are in fact brought in only to explain "belief." [49] They solve nothing with respect to the problem of the instinctive supposition which is made in all reasoning that leads to belief in matters of fact or existence. That original problem still remains unsolved.

VI. A CHART OF THE ARGUMENT, WITH COMMENTS

We have followed the guidance of the *Abstract* in respect to the "chief argument" which includes both the skeptical question and the so-called skeptical solution, and which has also indicated to us what Hume considered to be his other

[47] *Abstract*, p. 198.
[48] Pp. 33-39.
[49] Pp. 63-67.

"new discoveries" of some moment. We have noticed, too, the differences of weight or importance assigned to the less central topics, some being "hints," others "opinions." The order, too, in which the subjects were presented is enlightening in that regard, for in the main the same order is reproduced in the *Inquiry*. The following chart outlines the agreement and the points of difference:

THE ABSTRACT	THE INQUIRY
The Fundamental Theme: Reasoning from Cause and Effect, having to do with matters of fact and existence.—Book I of the *Treatise* is Hume's Logic	Section I: Of the Different Species of Philosophy: Moral Philosophy
First Proposition concerning Perception: Distinction between Impressions and Ideas	Section II: Of the Origin of Ideas
The Problem about the Causal Relation and Inference	Section IV: Skeptical Doubts Concerning the Operations of the Understanding
The Skeptical Solution: Some "Curious Discoveries" Custom Belief	Section V: Skeptical Solution of These Doubts Part I Part II
New Light on Probability	Section VI: Of Probability
The Idea of Necessity of Cause	Section VII: Of the Idea of Necessary Connection
Conclusion of the "Chief Argument": the philosophy is "very skeptical." "Hints" of further skepticism, e.g., about external existence of objects	Section XII: Of the Academical or Skeptical Philosophy Part I

Two "Peculiar Opinions"
    (1) regarding personal iden-   (Omitted)
       tity
    (2) regarding geometry with-   Parts II and III
       out metaphysics

Concerning Free Will   Section VIII: Of Liberty and
                                Necessity

Hume's Title to "Inventor":   Section III: Of the Associa-
His Use of the Principle of   tion of Ideas
Association of Ideas

Comment has been made already on the difference in regard to the principle of association of ideas, namely, that it
seemed of a "vast consequence" to the youthful Hume which
was lost, however, when he wrote the *Inquiry:* it was not by
any means the complete solution for his problem but explained only the peculiar character of belief in that "whole
operation" of the mind.

One further remark may be made concerning the penulti-
mate position of the topic of free will in the order of discussion in the *Abstract*. Hume may then have considered the
subject of free will as falling outside the book on the "logic"
of the understanding, and belonging properly to a "moral
philosophy" in the strict sense where it treats "of morals," as
in Book III of the original *Treatise*. Consequently, Hume,
the anonymous reviewer of Book I, may have been intimating
to the hoped-for readers of the *Treatise of Human Nature* in
its entirety (for the third volume must have been in prepara-
tion for the press, since it appeared in the very same year with
the *Abstract*) that the whole work contained, besides its
skeptical philosophy, something "more acceptable" for the
practical life of man as a "moral" being.

VII. THE PHILOSOPHICAL ESSAYS INCLUDED IN THE INQUIRY ADDITIONAL AND SUBSEQUENT TO THOSE ON THE TOPICS OUTLINED IN THE ABSTRACT: GENERAL CONSIDERATION

We are concerned here with three sections which form a sequence in the *Inquiry* and of which little or no "hint" was given in the *Abstract:* Sections IX, X, and XI, treating "Of the Reason of Animals," "Of Miracles," and "Of a Particular Providence and of a Future State." These follow upon the section on "Of Liberty and Necessity," and they may very properly be interpreted in the spirit of that section as offering something "more acceptable" than sheer intellectual skepticism. They are more than further illustrations or applications of "skeptical doubts." We must, indeed, take more seriously here the fact that Hume has offered a "skeptical solution" as well as doubts. These additional essays develop some consequences of that "solution." They prepare, too, for the final statement of Hume's position in Section XII, "Of the Academical or Skeptical Philosophy."

The eight years that elapsed between the publication of the *Abstract* and the third volume of the *Treatise* which dealt with morals and politics were by no means philosophically fruitless. Hume's work on his *Essays, Moral and Political* was actually constructive science. The "experimental reasoning," as he sometimes called the method of reasoning from experience, yielded significant results. Drawing upon literature and history which are the recorded experience of mankind, as well as upon his own observations of human affairs, Hume was able to make advances in the science of politics and in social and economic science which won signal recognition from the philosophers and the learned in his time as important contributions to modern enlightenment and knowledge. Morals, too, were shown to be the proper subject of *empirical* science: the moral virtues and values were learned by mankind in the course of experience of life in society. One of the things with which Hume increasingly concerned himself was liberty of the mind, and it is clear from the argument of his *History of England,* written later (1754-1761), as well as his moral and political essays, that he aimed to make his work teach a lesson in the value of such liberty.[1] Hume conceived of himself as a constructive moral philosopher and as *justifying* the experimental or empirical method of reasoning.

This constructive intent manifests itself in these additional essays that follow upon the essay on "Of Liberty and Necessity," and precede the concluding essay which states the distinctive features and the meaning of his "skeptical philosophy."

All such empirical knowledge as Hume was achieving in his essays on man, society, politics, economics, and history was based on the procedure which he had so acutely analyzed, namely, that we take the experienced conjunctions of the past to be a rule for the future and consequently infer causes or effects confidently and believe in their existence as matters of fact. There are regularities observable in nature, and man observing them and making use of his experience forms his ideas that there are laws of nature. But such regularity in the behavior of things is not at all confined to the phenomena of external nature. The life of man shows likewise a regular relationship between his passions and motives and his actual conduct. All study of man in society and in history depends upon some such regularity and constancy. Social and historical science are possible because of it. The very conduct of ordinary life is predicated upon it. Thus man's whole experience of action as well as his own observation leads him to envisage nature as a uniform order which can be understood according to laws and of which we can have science.

Here is the "human understanding"—remember that is in the title of this *Inquiry*—of man in his capacity as an "active being." This is the "understanding" by which man lives and works and acquires his science of nature as well as of society

---

[1] See *Hume's Political Essays,* xiv-xvi, xxii-xxv, xxix ff. and also pp. 142 f. and 156, where Hume indicates his concern for liberty of thought and speech.

and history. Grant the "skeptical doubts" so relentlessly presented in Section IV. Man as a "reasonable being" cannot ignore them but must understand them thoroughly. The challenging question of that Section still remains unanswered: what reason have we, what logic is there, for presupposing as we always do in our science as well as our behavior that the course of nature must be uniform, that the past can be made a rule for the future, or that the future must resemble the past? No reason can be given for such a presupposition on our part. Yet it is the very assumption on which we proceed in action and in the advancement of science. It cannot be justified by any argument. Yet it is justified, so to speak, in its fruits. It is too essential, too indispensable to human existence, to be doubted in practice. In fact, as Hume had blurted out in the *Abstract,* we "employ our reason [this reasoning where we use our past experience] only because we cannot help it." [2] And our philosophy of human nature must do justice to this aspect of our nature as well as to the intellectual aspect.

What we see here is the aspect of Hume himself as a practicing empiricist. He is no different from other men and he proceeds on the same general supposition as they do regarding the using of past experience in order to live and gain useful knowledge. He has no doubt about the value of empirical science. It may be rated as having only probability, but the important lesson to learn may be precisely this—that the life of man is guided only by probability and not by the kind of reason which is responsible for the knowledge of purely mathematical science. The thing is to appreciate what we have, in the case of empirical science and in moral and practical conduct, and not to dwell exclusively on the fact that it lacks the admired certainty of pure reason.

Hence Hume is very insistent, in Sections IX, X, and XI of the *Inquiry,* upon the reality for us of uniform nature and of a regularity in the affairs of man as well as in the physical

2 *Abstract,* p. 194.

world. If this regular order is further impugned, if besides the essential question concerning the *logic* of our use of experience there is a further doubt concerning such order as appears to be the fact, then nothing stands between us and an utter skepticism. There is nothing whatsoever to depend upon for the conduct of life. Nor is there any trustworthy knowledge possible about social and political affairs. Man sinks, then, into a Pyrrhonistic skepticism.

"Academical skepticism" is Hume's name for the philosophy which contains *both* the radical and unanswered question concerning the supposition involved in the procedure of reasoning from experience *and* this "solution" which has reference not only to the practical use of the beliefs attained by the employment of such reasoning but also to the various empirical sciences likewise attained—the sciences of nature and of society, politics, economics, and others that may still be developed. Hume's philosophy comprises a skepticism and an empiricism.

VIII. THE ESSAY ON THE REASON OF ANIMALS

We consider now the several essays and what they disclose. They are all both illustrative of the primary skeptical doubt and of developing the consequences of the "skeptical solution," that is, the "Academical skepticism."

There was only a phrase in the *Abstract* which anticipates the ideas of this Section IX; and since Hume himself in the earlier work made no special point of the matter it was not included in our Chart of the Argument (p. xxxvi). The phrase was that about employing our reasoning from cause and effect "only because we cannot help it." This echoes the unforgettable words of the *Treatise* that nature has determined us to think as well as to eat and breathe. And nature has provided thus for the subsistence of animals as well as man. The *Inquiry* develops the theme in this fashion, that "the experimental reasoning itself, which we possess in common with beasts, and on which the whole conduct of life depends, is nothing but a species of instinct . . . that acts in us unknown to ourselves." [1]

This is a constructive suggestion which has since Hume's day been identified with "naturalism" and sometimes with "pragmatism" or "instrumentalism." The philosophy of John Dewey is an expression of this view of the naturalistic foundation of "experimental reasoning." The connection of the theory with the biological aspect of human existence is clear in the essay which provides the title for the book of essays, *The Influence of Darwin in Modern Philosophy*.[2] The position is consummately worked out in *Essays in Experimental Logic*,[3] in *Experience and Nature*,[4] and *Logic: The Theory of Inquiry*.[5]

IX. THE ESSAY ON MIRACLES

Something had been written on the subject of miracles at the time of the publication of the *Treatise*, but it had been withheld. As we have suggested, the publication of Hume's thoughts could readily have distracted from the chief point of the new philosophy by arousing religious animus. Hume tried it later, nonetheless, and he obviously used his experience and literary skill to present the matter so as to enlighten and not merely antagonize. A remark which he made in another connection to his admirer, Montesquieu, is *apropos*. Hume had become involved in a discussion with another party about the interpretation of some data cited in his essay on "The Populousness of Ancient Nations," and he wrote to Montesquieu: "I should be much afraid that I am entirely refuted had I not all along in my Essay kept on the skeptical or doubtful side, which in most subjects gives a man so much

---

[1] Pp. 115-116.
[2] Holt, New York, 1910.
[3] The University of Chicago Press, Chicago, 1916.
[4] Open Court, Chicago, 1925.
[5] Holt, New York, 1938.

the advantage of the ground that it is very difficult to force [that is, refute] him." [1] This characterization of his own tactics may well apply to the cases where Hume treats of religious subjects. He is canny and keeps to the skeptical or doubtful side *with regard to his own opinions.* He does not want to put himself into a position where he could even seem to be refuted. Actually his later experience with James Beattie shows that Hume did not succeed, for Beattie maneuvered those most carefully designed discussions of Hume in such a way that he was put at a hopeless disadvantage.

PART I

Hume discusses miracles from the point of view of a philosophical empiricist. The court of appeal is "the experienced order of nature." There is a measure of constancy and uniformity in our experience. The regularities are the laws of nature. We act and live in accordance with them, as we know them. Our beliefs as to fact or existence are reached by inferences relying upon such regular experience. No one of those facts or existences can, however, be demonstrated by reason in the strict sense of the term. But where our experience proves to be perfectly uniform, without any contrary cases to disturb our thought, Hume allows the term "proof" to be employed. We can "prove" the existence of causes or effects remote from our present perception. When there are contrary conjunctions of objects, the contrary cases prevent the reasoning from being a proof, for the inference is then only a probability. But this must be noted, that whatever *logical* value be assigned to the inferences made on the ground of past experience, man always does *believe* them, with greater or less certainty or firmness of conviction as the case might be. Man believes and acts from probability as well as from proof.

Now a miracle is the idea of an event or a phenomenon which shocks this whole natural structure of man's experience and his thinking, belief, life, and conduct. "A miracle is a

[1] Hume to Montesquieu, 26 June 1753, Masson edit., tIII, pp. 1460-1461.

violation of the laws of nature; and as a firm and unalterable experience has established these laws, the proof against a miracle, from the very nature of the fact, is as entire as any argument from experience can possibly be imagined . . . . There must, therefore, be a uniform experience against every miraculous event, otherwise the event would not merit that appellation . . . . The plain consequence is (and it is a general maxim worthy of our attention) that no testimony is sufficient to establish a miracle unless the testimony be of such a kind that its falsehood would be more miraculous than the fact which it endeavors to establish." [1] So far the objection is in terms of sheer principle, without any examination of evidence or testimony.

PART II

Is there any particular testimony sufficient to establish a miracle? Hume approaches this question in the spirit of the historian and examines a number of cases on record, and concludes:

Upon the whole, then, it appears that no testimony for any kind of miracle has ever amounted to a probability, much less to a proof; and that, even supposing it amounted to a proof, it would be opposed by another proof derived from the very nature of the fact which it would endeavor to establish. It is experience only which gives authority to human testimony, and it is the same experience which assures us of the laws of nature. . . . and therefore we may establish it as a maxim that no human testimony can have such force as to prove a miracle and make it a just foundation for any such system of religion.

Hume goes on to say at once:

I beg the limitations here made may be remarked, when I say that a miracle can never be proved so as to be the foundation of a system of religion. For I own that otherwise there may possibly be miracles or violations of the usual course of nature, of such a kind as to admit of proof

[1] Pp. 122-123.

from human testimony, though perhaps it will be impossible to find any such in all the records of history.[1]

Of course the *possibility* is always there that the "usual course of nature" may change—this is the prime discovery of Hume's philosophy and the very ground of his own "skepticism" (Section IV). Here he, too, must remember his skepticism and acknowledge the metaphysical *possibility* of a miracle, though he remains very doubtful of finding any testimony from history.

Now Hume is here raising another skeptical question and it is about religion in particular: it is whether man believes "the system" of his religion on the ground of any historical evidence of miracles. This question opens up a further one which is treated in the next section: does man come to believe in a providential God or "divine existence" on the ground of his *regular* experience of nature? These are two alternative ways by which mankind have been supposed to reach their beliefs about God and their "system of religion."

Hume's parting word on miracles is ironical and elusive:

> . . . upon the whole, we may conclude that the Christian religion not only was at first attended with miracles, but even at this day cannot be believed by any reasonable person without one. Mere reason is insufficient to convince us of its veracity. And whoever is moved by *faith* to assent to it is conscious of a continued miracle in his own person which subverts all the principles of his understanding and gives him a determination to believe what is most contrary to custom and experience.[2]

In our time we have become accustomed to hearing professed Christians say the very same things as Hume. They agree with him that what they believe is not a reasonable conclusion from evidence or from history. They teach that it is by faith alone that religion comes, not by reason and philosophy. Thus Hume's irony is quite acceptable in their

---

[1] P. 137; see also A. E. Taylor's criticism of Hume on miracles (*David Hume and the Miraculous*, Cambridge, 1927).

[2] Pp. 140-141.

sight. A Kierkegaard, for instance, has familiarized us with such a point of view.[3] Christianity came as something miraculous and it is a continued miracle in one's own person, determining one to believe what is "absurd," as judged by experience and reason. Hume does not "approve" of this or recommend it. He is open-minded enough, however, to discern and to recognize the possibility in others of such a "faith."

X. THE ESSAY ON A PARTICULAR PROVIDENCE AND A FUTURE STATE

Hume was very much interested in the religious question, and especially in the claims of philosophers to be able to prove by argument the existence of God. The belief in "divine existence" has been widely established among mankind. The first question is how men come by it, or what there is that induces them to believe in the existence of a being other than the persons and things that populate the natural world? What is the evidence cited? What does it prove, or possibly fail to prove? Hume was destined to stay by these questions for quite a few years and to produce eventually a masterpiece on the subject, the *Dialogues Concerning Natural Religion,* which was never published during his lifetime.

The essay in the *Inquiry* is in the form of a dialogue between a "friend who loves skeptical paradoxes" and Hume himself. The "friend" takes a negative attitude toward the view that there is a "particular," that is, a special Providence of God, and that there is a future existence for man because of the dispensation of that providence. Hume interrogates him and raises the objections of the common man, so to speak. We have here a case where Hume is showing the force of the skeptical objections and yet refraining from an atheism or even from a denial of any meaning to the idea of divine

[3] See Kierkegaard: *Philosophical Fragments,* tr. David Swenson (Princeton University Press), especially the "Interlude" and the Contemporary Disciple" and "Disciple at Second Hand" chapters.

existence. The essay illustrates his "academical philosophy," with these two voices of the reasoning philosopher keen about difficulties and the practical man who shares the life and common beliefs of other men.

This essay, Hume explains in the beginning, discloses some "principles of which I can by no means approve, yet, as they seem to be curious and to bear some relation to the chain of reasoning carried on throughout this inquiry, I shall here copy them . . .[1] The relevance is this: The discussion is about ancient "argument from design." It had been perfected by the Stoics, and when Cicero devoted himself to philosophical writings after retirement from politics, he reproduced many of the Stoic arguments in his own version of the "academical philosophy," of which he was a follower. This Ciceronian version was well known to most of the modern philosophers from their own "liberal education" in the humanities. Hume had very early seen that the argument was an instance of causal reasoning from experience. It is surely referred to in the *Abstract* where he speaks of probable reasoning as being involved "even in most of our philosophical speculations."[2] It is true that some philosophers had claimed that reason *demonstrates* the existence and nature of God. But Hume's discovery that *no* matter of fact or existence can be demonstrated by pure reason eliminated that possibility. The only tenable argument is one by analogy with experience: "the chief or sole argument for a divine existence (which I never questioned) is derived from the order of nature, where there appear such marks of intelligence and design . . ." that one cannot but infer a designing cause similar to man.[3] The skeptic proceeds to examine that reasoning with an eye to its cogency and precision.

But before we look further into the discussion we should note that both parties accept the *reality* of the order of nature. This, we have pointed out, is the empiricist's assump-

[1] P. 142.
[2] *Abstract*, p. 184.
[3] P. 145.

tion for all his reasoning. On that assumption he achieves empirical science. You may say, the friend rejoins, that "I deny a providence," but "surely I deny not the course itself of events, which lies open to everyone's inquiry and examination." [4] Consequently, this particular discussion is widely different in its attitude from the preceding one that treated of miracles. The argument for the existence of God is based on the *regular*, and not on any supposedly miraculous, order of nature. Hume treats the subject with the greatest respect and "curiosity," and without the irony employed in the case of miracles.

The skeptic takes the ordinary procedure of causal inference as a *standard* by which to measure the validity of the argument by analogy. He treats the "religious hypothesis" as only an hypothesis, "a particular method of accounting for the visible phenomena of the universe." [5] What men actually seem to do is to conceive of a cause of the "experienced order of nature" which is more perfect, so to speak, than the evidence warrants, and whose assumed goodness is then made a warrant for a belief that the acknowledged ills and disorder (for the order is not perfect) are remedied in another existence. This is adding supposition upon supposition beyond the evidence. [6] Hume reminds his skeptical "friend" that religious men stress "the infinite difference" between man and his works of design which are familiar to us and the God of religion, and this hints at the possibility that the religious view does not originate at all in the argument from the order of nature but has some other source. [7] And there is a further question only dealt with adequately in the later *Dialogues*, viz., what it is we *are* warranted in believing with respect to the *raison d'être* of the order of nature.

Meantime Hume shows in the present Section that he is

[4] P. 149.
[5] P. 148.
[6] This is a very brief resumé of pp. 146-151.
[7] Pp. 151-155.

somewhat concerned about the moral effects of the "religious hypothesis" and "system." Not only have religious philosophers piled hypothesis upon hypothesis, a future life upon the hypothesis of God's existence, but they have also claimed that moral virtues and conduct depend upon such suppositions and that mankind could not develop them otherwise. Hume believes, however, that morality has a sufficient foundation in experience where man learns "that in the present order of things virtue is attended with more peace of mind than vice, and meets with a more favorable reception from the world. . . . according to the past experience of mankind, friendship is the chief joy of human life, and moderation the only source of tranquillity and happiness." [8] The injection of the religious system into the affair may actually be detrimental to sound and reasonable conduct by introducing other standards than those naturally reached. Hume puts his faith in the common beliefs and valuations of men which have been developed in the course of their own experience, and he is dubious about religious guarantees or authority. John Stuart Mill, in his *Utilitarianism*, carried on the spirit of Hume's work.

It is characteristic of Hume's own moderate skepticism, however, that he should remind his friend, the lover of paradoxes, that the strict and precise reasoner cannot lay down the law to the thinking or beliefs of others in matters moral and political. He disagrees with his friend's conclusion:

You conclude that religious doctrines and reasonings *can* have no influence on life because they *ought* to have no influence, never considering that men reason not in the same manner you do, but draw many consequences from the belief of a divine existence . . . Whether this reasoning of theirs be just or not is no matter. Its influence on their life and conduct must still be the same. And those who attempt to disabuse them of such prejudices may, for aught I know, be good reasoners, but I cannot allow them to be good citizens and politicians, since they free men

[8] P. 149.

from one restraint upon their passions and make the infringement of the laws of society in one respect more easy and secure.[9]

What is Hume's meaning here? Is the friend a bad citizen deserving of punishment or coercion? That is certainly not the intention of Hume. Should the skeptic be silent and leave his free thoughts unexpressed? Not a philosophical skeptic. "After all, I may perhaps agree to your general conclusion in favor of liberty, though upon different premises from those on which you endeavor to found it." [10] The reasons are that speculative philosophers are not fanatical, and that restraints upon speculation and critical philosophy also affect the sciences and the state itself, "paving the way for persecution and oppression in points where the generality of mankind are more deeply interested and concerned." [11]

As has been said several times in the course of this Introduction, Hume himself was "deeply interested and concerned" with religion. The present essay of the *Inquiry* ends inconclusively with a problem which Hume proceeded afterward to deal with to the best of his ability as a philosopher in the *Dialogues Concerning Natural Religion*.

XI. CONCLUSION: HUME'S PHILOSOPHICAL SKEPTICISM

The essay treating "Of a Particular Providence" runs out into other topics than those which are central to the inquiry concerning the human understanding. That shows, however, the scope of the "academical philosophy" which is defined in the last essay of the *Inquiry*. There is a certain inconclusiveness in all these essays. They start us on themes that remain to be worked out. The *Inquiry*, as we said at the beginning, is a "first reader" in Hume, but it does not give us the "complete" Hume. For that we must consult, too, those *Dialogues* and then the companion-piece into whose territory we have

---

9 Pp. 155-156.
10 P. 156.
11 P. 156.

already trenched, the *Inquiry Concerning the Principles of Morals* and the *Essays, Moral and Political.* These reveal Hume the practicing empiricist, as he applies his philosophy to the topics of wide human interest which were as much his concern as the question of the logic involved in human understanding. But lest we fall into the error of his contemporaries and see his only virtue residing in his moral and political philosophy, we should proceed to read Hume in his first masterpiece, the *Treatise of Human Nature,* and especially the First Book. That is the work that has illumined the greatest minds and enabled them to see the essential problem and the "chief argument" of Hume's philosophical skepticism. It is the problem of knowledge in view of our existence in time, and why we think that we are entitled to treat the unknown future as conformable to the past of our experience. Hume left that problem to the philosophical conscience of the modern world.

CHARLES W. HENDEL

YALE UNIVERSITY
July 8, 1955

SELECTED BIBLIOGRAPHY

Hume's Works and Letters

A Treatise of Human Nature, Books I and II (1739), and Book III (1740).

Essays, Moral and Political (vol. I: 1741; vol. II: 1742).

An Enquiry Concerning Human Understanding (1748).
(First published as *Philosophical Essays Concerning Human Understanding*.)
Second edition with additions and corrections, 1750.

An Enquiry Concerning the Principles of Morals (1751).

Political Discourses (1752).

History of England (1754-62).

Four Dissertations (1757):
  (1) Natural History of Religion
  (2) Of the Passions
  (3) Of Tragedy
  (4) Of the Standard of Taste

Dialogues Concerning Natural Religion (1779).

The Letters of David Hume, edited by J. Y. T. Greig. Oxford, 1932.

The Letters of David Hume, edited by R. Klibansky and E. C. Mossner. Oxford, 1952.

Collected Works

The Philosophical Works of David Hume. 4 vols. Adam Black and William Tait, Edinburgh, 1826.

The Philosophical Works of David Hume. 4 vols. Little, Brown and Company, Boston, 1854.

The Philosophical Works of David Hume, edited by T. H. Green and T. H. Grose. 4 vols. Longmans, Green and Company, London, 1898.

CURRENT EDITIONS OF HUME'S WORKS

An Abstract of a Treatise of Human Nature (1740), edited with an Introduction by J. M. Keynes and P. Sraffa, Cambridge, 1938.

David Hume's Political Essays, edited by C. W. Hendel. The Liberal Arts Press, New York, 1953.

Hume's Dialogues Concerning Natural Religion, edited with an Introduction by Norman Kemp Smith. Oxford, 1935.

Hume's Enquiries, edited by L. A. Selby-Bigge. Oxford, 1902.

Hume's Moral and Political Philosophy, edited by Henry D. Aiken. Hafner Publishing Company, New York, 1948.

Hume's Treatise, edited with an analytical index by L. A. Selby-Bigge. Oxford, 1941.

Selections from Hume, edited by C. W. Hendel. Scribner's, New York, 1927.

WORKS ON HUME

Burton, J. H., *Life and Correspondence of David Hume.* 2 vols. Edinburgh, 1846.

Church, R. W., *Hume's Theory of the Understanding.* Ithaca, N. Y., 1935.

Greig, J. Y. T., *David Hume.* New York, 1931.·

Hendel, C. W., *Studies in the Philosophy of David Hume.* Princeton, 1925.

Huxley, T. H., *Hume.* London, 1879.

Kemp Smith, Norman, *The Philosophy of Hume.* London, 1941.

Kuypers, M. S., *Studies in the Eighteenth Century Background of Hume's Empiricism.* Minneapolis, 1930.

Kydd, Rachel M., *Reason and Conduct in Hume's Treatise.* Oxford, 1946.

Laing, B. M., *David Hume.* London, 1932.

Laird, John, *Hume's Philosophy of Human Nature.* London, 1932.

MacNabb, D. I. C., *David Hume: His Theory of Knowledge and Morality.* "Hutchinson's University Library," 1951.

Maund, Constance, *Hume's Theory of Knowledge.* Macmillan, 1937.

Morris, C. R., *Locke, Berkeley, Hume.* Oxford, 1931.

Mossner, E. C., *The Life of David Hume.* Austin, Texas, 1941.

———— *Forgotten Hume: Le Bon David.* New York, 1943.

———— "Was Hume a Tory Historian?" *Journal of the History of Ideas,* II, 225-36. Lancaster, 1941.

Oake, Roger B., "Montesquieu and Hume," *Modern Language Quarterly,* II, 25-41. Seattle, 1941.

Passmore, J. A., *Hume's Intentions.* Cambridge, 1952.

Price, H. H., *Hume's Theory of the External World.* Oxford, 1940.

Ross, W. D., *Human Nature and Utility in Hume's Social Philosophy.* Berea, Ky., 1942.

Sabine, George H., *A History of Political Theory.* New York, 1937; revised edition, 1950.

Shearer, Edna A., *Hume's Place in Ethics.* Bryn Mawr, 1915.

Smith, A. H., *A Treatise on Knowledge.* Oxford, 1943.

Stephen, Leslie, *History of English Thought in the Eighteenth Century.* London, 1876.

Taylor, A. E., *David Hume and the Miraculous.* Cambridge, 1927.

NOTE ON THE TEXT

The present edition of the *Inquiry Concerning Human Understanding* is reprinted from the first edition of Hume's collected philosophical writings, published in 1826 by Adam Black and William Tait. The text follows the version published in 1777 which contains the author's last corrections made a short time before his death in 1776. The editor of *The Philosophical Works* states that "the text of that edition [1777] has been faithfully adhered to in the present; but as it has been thought an interesting object of curiosity to trace the successive variations of sentiment and taste in a mind like that of Hume, and to mark the gradual and most observable increase of caution in his expression of those sentiments, it has been the care of the present Editor to compare the former editions, . . . and where any alterations were discovered, not merely verbal, but illustrative of the philosophical opinions of the author, to add these as notes to the passages where they occur."

These notes have been retained and supplemented in the present edition, and compared with the notes in Hume's *Essays* (1912), edited by T. H. Green and T. H. Grose.

It is customary to designate by letter the various editions published during Hume's lifetime. The references in the footnotes are to the listings given in the 1826 edition, which are reprinted on the next page.

The present edition also includes a reprint of the author's own *Abstract of the Treatise*. (For further information about this interesting essay, see Professor Hendel's Introduction, pp. xviiff.)

The publishers' editorial staff has supplied translations of foreign-language passages and helpful supplementary notes, which have been bracketed. Spelling and punctuation have been revised throughout to conform to present-day American usage.

O. P.

Essays, Moral and Political. Edinburgh, Kincaid, 1741. *(A)*

Essays, Moral and Political, Vol. II. Edinburgh, Kincaid, 1742. *(B)*

Essays, Moral and Political. Second edition, corrected. Edinburgh, Kincaid, 1742. *(C)*

Essays, Moral and Political. By D. Hume, Esq. Third edition, corrected, with additions. London, Millar, 1748. *(D)*

Three Essays, Moral and Political, never before published, which completes the former edition. By D. Hume, Esq. London, Millar, 1748. *(E)*

Political Discourses. By D. Hume, Esq. Edinburgh, Kincaid, 1752. *To this edition there is sometimes added "a list of Scotticisms." (F)*

Political Discourses. By D. Hume, Esq. Second edition. Edinburgh, Kincaid, 1752. *Merely a reprint of the preceding. (G)*

Essays and Treatises on several Subjects. By D. Hume, Esq. Vol. IV containing Political Discourses. Third edition, with additions and corrections. London, Millar, 1754. *(H)*

Four Dissertations: 1st, Natural History of Religion; 2nd, Of the Passions; 3rd, Of Tragedy; 4th, Of the Standard of Taste. By D. Hume, Esq. London, Millar, 1757. *(I)*

Philosophical Essays concerning Human Understanding. By the Author of the Essays, Moral and Political. London, Millar, 1748. *(K)*

Philosophical Essays concerning Human Understanding. By D. Hume, Esq. Second edition, with additions and corrections. London, Millar, 1750. *(L)*

An Enquiry concerning the Principles of Morals. By D. Hume, Esq. London, Millar, 1751. *(M)*

Essays and Treatises on several Subjects. By D. Hume, Esq. London, Millar, 1768. 2 vols. *(N)*

Essays and Treatises on several Subjects. By D. Hume, Esq. London, Cadell, 1777. 2 vols. *(O)*

HUME'S AUTOBIOGRAPHY:
"MY OWN LIFE"

MY OWN LIFE

IT IS DIFFICULT for a man to speak long of himself without vanity; therefore, I shall be short. It may be thought an instance of vanity that I pretend at all to write my life, but this narrative shall contain little more than the history of my writings, as, indeed, almost all my life has been spent in literary pursuits and occupations. The first success of most of my writings was not such as to be an object of vanity.

I was born the 26th of April, 1711, old style, at Edinburgh. I was of a good family, both by father and mother. My father's family is a branch of the Earl of Home's or Hume's; and my ancestors had been proprietors of the estate, which my brother possesses, for several generations. My mother was daughter of Sir David Falconer, President of the College of Justice; the title of Lord Halkerton came by succession to her brother.

My family, however, was not rich; and, being myself a younger brother, my patrimony, according to the mode of my country, was of course very slender. My father, who passed for a man of parts, died when I was an infant, leaving me, with an elder brother and a sister, under the care of our mother, a woman of singular merit, who, though young and handsome, devoted herself entirely to the rearing and educating of her children. I passed through the ordinary course of education with success, and was seized very early with a passion for literature, which has been the ruling passion of my life and the great source of my enjoyments. My studious disposition, my sobriety, and my industry gave my family a notion that the law was a proper profession for me, but I found an unsurmountable aversion to everything but the pursuits of philosophy and general learning; and while they fancied I was poring upon Voet [1] and Vinnius,[2] Cicero and Vergil were the authors which I was secretly devouring.

My very slender fortune, however, being unsuitable to this plan of life, and my health being a little broken by my ardent application, I was tempted, or rather forced, to make a very feeble trial for entering into a more active scene of life. In 1734, I went to Bristol with some recommendations to eminent merchants, but in a few months found that scene totally unsuitable to me. I went over to France with a view of prosecuting my studies in a country retreat; and I there laid that plan of life which I have steadily and successfully pursued. I resolved to make a very rigid frugality supply my deficiency of fortune, to maintain unimpaired my independence, and to regard every object as contemptible except the improvement of my talents in literature.

During my retreat in France, first at Rheims, but chiefly at La Flèche, in Anjou, I composed my *Treatise of Human Nature*. After passing three years very agreeably in that country, I came over to London in 1737. In the end of 1738, I published my *Treatise,* and immediately went down to my mother and my brother, who lived at his country house, and was employing himself very judiciously and successfully in the improvement of his fortune.

Never literary attempt was more unfortunate than my *Treatise of Human Nature*. It fell *deadborn from the press,* without reaching such distinction as even to excite a murmur among the zealots. But being naturally of a cheerful and sanguine temper, I very soon recovered the blow and prosecuted with great ardor my studies in the country. In 1742, I printed at Edinburgh the first part of my essays; the work was favorably received, and soon made me entirely forget my former disappointment. I continued with my mother and brother in the country, and in that time recovered the

---

1 [Gisbert Voet (1588-1676), a Dutch Calvinist theologian who was opposed to Arminianism and Cartesianism.—Ed.]

2 [Reference is apparently to Charles Viner (1678-1756), a leading English jurist in Hume's time and author of several legal works.—Ed.]

knowledge of the Greek language, which I had too much neglected in my early youth.

In 1745, I received a letter from the Marquis of Annandale, inviting me to come and live with him in England; I found also that the friends and family of that young nobleman were desirous of putting him under my care and direction, for the state of his mind and health required it. I lived with him a twelvemonth. My appointments during that time made a considerable accession to my small fortune. I then received an invitation from General St. Clair to attend him as a secretary to his expedition which was at first meant against Canada, but ended in an incursion on the coast of France. Next year, to wit, 1747, I received an invitation from the General to attend him in the same station in his military embassy to the courts of Vienna and Turin. I then wore the uniform of an officer, and was introduced at these courts as aide-de-camp to the General, along with Sir Harry Erskine and Captain Grant, now General Grant. These two years were almost the only interruptions which my studies have received during the course of my life. I passed them agreeably and in good company; and my appointments, with my frugality, had made me reach a fortune which I called independent, though most of my friends were inclined to smile when I said so; in short, I was now master of near a thousand pounds.

I had always entertained a notion that my want of success in publishing the *Treatise of Human Nature* had proceeded more from the manner than the matter, and that I had been guilty of a very usual indiscretion in going to the press too early. I, therefore, cast the first part of that work anew in the *Inquiry Concerning Human Understanding,* which was published while I was at Turin. But this piece was at first little more successful than the *Treatise of Human Nature.* On my return from Italy, I had the mortification to find all England in a ferment on account of Dr. Middleton's [3] *Free Inquiry,*

---

[3] [Reference is to Conyers Middleton (1683-1750), an English divine who questioned the historical accuracy of the Bible and proposed "free inquiry"; he was later accused of being a freethinker.—Ed.]

while my performance was entirely overlooked and neglected. A new edition, which had been published at London, of my *Essays, Moral and Political* met not with a much better reception.

Such is the force of natural temper that these disappointments made little or no impression on me. I went down in 1749, and lived two years with my brother at his country house, for my mother was now dead. I there composed the second part of my essays, which I called *Political Discourses,* and also my *Inquiry Concerning the Principles of Morals,* which is another part of my *Treatise* that I cast anew. Meanwhile my bookseller A. Millar informed me that my former publications (all but the unfortunate *Treatise*) were beginning to be the subject of conversation, that the sale of them was gradually increasing, and that new editions were demanded. Answers by Reverends and Right Reverends came out two or three in a year, and I found, by Dr. Warburton's [4] railing, that the books were beginning to be esteemed in good company. However, I had fixed a resolution which I inflexibly maintained, never to reply to anybody; and not being very irascible in my temper, I have easily kept myself clear of all literary squabbles. These symptoms of a rising reputation gave me encouragement, as I was ever more disposed to see the favorable than unfavorable side of things—a turn of mind which it is more happy to possess than to be born to an estate of ten thousand a year.

In 1751, I removed from the country to the town, the true scene for a man of letters. In 1752 were published at Edinburgh, where I then lived, my *Political Discourses,* the only work of mine that was successful on the first publication. It was well received abroad and at home. In the same year was published at London my *Inquiry Concerning the Principles of Morals,* which in my own opinion (who ought not to judge on that subject) is of all my writings, historical, philosophical,

---

4 [William Warburton (1698-1779), Bishop of Gloucester, who in several works defended the doctrine of revelation and bitterly attacked philosophical skepticism, a.o., of Hume and Bolingbroke.—Ed.]

or literary, incomparably the best. It came unnoticed and un-
observed into the world.

In 1752, the Faculty of Advocates chose me their librarian,
an office from which I received little or no emolument, but
which gave me the command of a large library. I then formed
the plan of writing the *History of England;* but being
frightened with the notion of continuing a narrative through
a period of 1700 years, I commenced with the accession of the
House of Stuart, an epoch when, I thought, the misrepre-
sentations of faction began chiefly to take place. I was, I own,
sanguine in my expectations of the success of this work. I
thought that I was the only historian that had at once
neglected present power, interest, and authority, and the cry
of popular prejudices; and as the subject was suited to every
capacity, I expected proportional applause. But miserable
was my disappointment: I was assailed by one cry of reproach,
disapprobation, and even detestation; English, Scotch, and
Irish, Whig and Tory, Churchman and Sectary, Freethinker
and Religionist, Patriot and Courtier united in their rage
against the man who had presumed to shed a generous tear
for the fate of Charles I and the Earl of Strafford; and after
the first ebullitions of their fury were over, what was still
more mortifying, the book seemed to sink into oblivion. Mr.
Millar told me that in a twelvemonth he sold only forty-five
copies of it. I scarcely, indeed, heard of one man in the three
kingdoms, considerable for rank or letters, that could endure
the book. I must only except the primate of England, Dr.
Herring, and the primate of Ireland, Dr. Stone, which seem
two odd exceptions. These dignified prelates separately sent
me messages not to be discouraged.

I was however, I confess, discouraged; and had not the war
been at that time breaking out between France and England,
I had certainly retired to some provincial town of the former
kingdom, have changed my name, and never more have returned to my native country. But as this scheme was not now
practicable, and the subsequent volume was considerably advanced, I resolved to pick up courage and to persevere.

In this interval, I published at London my *Natural History of Religion,* along with some other small pieces. Its public entry was rather obscure, except only that Dr. Hurd wrote a pamphlet against it, with all the illiberal petulance, arrogance, and scurrility which distinguish the Warburtonian school. This pamphlet gave me some consolation for the otherwise indifferent reception of my performance.

In 1756, two years after the fall of the first volume, was published the second volume of my *History,* containing the period from the death of Charles I till the Revolution. This performance happened to give less displeasure to the Whigs, and was better received. It not only rose itself, but helped to buoy up its unfortunate brother.

But though I had been taught, by experience, that the Whig party were in possession of bestowing all places, both in the state and in literature, I was so little inclined to yield to their senseless clamor that in above a hundred alterations, which further study, reading or reflection engaged me to make in the reigns of the two first Stuarts, I have made all of them invariably to the Tory side. It is ridiculous to consider the English constitution before that period as a regular plan of liberty.

In 1759, I published my History of the House of Tudor. The clamor against this performance was almost equal to that against the History of the two first Stuarts. The reign of Elizabeth was particularly obnoxious. But I was now callous against the impressions of public folly, and continued very peaceably and contentedly in my retreat at Edinburgh to finish, in two volumes, the more early part of the English history, which I gave to the public in 1761, with tolerable, and but tolerable, success.

But, notwithstanding this variety of winds and seasons to which my writings had been exposed, they had still been making such advances that the copy-money given me by the booksellers much exceeded anything formerly known in England; I was become not only independent, but opulent. I retired to my native country of Scotland, determined never more to set my foot out of it, and retaining the satisfaction of never having preferred a request to one great man, or even making advances of friendship to any of them. As I was now turned to fifty, I thought of passing all the rest of my life in this philosophical manner, when I received, in 1763, an invitation from the Earl of Hertford, with whom I was not in the least acquainted, to attend him on his embassy to Paris, with a near prospect of being appointed secretary to the embassy, and, in the meanwhile, of performing the functions of that office. This offer, however inviting, I at first declined, both because I was reluctant to begin connections with the great, and because I was afraid that the civilities and gay company of Paris would prove disagreeable to a person of my age and humor; but on his Lordship's repeating the invitation, I accepted of it. I have every reason, both of pleasure and interest, to think myself happy in my connections with that nobleman, as well as afterwards with his brother, General Conway.

Those who have not seen the strange effects of modes will never imagine the reception I met with at Paris from men and women of all ranks and stations. The more I resiled from their excessive civilities, the more I was loaded with them. There is, however, a real satisfaction in living at Paris, from the great number of sensible, knowing, and polite company with which that city abounds above all places in the universe. I thought once of settling there for life.

I was appointed secretary to the embassy; and, in summer 1765, Lord Hertford left me, being appointed Lord Lieutenant of Ireland. I was *chargé d'affaires* till the arrival of the Duke of Richmond, toward the end of the year. In the beginning of 1766, I left Paris, and next summer went to Edinburgh, with the same view as formerly, of burying myself in a philosophical retreat. I returned to that place, not richer, but with much more money and a much larger income, by means of Lord Hertford's friendship, than I left it; and I was desirous of trying what superfluity could produce, as I had formerly made an experiment of a competency.

But, in 1767, I received from Mr. Conway an invitation to be Undersecretary; and this invitation, both the character of the person, and my connections with Lord Hertford, prevented me from declining. I returned to Edinburgh in 1769, very opulent (for I possessed a revenue of £1000 a year), healthy and, though somewhat stricken in years, with the prospect of enjoying long my ease and of seeing the increase of my reputation.

In spring 1775, I was struck with a disorder in my bowels, which at first gave me no alarm, but has since, as I apprehend it, become mortal and incurable. I now reckon upon a speedy dissolution. I have suffered very little pain from my disorder and, what is more strange, have, notwithstanding the great decline of my person, never suffered a moment's abatement of my spirits, insomuch that were I to name the period of my life which I should most choose to pass over again, I might be tempted to point to this later period. I possess the same ardor as ever in study, and the same gaiety in company. I consider, besides, that a man of sixty-five, by dying, cuts off only a few years of infirmities; and though I see many symptoms of my literary reputation's breaking out at last with additional luster, I knew that I could have but few years to enjoy it. It is difficult to be more detached from life than I am at present.

To conclude historically with my own character. I am, or rather was (for that is the style I must now use in speaking of myself, which emboldens me the more to speak my sentiments)—I was, I say, a man of mild dispositions, of command of temper, of an open, social, and cheerful humor, capable of attachment, but little susceptible of enmity, and of great moderation in all my passions. Even my love of literary fame, my ruling passion, never soured my temper, notwithstanding my frequent disappointments. My company was not unacceptable to the young and careless, as well as to the studious and literary; and as I took a particular pleasure in the company of modest women, I had no reason to be displeased with the reception I met with from them. In a word, though most men anywise eminent have found reason to complain of calumny, I never was touched or even attacked by her baleful tooth; and though I wantonly exposed myself to the rage of both civil and religious factions, they seemed to be disarmed in my behalf of their wonted fury. My friends never had occasion to vindicate any one circumstance of my character and conduct; not but that the zealots, we may well suppose, would have been glad to invent and propagate any story to my disadvantage, but they could never find any which they thought would wear the face of probability. I cannot say there is no vanity in making this funeral oration of myself, but I hope it is not a misplaced one; and this is a matter of fact which is easily cleared and ascertained.

April 18, 1776.

AN INQUIRY CONCERNING
HUMAN UNDERSTANDING

SECTION I

OF THE DIFFERENT SPECIES OF PHILOSOPHY

MORAL PHILOSOPHY or the science of human nature may be treated after two different manners, each of which has its peculiar merit and may contribute to the entertainment, instruction, and reformation of mankind. The one considers man chiefly as born for action and as influenced in his measures by taste and sentiment, pursuing one object and avoiding another according to the value which these objects seem to possess, and according to the light in which they present themselves. As virtue, of all objects, is allowed to be the most valuable, this species of philosophers paint her in the most amiable colors, borrowing all helps from poetry and eloquence and treating their subject in an easy and obvious manner, and such as is best fitted to please the imagination and engage the affections. They select the most striking observations and instances from common life, place opposite characters in a proper contrast, and, alluring us into the paths of virtue by the views of glory and happiness, direct our steps in these paths by the soundest precepts and most illustrious examples. They make us feel the difference between vice and virtue; they excite and regulate our sentiments; and so they can but bend our hearts to the love of probity and true honor, they think that they have fully attained the end of all their labors.

The other species of philosophers consider man in the light of a reasonable rather than an active being, and endeavor to form his understanding more than cultivate his manners. They regard human nature as a subject of speculation, and with a narrow scrutiny examine it in order to find those principles which regulate our understanding, excite our sentiments, and make us approve or blame any particular object, action, or behavior. They think it a reproach to all literature that philosophy should not yet have fixed, beyond controversy, the foundation of morals, reasoning, and criticism, and should forever talk of truth and falsehood, vice and virtue, beauty and deformity, without being able to determine the source of those distinctions. While they attempt this arduous task, they are deterred by no difficulties; but, proceeding from particular instances to general principles, they still push on their inquiries to principles more general, and rest not satisfied till they arrive at those original principles by which, in every science, all human curiosity must be bounded. Though their speculations seem abstract, and even unintelligible to common readers, they aim at the approbation of the learned and the wise, and think themselves sufficiently compensated for the labor of their whole lives if they can discover some hidden truths which may contribute to the instruction of posterity.

It is certain that the easy and obvious philosophy will always, with the generality of mankind, have the preference above the accurate and abstruse; and by many will be recommended, not only as more agreeable, but more useful, than the other. It enters more into common life, molds the heart and affections, and, by touching those principles which actuate men, reforms their conduct and brings them nearer to that model of perfection which it describes. On the contrary, the abstruse philosophy, being founded on a turn of mind which cannot enter into business and action, vanishes when the philosopher leaves the shade and comes into open day, nor can its principles easily retain any influence over our conduct and behavior. The feelings of our heart, the agitation of our passions, the vehemence of our affections dissipate all its conclusions and reduce the profound philosopher to a mere plebeian.

This also must be confessed, that the most durable as well as justest fame has been acquired by the easy philosophy, and that abstract reasoners seem hitherto to have enjoyed only a momentary reputation, from the caprice or ignorance of their own age, but have not been able to support their renown with more equitable posterity. It is easy for a profound philosopher to commit a mistake in his subtile reasonings—and one mistake is the necessary parent of another, while he pushes on his consequences, and is not deterred from embracing any conclusion by its unusual appearance or its contradiction to popular opinion. But a philosopher who purposes only to represent the common sense of mankind in more beautiful and more engaging colors, if by accident he falls into error, goes no farther; but, renewing his appeal to common sense and the natural sentiments of the mind, returns into the right path and secures himself from any dangerous illusions. The fame of Cicero flourishes at present, but that of Aristotle is utterly decayed. La Bruyère passes the seas and still maintains his reputation, but the glory of Malebranche is confined to his own nation and to his own age. And Addison, perhaps, will be read with pleasure when Locke shall be entirely forgotten.[1]

The mere philosopher is a character which is commonly but little acceptable in the world, as being supposed to contribute nothing either to the advantage or pleasure of society, while he lives remote from communication with mankind and is wrapped up in principles and notions equally remote from their comprehension. On the other hand, the mere ignorant is still more despised, nor is anything deemed a surer sign of an illiberal genius, in an age and nation where the sciences flourish, than to be entirely destitute of all relish for those noble entertainments. The most perfect character is supposed to lie between those extremes: retaining an equal ability and taste for books, company, and business; preserving in conversation that discernment and delicacy which arise from polite letters; and, in business, that probity and accuracy which are the natural result of a just philosophy. In order to diffuse and cultivate so accomplished a character, nothing can be more useful than compositions of the easy style and man-

---

[1] This is not intended any way to detract from the merit of Mr. Locke, who was really a great philosopher and a just and modest reasoner. It is only meant to show the common fate of such abstract philosophy. [Note in Editions K and L.]

ner which draw not too much from life, require no deep application or retreat to be comprehended, and send back the
student among mankind full of noble sentiments and wise
precepts applicable to every exigency of human life. By means
of such compositions virtue becomes amiable, science agreeable, company instructive, and retirement entertaining.

Man is a reasonable being, and, as such, receives from
science his proper food and nourishment. But so narrow are
the bonds of human understanding that little satisfaction can
be hoped for in this particular, either from the extent or
security of his acquisitions. Man is a sociable no less than a
reasonable being. But neither can he always enjoy company
agreeable and amusing or preserve the proper relish for them.
Man is also an active being, and, from that disposition as well
as from the various necessities of human life, must submit to
business and occupation; but the mind requires some relaxa-
tion and cannot always support its bent to care and industry.
It seems, then, that nature has pointed out a mixed kind of
life as most suitable to the human race, and secretly admon-
ished them to allow none of these biases to *draw* too much,
so as to incapacitate them for other occupations and entertainments. Indulge your passion for science, says she, but let your
science be human and such as may have a direct reference to
action and society. Abstruse thought and profound researches
I prohibit and will severely punish by the pensive melancholy
which they introduce, by the endless uncertainty in which
they involve you, and by the cold reception your pretended
discoveries shall meet with when communicated. Be a philosopher, but, amidst all your philosophy, be still a man.

Were the generality of mankind contented to prefer the
easy philosophy to the abstract and profound, without throw-
ing any blame or contempt on the latter, it might not be
improper, perhaps, to comply with this general opinion and
allow every man to enjoy, without opposition, his own taste
and sentiment. But as the matter is often carried further, even
to the absolute rejecting of all profound reasonings or what
is commonly called "metaphysics," we shall now proceed to
consider what can reasonably be pleaded in their behalf.

We may begin with observing that one considerable advantage which results from the accurate and abstract philosophy is its subservience to the easy and humane, which, without the former, can never attain a sufficient degree of exactness in its sentiments, precepts, or reasonings. All polite letters are nothing but pictures of human life in various attitudes and situations, and inspire us with different sentiments of praise or blame, admiration or ridicule, according to the qualities of the object which they set before us. An artist must be better qualified to succeed in this undertaking who, besides a delicate taste and a quick apprehension, possesses an accurate knowledge of the internal fabric, the operations of the understanding, the workings of the passions, and the various species of sentiment which discriminate vice and virtue. How painful soever this inward search or inquiry may appear, it becomes in some measure requisite to those who would describe with success the obvious and outward appearances of life and manners. The anatomist presents to the eye the most hideous and disagreeable objects, but his science is useful to the painter in delineating even a Venus or a Helen. While the latter employs all the richest colors of his art and gives his figures the most graceful and engaging airs, he must still carry his attention to the inward structure of the human body, the position of the muscles, the fabric of the bones, and the use and figure of every part or organ. Accuracy is, in every case, advantageous to beauty, and just reasoning to delicate sentiment. In vain would we exalt the one by depreciating the other.

Besides, we may observe in every art or profession, even those which most concern life or action, that a spirit of accuracy, however acquired, carries all of them nearer their perfection and renders them more subservient to the interests of society. And though a philosopher may live remote from business, the genius of philosophy, if carefully cultivated by several, must gradually diffuse itself throughout the whole society and bestow a similar correctness on every art or calling. The politician will acquire greater foresight and subtilty in the subdividing and balancing of power, the lawyer more method and finer principles in his reasonings, and the general more regularity in his discipline and more caution in his plans and operations. The stability of modern governments above the ancient and the accuracy of modern philosophy have improved, and probably will still improve, by similar gradations.

Were there no advantage to be reaped from these studies beyond the gratification of an innocent curiosity, yet ought not even this to be despised as being an accession to those few safe and harmless pleasures which are bestowed on the human race. The sweetest and most inoffensive path of life leads through the avenues of science and learning; and whoever can either remove any obstructions in this way or open up any new prospect ought so far to be esteemed a benefactor to mankind. And though these researches may appear painful and fatiguing, it is with some minds as with some bodies, which, being endowed with vigorous and florid health, require severe exercise and reap a pleasure from what, to the generality of mankind, may seem burdensome and laborious. Obscurity, indeed, is painful to the mind as well as to the eye, but to bring light from obscurity, by whatever labor, must needs be delightful and rejoicing.

But this obscurity, in the profound and abstract philosophy, is objected to, not only as painful and fatiguing, but as the inevitable source of uncertainty and error. Here, indeed, lies the justest and most plausible objection against a considerable part of metaphysics, that they are not properly a science, but arise either from the fruitless efforts of human vanity, which would penetrate into subjects utterly inaccessible to the understanding, or from the craft of popular superstitions, which, being unable to defend themselves on fair ground, raise these entangling brambles to cover and protect their weakness. Chased from the open country, these robbers fly into the forest and lie in wait to break in upon every unguarded avenue of the mind, and overwhelm it with religious fears and prejudices. The stoutest antagonist, if he remit his watch a moment, is oppressed, and many, through cowardice and folly, open the gates to the enemies and willingly receive them with reverence and submission as their legal sovereigns.

But is this a sufficient reason why philosophers should desist from such researches and leave superstition still in possession of her retreat? Is it not proper to draw an opposite conclusion and perceive the necessity of carrying the war into the most secret recesses of the enemy? In vain do we hope that men, from frequent disappointment, will at last abandon such airy sciences and discover the proper province of human reason; for, besides that many persons find too sensible an interest in perpetually recalling such topics—besides this, I say, the motive of blind despair can never reasonably have place in the sciences, since, however unsuccessful former attempts may have proved, there is still room to hope that the industry, good fortune, or improved sagacity of succeeding generations may reach discoveries unknown to former ages. Each adventurous genius will still leap at the arduous prize and find himself stimulated rather than discouraged by the failures of his predecessors, while he hopes that the glory of achieving so hard an adventure is reserved for him alone. The only method of freeing learning at once from these abstruse questions is to inquire seriously into the nature of human understanding and show, from an exact analysis of its powers and capacity, that it is by no means fitted for such remote and abstruse subjects. We must submit to this fatigue in order to live at ease ever after, and must cultivate true metaphysics with some care in order to destroy the false and adulterated. Indolence, which to some persons affords a safeguard against this deceitful philosophy, is, with others, overbalanced by curiosity; and despair, which at some moments prevails, may give place afterwards to sanguine hopes and expectations. Accurate and just reasoning is the only catholic remedy fitted for all persons and all dispositions, and is alone able to subvert that abstruse philosophy and metaphysical jargon which, being mixed up with popular superstition, renders it in a manner impenetrable to careless reasoners and gives it the air of science and wisdom.

Besides this advantage of rejecting, after deliberate inquiry, the most uncertain and disagreeable part of learning, there are many positive advantages which result from an accurate scrutiny into the powers and faculties of human nature. It is remarkable, concerning the operations of the mind, that, though most intimately present to us, yet, whenever they become the object of reflection, they seem involved in obscurity, nor can the eye readily find those lines and boundaries which discriminate and distinguish them. The objects are too fine to remain long in the same aspect or situation, and must be apprehended in an instant by a superior penetration derived from nature and improved by habit and reflection. It becomes, therefore, no inconsiderable part of science barely to know the different operations of the mind, to separate them from each other, to class them under their proper heads, and to correct all that seeming disorder in which they lie involved when made the object of reflection and inquiry. This task of ordering and distinguishing, which has no merit when performed with regard to external bodies, the objects of our senses, rises in its value when directed toward the operations of the mind, in proportion to the difficulty and labor which we meet with in performing it. And if we can go no further than this mental geography, or delineation of the distinct parts and powers of the mind, it is at least a satisfaction to go so far; and the more obvious this science may appear (and it is by no means obvious), the more contemptible still must the ignorance of it be esteemed in all pretenders to learning and philosophy.

Nor can there remain any suspicion that this science is uncertain and chimerical, unless we should entertain such a skepticism as is entirely subversive of all speculation, and even action. It cannot be doubted that the mind is endowed with several powers and faculties, that these powers are distinct from each other, that what is really distinct to the immediate perception may be distinguished by reflection, and, consequently, that there is a truth and falsehood in all propositions on this subject, and a truth and falsehood which lie not beyond the compass of human understanding. There are many obvious distinctions of this kind, such as those between the will and understanding, the imagination and passions, which fall within the comprehension of every human creature; and the finer and more philosophical distinctions are no less real and certain, though more difficult to be comprehended. Some instances, especially late ones, of success in these inquiries may give us a juster notion of the certainty and solidity of this branch of learning. And shall we esteem it worthy the labor of a philosopher to give us a true system of the planets and adjust the position and order of those remote bodies, while we affect to overlook those who, with so much success, delineate the parts of the mind in which we are so intimately concerned? [2]

[2] That faculty by which we discern truth and falsehood, and that by which we perceive vice and virtue, had long been confounded with each other; and all morality was supposed to be built on eternal and immutable relations which, to every intelligent mind, were equally invariable as any proposition concerning quantity or number. But a late philosopher [Francis Hutcheson] has taught us, by the most convincing arguments, that morality is nothing in the abstract nature of things, but is entirely relative to the sentiment or mental taste of each particular being, in the same manner as the distinctions of sweet and bitter, hot and cold arise from the particular feeling of each sense or organ. Moral perceptions, therefore, ought not to be classed with the operations of the understanding, but with the tastes or sentiments.

It had been usual with philosophers to divide all the passions of the mind into two classes, the selfish and benevolent, which were supposed to stand in constant opposition and contrariety; nor was it thought that the latter could ever attain their proper object but at the expense of the former. Among the selfish passions were ranked avarice, ambition, revenge; among the benevolent, natural affection, friendship, public spirit. Philosophers may now perceive the impropriety of this division. [See Butler's *Sermons*.] It has been proved, beyond all controversy, that even the passions commonly esteemed selfish carry the mind beyond self directly to the object; that though the satisfaction of these passions gives us enjoyment, yet the prospect of this enjoyment is not the cause of the passion, but, on the contrary, the passion is antecedent to the enjoyment, and without the former the latter could never possibly exist; that the case is precisely the same with the passions denominated benevolent, and consequently that a man is no more interested when he seeks his own glory than when the happiness of his friend is the object of his wishes; nor is he any more disinterested when he sacrifices his ease and quiet to public

But may we not hope that philosophy, if cultivated with care and encouraged by the attention of the public, may carry its researches still further and discover, at least in some degree, the secret springs and principles by which the human mind is actuated in its operation? Astronomers had long contented themselves with proving, from the phenomena, the true motions, order, and magnitude of the heavenly bodies, till a philosopher at last arose [3] who seems, from the happiest reasoning, to have also determined the laws and forces by which the revolutions of the planets are governed and directed. The like has been performed with regard to other parts of nature. And there is no reason to despair of equal success in our inquiries concerning the mental powers and economy if prosecuted with equal capacity and caution. It is probable that one operation and principle of the mind depends on another, which again may be resolved into one more general and universal: And how far these researches may possibly be carried, it will be difficult for us, before or even after a careful trial, exactly to determine. This is certain, that attempts of this kind are every day made, even by those who philosophize the most negligently; and nothing can be more requisite than to enter upon the enterprise with thorough care and attention that, if it lie within the compass of human understanding, it may at last be happily achieved; if not, it may, however, be rejected with some confidence and security. This last conclusion, surely, is not desirable, nor ought it to be embraced too rashly. For how much must we diminish from the beauty and value of this species of philosophy, upon such a supposition? Moralists have hitherto been accustomed, when they considered the vast multitude and diversity of those actions that excite our approbation or dislike, to search for some common principle on which this variety of senti-

---

good than when he labors for the gratification of avarice or ambition. Here, therefore, is a considerable adjustment in the boundaries of the passions, which had been confounded by the negligence or inaccuracy of former philosophers. These two instances may suffice to show us the nature and importance of that species of philosophy. [Note in Editions K and L.]

[3] [Reference is to Isaac Newton (1641-1727).—Ed.]

ments might depend. And though they have sometimes carried the matter too far, by their passion for some one general principle, it must, however, be confessed that they are excusable in expecting to find some general principles into which all the vices and virtues were justly to be resolved. The like has been the endeavor of critics, logicians, and even politicians; nor have their attempts been wholly unsuccessful, though perhaps longer time, greater accuracy, and more ardent application may bring these sciences still nearer their perfection. To throw up at once all pretensions of this kind may justly be deemed more rash, precipitate, and dogmatical than even the boldest and most affirmative philosophy that has ever attempted to impose its crude dictates and principles on mankind.

What though these reasonings concerning human nature seem abstract and of difficult comprehension, this affords no presumption of their falsehood. On the contrary, it seems impossible that what has hitherto escaped so many wise and profound philosophers can be very obvious and easy. And whatever pains these researches may cost us, we may think ourselves sufficiently rewarded, not only in point of profit but of pleasure, if, by that means, we can make any addition to our stock of knowledge in subjects of such unspeakable importance.

But as, after all, the abstractedness of these speculations is no recommendation, but rather a disadvantage, to them, and as this difficulty may perhaps be surmounted by care and art and the avoiding of all unnecessary detail, we have, in the following *Inquiry*, attempted to throw some light upon subjects from which uncertainty has hitherto deterred the wise, and obscurity the ignorant. Happy if we can unite the boundaries of the different species of philosophy by reconciling profound inquiry with clearness, and truth with novelty! And still more happy, if, reasoning in this easy manner, we can undermine the foundations of an abstruse philosophy which seems to have hitherto served only as a shelter to superstition and a cover to absurdity and error!

SECTION II

OF THE ORIGIN OF IDEAS

EVERYONE WILL readily allow that there is a considerable difference between the perceptions of the mind when a man feels the pain of excessive heat or the pleasure of moderate warmth, and when he afterwards recalls to his memory this sensation or anticipates it by his imagination. These faculties may mimic or copy the perceptions of the senses, but they never can entirely reach the force and vivacity of the original sentiment. The utmost we say of them, even when they operate with greatest vigor, is that they represent their object in so lively a manner that we could *almost* say we feel or see it. But, except the mind be disordered by disease or madness, they never can arrive at such a pitch of vivacity as to render these perceptions altogether undistinguishable. All the colors of poetry, however splendid, can never paint natural objects in such a manner as to make the description be taken for a real landscape. The most lively thought is still inferior to the dullest sensation.

We may observe a like distinction to run through all the other perceptions of the mind. A man in a fit of anger is actuated in a very different manner from one who only thinks of that emotion. If you tell me that any person is in love, I easily understand your meaning and form a just conception of his situation, but never can mistake that conception for the real disorders and agitations of the passion. When we reflect on our past sentiments and affections, our thought is a faithful mirror and copies its objects truly, but the colors which it employs are faint and dull in comparison of those in which our original perceptions were clothed. It requires no nice discernment or metaphysical head to mark the distinction between them.

Here, therefore, we may divide all the perceptions of the

mind into two classes or species, which are distinguished by their different degrees of force and vivacity. The less forcible and lively are commonly denominated "thoughts" or "ideas." The other species want a name in our language, and in most others; I suppose, because it was not requisite for any but philosophical purposes to rank them under a general term or appellation. Let us, therefore, use a little freedom and call them "impressions," employing that word in a sense some-what different from the usual. By the term "impression," then, I mean all our more lively perceptions, when we hear, or see, or feel, or love, or hate, or desire, or will. And impressions are distinguished from ideas, which are the less lively perceptions of which we are conscious when we reflect on any of those sensations or movements above mentioned.

Nothing, at first view, may seem more unbounded than the thought of man, which not only escapes all human power and authority, but is not even restrained within the limits of nature and reality. To form monsters and join incongruous shapes and appearances costs the imagination no more trouble than to conceive the most natural and familiar objects. And while the body is confined to one planet, along which it creeps with pain and difficulty, the thought can in an instant transport us into the most distant regions of the universe, or even beyond the universe into the unbounded chaos where nature is supposed to lie in total confusion. What never was seen or heard of, may yet be conceived, nor is anything be-yond the power of thought except what implies an absolute contradiction.

But though our thought seems to possess this unbounded liberty, we shall find upon a nearer examination that it is really confined within very narrow limits, and that all this creative power of the mind amounts to no more than the faculty of compounding, transposing, augmenting, or diminishing the materials afforded us by the senses and experience. When we think of a golden mountain, we only join two consistent ideas, "gold" and "mountain," with which we were formerly acquainted. A virtuous horse we can conceive, because, from our own feeling, we can conceive virtue; and this we may unite to the figure and shape of a horse, which is an animal familiar to us. In short, all the materials of thinking are derived either from our outward or inward sentiment; the mixture and composition of these belongs alone to the mind and will, or, to express myself in philosophical language, all our ideas or more feeble perceptions are copies of our impressions or more lively ones.

To prove this, the two following arguments will, I hope, be sufficient. *First,* when we analyze our thoughts or ideas, however compounded or sublime, we always find that they resolve themselves into such simple ideas as were copied from a precedent feeling or sentiment. Even those ideas which at first view seem the most wide of this origin are found, upon a nearer scrutiny, to be derived from it. The idea of God, as meaning an infinitely intelligent, wise, and good Being, arises from reflecting on the operations of our own mind and augmenting, without limit, those qualities of goodness and wisdom. We may prosecute this inquiry to what length we please; where we shall always find that every idea which we examine is copied from a similar impression. Those who would assert that this position is not universally true, nor without exception, have only one, and that an easy, method of refuting it by producing that idea which, in their opinion, is not derived from this source. It will then be incumbent on us, if we would maintain our doctrine, to produce the impression or lively perception which corresponds to it.

Secondly, if it happen, from a defect of the organ, that a man is not susceptible of any species of sensation, we always find that he is as little susceptible of the correspondent idea. A blind man can form no notion of colors, a deaf man of sounds. Restore either of them that sense in which he is deficient by opening this new inlet for his sensations, you also open an inlet for the ideas, and he finds no difficulty in conceiving these objects. The case is the same if the object proper for exciting any sensation has never been applied to the organ. A Laplander or Negro has no notion of the relish of wine. And though there are few or no instances of a like deficiency in the mind where a person has never felt or is wholly incapable of a sentiment or passion that belongs to his species, yet we find the same observation to take place in a less degree. A man of mild manners can form no idea of inveterate revenge or cruelty, nor can a selfish heart easily conceive the heights of friendship and generosity. It is readily allowed that other beings may possess many senses of which we can have no conception, because the ideas of them have never been introduced to us in the only manner by which an idea can have access to the mind, to wit, by the actual feeling and sensation.

There is, however, one contradictory phenomenon which may prove that it is not absolutely impossible for ideas to arise independent of their correspondent impressions. I believe it will readily be allowed that the several distinct ideas of color, which enter by the eye, or those of sound, which are conveyed by the ear, are really different from each other, though at the same time resembling. Now, if this be true of different colors, it must be no less so of the different shades of the same color; and each shade produces a distinct idea, independent of the rest. For if this should be denied, it is possible, by the continual gradation of shades, to run a color insensibly into what is most remote from it; and if you will not allow any of the means to be different, you cannot, without absurdity, deny the extremes to be the same. Suppose, therefore, a person to have enjoyed his sight for thirty years and to have become perfectly acquainted with colors of all kinds, except one particular shade of blue, for instance, which it never has been his fortune to meet with; let all the different shades of that color, except that single one, be placed before him, descending gradually from the deepest to the lightest, it is plain that he will perceive a blank where that shade is wanting, and will be sensible that there is a greater distance in that place between the contiguous colors than in any other. Now I ask whether it be possible for him, from his own imagination, to supply this deficiency and raise up to himself the idea of that particular shade, though it had never been conveyed to him by his senses? I believe there are few but will be of opinion that he can; and this may serve as a proof that the simple ideas are not always, in every instance, derived from the correspondent impressions, though this instance is so singular that it is scarcely worth our observing, and does not merit that for it alone we should alter our general maxim.

Here, therefore, is a proposition which not only seems in itself simple and intelligible, but, if a proper use were made of it, might render every dispute equally intelligible, and banish all that jargon which has so long taken possession of metaphysical reasonings and drawn disgrace upon them. All ideas, especially abstract ones, are naturally faint and obscure. The mind has but a slender hold of them. They are apt to be confounded with other resembling ideas; and when we have often employed any term, though without a distinct meaning, we are apt to imagine it has a determinate idea annexed to it. On the contrary, all impressions, that is, all sensations either outward or inward, are strong and vivid. The limits between them are more exactly determined, nor is it easy to fall into any error or mistake with regard to them. When we entertain, therefore, any suspicion that a philosophical term is employed without any meaning or idea (as is but too frequent), we need but inquire, *from what impression is that supposed idea derived?* And if it be impossible to assign any, this will serve to confirm our suspicion. By bringing ideas in so clear a light, we may reasonably hope to remove all dispute which may arise concerning their nature and reality.[1]

---

1 It is probable that no more was meant by those who denied innate ideas than that all ideas were copies of our impressions, though it must be confessed that the terms which they employed were not chosen with such caution, nor so exactly defined, as to prevent all mistakes about their doctrine. For what is meant by "innate"? If "innate" be equivalent to "natural," then all the perceptions and ideas of the mind must be allowed to be innate or natural, in whatever sense we take the latter word, whether in opposition to what is uncommon, artificial, or miraculous. If by innate be meant contemporary to our birth, the dispute seems to be frivolous, nor is it worth while to inquire at what time thinking begins,

SECTION III

OF THE ASSOCIATION [1] OF IDEAS

IT IS EVIDENT that there is a principle of connection between the different thoughts or ideas of the mind, and that, in their appearance to the memory or imagination, they introduce each other with a certain degree of method and regularity. In our more serious thinking or discourse this is so observable that any particular thought which breaks in upon the regular tract or chain of ideas is immediately remarked and rejected. And even in our wildest and most wandering reveries, nay, in our very dreams, we shall find, if we reflect, that the imagination ran not altogether at adventures, but that there was still a connection upheld among the different ideas which succeeded each other. Were the loosest and freest conversation to be transcribed, there would immediately be observed something which connected it in all its transitions. Or where this is wanting, the person who broke the thread of discourse might still inform you that there had secretly re-

---

whether before, at, or after our birth. Again, the word "idea" seems to be commonly taken in a very loose sense by Locke and others, as standing for any of our perceptions, our sensations and passions, as well as thoughts. Now, in this sense, I should desire to know what can be meant by asserting that self-love, or resentment of injuries, or the passion between the sexes is not innate?

But admitting these terms "impressions" and "ideas" in the sense above explained, and understanding by "innate" what is original or copied from no precedent perception, then may we assert that all our impressions are innate, and our ideas not innate.

To be ingenuous, I must own it to be my opinion that Locke was betrayed into this question by the schoolmen, who, making use of undefined terms, draw out their disputes to a tedious length without ever touching the point in question. A like ambiguity and circumlocution seem to run through that philosopher's reasonings, on this as well as most other subjects.

[1] [Editions K and L: "Connection of Ideas."]

volved in his mind a succession of thought which had gradually led him from the subject of conversation. Among different languages, even when we cannot suspect the least connection or communication, it is found that the words expressive of ideas the most compounded do yet nearly correspond to each other—a certain proof that the simple ideas comprehended in the compound ones were bound together by some universal principle which had an equal influence on all mankind.

Though it be too obvious to escape observation that different ideas are connected together, I do not find that any philosopher has attempted to enumerate or class all the principles of association—a subject, however, that seems worthy of curiosity. To me there appear to be only three principles of connection among ideas, namely, *Resemblance, Contiguity* in time or place, and *Cause* or *Effect.*

That these principles serve to connect ideas will not, I believe, be much doubted. A picture naturally leads our thoughts to the original.[2] The mention of one apartment in a building naturally introduces an inquiry or discourse concerning the others;[3] and if we think of a wound, we can scarcely forbear reflecting on the pain which follows it.[4] But that this enumeration is complete, and that there are no other principles of association except these, may be difficult to prove to the satisfaction of the reader or even to a man's own satisfaction. All we can do, in such cases, is to run over several instances and examine carefully the principle which binds the different thoughts to each other, never stopping till we render the principle as general as possible.[5] The more instances we examine and the more care we employ, the more

[2] Resemblance. [3] Contiguity. [4] Cause and Effect.

[5] For instance, *Contrast* or *Contrariety* is also a connection among ideas, but it may perhaps be considered as a mixture of *Causation* and *Resemblance*. Where two objects are contrary, the one destroys the other; that is, the cause of its annihilation, and the idea of the annihilation of an object, implies the idea of its former existence.

assurance shall we acquire that the enumeration which we form from the whole is complete and entire.

This Section, as it stands in Editions K, L, and N, thus continues:

Instead of entering into a detail of this kind, which would lead us into many useless subtilities, we shall consider some of the effects of this connection upon the passions and imagination; where we may open up a field of speculation more entertaining, and perhaps more instructive, than the other.

As man is a reasonable being and is continually in pursuit of happiness, which he hopes to find in the gratification of some passion or affection, he seldom acts or speaks or thinks without a purpose and intention. He has still some object in view; and however improper the means may sometimes be which he chooses for the attainment of his end, he never loses view of an end, nor will he so much as throw away his thoughts or reflections where he hopes not to reap any satisfaction from them.

In all compositions of genius, therefore, it is requisite that the writer have some plan or object; and though he may be hurried from this plan by the vehemence of thought, as in an ode, or drop it carelessly, as in an epistle or essay, there must appear some aim or intention in his first setting out, if not in the composition of the whole work. A production without a design would resemble more the ravings of a madman than the sober efforts of genius and learning.

As this rule admits of no exception, it follows that in narrative compositions the events or actions which the writer relates must be connected together by some bond or tie: They must be related to each other in the imagination, and form a kind of *unity* which may bring them under one plan or view, and which may be the object or end of the writer in his first undertaking.

This connecting principle among the several events which form the subject of a poem or history may be very different according to the different designs of the poet or historian. Ovid has formed his plan upon the connecting principle of resemblance. Every fabulous transformation produced by the miraculous power of the gods falls within the compass of his work. There needs but this one circumstance, in any event, to bring it under his original plan or intention.

An annalist or historian who should undertake to write the history of Europe during any century would be influenced by the connection of contiguity in time or place. All events which happen in that portion of space and period of time are comprehended in his design, though in other respects different and unconnected. They have still a species of unity amidst all their diversity.

But the most usual species of connection among the different events which enter into any narrative composition is that of cause and effect; while the historian traces the series of actions according to their natural order, remounts to their secret springs and principles, and delineates their most remote consequences. He chooses for his subject a certain portion of that great chain of events which compose the history of mankind: each link in this chain he endeavors to touch in his narration; sometimes unavoidable ignorance renders all his attempts fruitless; sometimes he supplies by conjecture what is wanting in knowledge; and always he is sensible that the more unbroken the chain is which he presents to his readers, the more perfect is his production. He sees that the knowledge of causes is not only the most satisfactory, this relation or connection being the strongest of all others, but also the most instructive; since it is by this knowledge alone we are enabled to control events and govern futurity.

Here, therefore, we may attain some notion of that *unity* of *action* about which all critics after Aristotle have talked so much, perhaps to little purpose, while they directed not their taste or sentiment by the accuracy of philosophy. It appears that in all productions, as well as in the epic and tragic, there is a certain unity required, and that on no occasion our thoughts can be allowed to run at adventures if we would produce a work that will give any lasting entertainment to mankind. It appears, also, that even a biographer who should write the life of Achilles would connect the events by showing their mutual dependence and relation, as much as a poet who should make the anger of that hero the subject of his narration.[6] Not only in any limited portion of life a man's actions have a de-

---

[6] Contrary to Aristotle [cf. 1450a].

pendence on each other, but also during the whole period
of his duration from the cradle to the grave; nor is it possible to strike off one link, however minute, in this regular
chain without affecting the whole series of events which
follow. The unity of action, therefore, which is to be found
in biography or history differs from that of epic poetry, not
in kind, but in degree. In epic poetry, the connection
among the events is more close and sensible; the narration
is not carried on through such a length of time; and the
actors hasten to some remarkable period which satisfies the
curiosity of the reader. This conduct of the epic poet depends on that particular situation of the imagination and
of the passions which is supposed in that production. The
imagination both of writer and reader is more enlivened,
and the passions more inflamed than in history, biography,
or any species of narration that confine themselves to strict
truth and reality. Let us consider the effect of these two circumstances of an enlivened imagination and inflamed passions which belong to poetry, especially the epic kind,
above any other species of composition; and let us see for
what reason they require a stricter and closer unity in the
fable.

First, all poetry, being a species of painting, approaches
us nearer to the objects than any other species of narration,
throws a stronger light upon them, and delineates more
distinctly those minute circumstances which, though to the
historian they seem superfluous, serve mightily to enliven
the imagery and gratify the fancy. If it be not necessary, as
in the *Iliad,* to inform us each time the hero buckles his
shoes and ties his garters, it will be requisite, perhaps, to
enter into a greater detail than in the *Henriade,* where the
events are run over with such rapidity that we scarce have
leisure to become acquainted with the scene or action.
Were a poet, therefore, to comprehend in his subject any
great compass of time or series of events, and trace up the
death of Hector to its remote causes in the rape of Helen
or the judgment of Paris, he must draw out his poem to an
immeasurable length in order to fill this large canvas with
just painting and imagery. The reader's imagination, inflamed with such a series of poetical descriptions, and his
passions, agitated by a continual sympathy with the actors,
must flag long before the period of narration and must
sink into lassitude and disgust from the repeated violence
of the same movements.

Secondly, that an epic poet must not trace the causes to any great distance will further appear if we consider another reason, which is drawn from a property of the passions still more remarkable and singular. It is evident that in a just composition all the affections excited by the different events described and represented add mutual force to each other; and that, while the heroes are all engaged in one common scene, and each action is strongly connected with the whole, the concern is continually awake, and the passions make an easy transition from one object to another. The strong connection of the events, as it facilitates the passage of the thought or imagination from one to another, facilitates also the transfusion of the passions and preserves the affection still in the same channel and direction. Our sympathy and concern for Eve prepares the way for a like sympathy with Adam: the affection is preserved almost entire in the transition, and the mind seizes immediately the new object as strongly related to that which formerly engaged its attention. But were the poet to make a total digression from his subject and introduce a new actor no way connected with the personages, the imagination, feeling a breach in the transition, would enter coldly into the new scene; would kindle by slow degrees; and in returning to the main subject of the poem would pass, as it were, upon foreign ground and have its concern to excite anew in order to take party with the principal actors. The same inconvenience follows in a lesser degree where the poet traces his events to too great a distance and binds together actions which, though not altogether disjoined, have not so strong a connection as is requisite to forward the transition of the passions. Hence arises the artifice of oblique narration employed in the *Odyssey* and *Æneid*— where the hero is introduced, at first, near the period of his designs, and afterwards shows us, as it were in perspective, the more distant events and causes. By this means, the reader's curiosity is immediately excited; the events follow with rapidity, and in a very close connection; and the concern is preserved alive, and continually increases by means of the near relation of the objects, from the beginning to the end of the narration.

The same rule takes place in dramatic poetry; nor is it ever permitted in a regular composition to introduce an actor who has no connection, or but a small one, with the principal personages of the fable. The spectator's concern must not be diverted by any scenes disjoined and separated from the rest. This breaks the course of the passions, and prevents that communication of the several emotions by which one scene adds force to another, and transfuses the pity and terror which it excites upon each succeeding scene until the whole produces that rapidity of movement which is peculiar to the theater. How must it extinguish this warmth of affection to be entertained on a sudden with a new action and new personages no way related to the former; to find so sensible a breach or vacuity in the course of the passions, by means of this breach in the connection of ideas; and instead of carrying the sympathy of one scene into the following, to be obliged every moment to excite a new concern, and take party in a new scene of action?

But though this rule of unity of action be common to dramatic and epic poetry, we may still observe a difference betwixt them which may, perhaps, deserve our attention. In both these species of composition it is requisite the action be one and simple, in order to preserve the concern or sympathy entire and undiverted: but in epic or narrative poetry, this rule is also established upon another foundation, viz., the necessity that is incumbent on every writer to form some plan or design before he enter on any discourse or narration, and to comprehend his subject in some general aspect or united view which may be the constant object of his attention. As the author is entirely lost in dramatic compositions, and the spectator supposes himself to be really present at the actions represented, this reason has no place with regard to the stage; but any dialogue or conversation may be introduced which, without improbability, might have passed in that determinate portion of space represented by the theater. Hence, in all our English comedies, even those of Congreve, the unity of action is never strictly observed; but the poet thinks it sufficient if his personages be any way related to each other by blood, or by living in the same family; and he afterwards introduces them in particular scenes, where they display their humors and characters without much forwarding the main action. The double plots of Terence are licenses of the same kind, but in a lesser degree. And though this conduct be not perfectly regular, it is not wholly unsuitable to the nature of comedy, where the movements and passions are not raised to such a height as in tragedy; at the same time that the fiction or representation palliates, in some degree, such licenses. In a narrative poem, the first proposition or design confines the author to one subject; and any digressions of this nature would, at first view, be rejected as absurd and monstrous. Neither Boccace, La Fontaine, nor any author of that kind, though pleasantry be their chief object, have ever indulged them.

To return to the comparison of history and epic poetry, we may conclude from the foregoing reasonings that as a certain unity is requisite in all productions, it cannot be wanting to history more than to any other; that in history the connection among the several events which unites them into one body is the relation of cause and effect, the same which takes place in epic poetry; and that, in the latter composition, this connection is only required to be closer and more sensible on account of the lively imagination and strong passions which must be touched by the poet in his narration. The Peloponnesian war is a proper subject for history, the siege of Athens for an epic poem, and the death of Alcibiades for a tragedy.

As the difference, therefore, betwixt history and epic poetry consists only in the degrees of connection which bind together those several events of which their subject is composed, it will be difficult, if not impossible, by words to determine exactly the bounds which separate them from each other. That is a matter of taste more than of reasoning; and perhaps this unity may often be discovered in a subject where, at first view, and from an abstract consideration, we should least expect to find it.

It is evident that Homer, in the course of his narration, exceeds the first proposition of his subject; and that the anger of Achilles, which caused the death of Hector, is not the same with that which produced so many ills to the Greeks. But the strong connection betwixt these two movements, the quick transition from one to the other, the contrast betwixt the effects of concord and discord amongst the princes, and the natural curiosity we have to see Achilles in action after so long repose—all these causes carry on the reader, and produce a sufficient unity in the subject.

It may be objected to Milton that he has traced up his causes to too great a distance, and that the rebellion of the angels produces the fall of man by a train of events which is both very long and very casual. Not to mention that the creation of the world, which he has related at length, is no more the cause of that catastrophe than of the battle of

Pharsalia, or any other event that has ever happened. But if we consider, on the other hand, that all these events, the rebellion of the angels, the creation of the world, and the fall of man, *resemble* each other in being miraculous, and out of the common course of nature; that they are supposed to be *contiguous* in time; and that, being detached from all other events, and being the only original facts which revelation discovers, they strike the eye at once, and naturally recall each other to the thought or imagination—if we consider all these circumstances, I say, we shall find that these parts of the action have a sufficient unity to make them be comprehended in one fable or narration. To which we may add that the rebellion of the angels and the fall of man have a peculiar resemblance, as being counterparts to each other, and presenting to the reader the same moral of obedience to our Creator.

These loose hints I have thrown together in order to excite the curiosity of philosophers, and beget a suspicion at least if not a full persuasion that this subject is very copious, and that many operations of the human mind depend on the connection or association of ideas which is here explained. Particularly, the sympathy betwixt the passions and imagination will, perhaps, appear remarkable; while we observe that the affections, excited by one object, pass easily to another connected with it, but transfuse themselves with difficulty, or not at all, along different objects which have no manner of connection together. By introducing into any composition personages and actions foreign to each other, an injudicious author loses that communication of emotions by which alone he can interest the heart and raise the passions to their proper height and period. The full explication of this principle and all its consequences would lead us into reasonings too profound and too copious for these Essays. It is sufficient for us, at present, to have established this conclusion, that the three connecting principles of all ideas are the relations of *resemblance, contiguity,* and *causation.*

SECTION IV

SKEPTICAL DOUBTS CONCERNING THE OPERATIONS OF THE UNDERSTANDING

PART I

ALL THE OBJECTS of human reason or inquiry may naturally be divided into two kinds, to wit, "Relations of Ideas," and "Matters of Fact." Of the first kind are the sciences of Geometry, Algebra, and Arithmetic, and, in short, every affirmation which is either intuitively or demonstratively certain. *That the square of the hypotenuse is equal to the square of the two sides* is a proposition which expresses a relation between these figures. *That three times five is equal to the half of thirty* expresses a relation between these numbers. Propositions of this kind are discoverable by the mere operation of thought, without dependence on what is anywhere existent in the universe. Though there never were a circle or triangle in nature, the truths demonstrated by Euclid would forever retain their certainty and evidence.

Matters of fact, which are the second objects of human reason, are not ascertained in the same manner, nor is our evidence of their truth, however great, of a like nature with the foregoing. The contrary of every matter of fact is still possible, because it can never imply a contradiction and is conceived by the mind with the same facility and distinctness as if ever so conformable to reality. *That the sun will not rise tomorrow* is no less intelligible a proposition and implies no more contradiction than the affirmation *that it will rise*. We should in vain, therefore, attempt to demonstrate its falsehood. Were it demonstratively false, it would imply a contradiction and could never be distinctly conceived by the mind.

It may, therefore, be a subject worthy of curiosity to inquire what is the nature of that evidence which assures us of any real existence and matter of fact beyond the present testimony of our senses or the records of our memory. This part of philosophy, it is observable, had been little cultivated either by the ancients or moderns; and, therefore, our doubts and errors in the prosecution of so important an inquiry may be the more excusable while we march through such difficult paths without any guide or direction. They may even prove useful by exciting curiosity and destroying that implicit faith and security which is the bane of all reasoning and free inquiry. The discovery of defects in the common philosophy, if any such there be, will not, I presume, be a discouragement, but rather an incitement, as is usual, to attempt something more full and satisfactory than has yet been proposed to the public.

All reasonings concerning matter of fact seem to be founded on the relation of *cause* and *effect*. By means of that relation alone we can go beyond the evidence of our memory and senses. If you were to ask a man why he believes any matter of fact which is absent, for instance, that his friend is in the country or in France, he would give you a reason, and this reason would be some other fact: as a letter received from him or the knowledge of his former resolutions and promises. A man finding a watch or any other machine in a desert island would conclude that there had once been men in that island. All our reasonings concerning fact are of the same nature. And here it is constantly supposed that there is a connection between the present fact and that which is inferred from it. Were there nothing to bind them together, the inference would be entirely precarious. The hearing of an articulate voice and rational discourse in the dark assures us of the presence of some person. Why? Because these are the effects of the human make and fabric, and closely connected with it. If we anatomize all the other reasonings of this nature, we shall find that they are founded on the relation of cause and effect, and that this relation is either near or remote, direct or collateral. Heat and light are collateral effects·

of fire, and the one effect may justly be inferred from the other.

If we would satisfy ourselves, therefore, concerning the nature of that evidence which assures us of matters of fact, we must inquire how we arrive at the knowledge of cause and effect.

I shall venture to affirm, as a general proposition which admits of no exception, that the knowledge of this relation is not, in any instance, attained by reasonings *a priori*, but arises entirely from experience, when we find that any particular objects are constantly conjoined with each other. Let an object be presented to a man of ever so strong natural reason and abilities—if that object be entirely new to him, he will not be able, by the most accurate examination of its sensible qualities, to discover any of its causes or effects. Adam, though his rational faculties be supposed, at the very first, entirely perfect, could not have inferred from the fluidity and transparency of water that it would suffocate him, or from the light and warmth of fire that it would consume him. No object ever discovers, by the qualities which appear to the senses, either the causes which produced it or the effects which will arise from it; nor can our reason, unassisted by experience, ever draw any inference concerning real existence and matter of fact.

This proposition, *that causes and effects are discoverable, not by reason, but by experience,* will readily be admitted with regard to such objects as we remember to have once been altogether unknown to us, since we must be conscious of the utter inability which we then lay under of foretelling what would arise from them. Present two smooth pieces of marble to a man who has no tincture of natural philosophy; he will never discover that they will adhere together in such a manner as to require great force to separate them in a direct line, while they make so small a resistance to a lateral pressure. Such events as bear little analogy to the common course of nature are also readily confessed to be known only by experience, nor does any man imagine that the explosion of gunpowder or the attraction of a loadstone could ever be discovered by arguments *a priori*. In like manner, when an effect is supposed to depend upon an intricate machinery or secret structure of parts, we make no difficulty in attributing all our knowledge of it to experience. Who will assert that he can give the ultimate reason why milk or bread is proper nourishment for a man, not for a lion or tiger?

But the same truth may not appear at first sight to have the same evidence with regard to events which have become familiar to us from our first appearance in the world, which bear a close analogy to the whole course of nature, and which are supposed to depend on the simple qualities of objects without any secret structure of parts. We are apt to imagine that we could discover these effects by the mere operation of our reason without experience. We fancy that, were we brought on a sudden into this world, we could at first have inferred that one billiard ball would communicate motion to another upon impulse, and that we needed not to have waited for the event in order to pronounce with certainty concerning it. Such is the influence of custom that where it is strongest it not only covers our natural ignorance but even conceals itself, and seems not to take place, merely because it is found in the highest degree.

But to convince us that all the laws of nature and all the operations of bodies without exception are known only by experience, the following reflections may perhaps suffice. Were any object presented to us, and were we required to pronounce concerning the effect which will result from it without consulting past observation, after what manner, I beseech you, must the mind proceed in this operation? It must invent or imagine some event which it ascribes to the object as its effect; and it is plain that this invention must be entirely arbitrary. The mind can never possibly find the effect in the supposed cause by the most accurate scrutiny and examination. For the effect is totally different from the cause, and consequently can never be discovered in it. Motion in the second billiard ball is a quite distinct event from motion in the first, nor is there anything in the one to suggest the smallest hint of the other. A stone or piece of metal raised into the air and left without any support immediately falls. But to consider the matter *a priori,* is there anything we discover in this situation which can beget the idea of a downward rather than an upward or any other motion in the stone or metal?

And as the first imagination or invention of a particular effect in all natural operations is arbitrary where we consult not experience, so must we also esteem the supposed tie or connection between the cause and effect which binds them together and renders it impossible that any other effect could result from the operation of that cause. When I see, for instance, a billiard ball moving in a straight line toward another, even suppose motion in the second ball should by accident be suggested to me as the result of their contact or impulse, may I not conceive that a hundred different events might as well follow from that cause? May not both these balls remain at absolute rest? May not the first ball return in a straight line or leap off from the second in any line or direction? All these suppositions are consistent and conceivable. Why, then, should we give the preference to one which is no more consistent or conceivable than the rest? All our reasonings *a priori* will never be able to show us any foundation for this preference.

In a word, then, every effect is a distinct event from its cause. It could not, therefore, be discovered in the cause, and the first invention or conception of it, *a priori,* must be entirely arbitrary. And even after it is suggested, the conjunction of it with the cause must appear equally arbitrary, since there are always many other effects which, to reason, must seem fully as consistent and natural. In vain, therefore, should we pretend to determine any single event or infer any cause or effect without the assistance of observation and experience.

Hence we may discover the reason why no philosopher who is rational and modest has ever pretended to assign the ultimate cause of any natural operation, or to show distinctly the action of that power which produces any single effect in the universe. It is confessed that the utmost effort of human reason is to reduce the principles productive of natural phenomena to a greater simplicity, and to resolve the many particular effects into a few general causes, by means of reasonings from analogy, experience, and observation. But as to the causes of these general causes, we should in vain attempt their discovery, nor shall we ever be able to satisfy ourselves by any particular explication of them. These ultimate springs and principles are totally shut up from human curiosity and inquiry. Elasticity, gravity, cohesion of parts, communication of motion by impulse—these are probably the ultimate causes and principles which we shall ever discover in nature; and we may esteem ourselves sufficiently happy if, by accurate inquiry and reasoning, we can trace up the particular phenomena to, or near to, these general principles. The most perfect philosophy of the natural kind only staves off our ignorance a little longer, as perhaps the most perfect philosophy of the moral or metaphysical kind serves only to discover larger portions of it. Thus the observation of human blindness and weakness is the result of all philosophy, and meets us, at every turn, in spite of our endeavors to elude or avoid it.

Nor is geometry, when taken into the assistance of natural philosophy, ever able to remedy this defect or lead us into the knowledge of ultimate causes by all that accuracy of reasoning for which it is so justly celebrated. Every part of mixed mathematics proceeds upon the supposition that certain laws are established by nature in her operations, and abstract reasonings are employed either to assist experience in the discovery of these laws or to determine their influence in particular instances where it depends upon any precise degree of distance and quantity. Thus it is a law of motion, discovered by experience, that the moment or force of any body in motion is in the compound ratio or proportion of its solid contents and its velocity, and, consequently, that a small force may remove the greatest obstacle or raise the greatest weight if by any contrivance or machinery we can increase the velocity of that force so as to make it an overmatch for its antagonist. Geometry assists us in the application of this law by giving us the just dimensions of all the parts and figures which can enter into any species of machine, but still the discovery of the law itself is owing merely to experience; and all the abstract reasonings in the world could never lead us one step toward the knowledge of it. When we reason *a priori* and consider merely any object or cause as it appears to the mind, independent of all observation, it never could suggest to us the notion of any distinct object, such as its effect, much less show us the inseparable and inviolable connection between them. A man must be very sagacious who could discover by reasoning that crystal is the effect of heat, and ice of cold, without being previously acquainted with the operation of these qualities.

PART II

But we have not yet attained any tolerable satisfaction with regard to the question first proposed. Each solution still gives rise to a new question as difficult as the foregoing and leads us on to further inquiries. When it is asked, *What is the nature of all our reasonings concerning matter of fact?* the proper answer seems to be, That they are founded on the relation of cause and effect. When again it is asked, *What is the foundation of all our reasonings and conclusions concerning that relation?* it may be replied in one word, *experience*. But if we still carry on our sifting humor and ask, *What is the foundation of all conclusions from experience?* this implies a new question which may be of more difficult solution and explication. Philosophers that give themselves airs of superior wisdom and sufficiency have a hard task when they encounter persons of inquisitive dispositions, who push them from every corner to which they retreat, and who are sure at last to bring them to some dangerous dilemma. The best expedient to prevent this confusion is to be modest in our pretensions and even to discover the difficulty ourselves before it is objected to us. By this means we may make a kind of merit of our very ignorance.

I shall content myself in this section with an easy task and shall pretend only to give a negative answer to the question here proposed. I say, then, that even after we have experience of the operations of cause and effect, our conclusions from that experience are *not* founded on reasoning or any process of the understanding. This answer we must endeavor both to explain and to defend.

It must certainly be allowed that nature has kept us at a great distance from all her secrets and has afforded us only the knowledge of a few superficial qualities of objects, while she conceals from us those powers and principles on which the influence of these objects entirely depends. Our senses inform us of the color, weight, and consistency of bread, but neither sense nor reason can ever inform us of those qualities which fit it for the nourishment and support of the human body. Sight or feeling conveys an idea of the actual motion of bodies, but as to that wonderful force or power which would carry on a moving body forever in a continued change of place, and which bodies never lose but by communicating it to others, of this we cannot form the most distant conception. But notwithstanding this ignorance of natural powers [1] and principles, we always presume when we see like sensible qualities that they have like secret powers, and expect that effects similar to those which we have experienced will follow from them. If a body of like color and consistency with that bread which we have formerly eaten be presented to us, we make no scruple of repeating the experiment and foresee with certainty like nourishment and support. Now this is a process of the mind or thought of which I would willingly know the foundation. It is allowed on all hands that there is no known connection between the sensible qualities and the

[1] The word "power" is here used in a loose and popular sense. The more accurate explication of it would give additional evidence to this argument. See Section VII. [This note was added in Edition L.]

secret powers, and, consequently, that the mind is not led to form such a conclusion concerning their constant and regular conjunction by anything which it knows of their nature. As to past *experience,* it can be allowed to give *direct* and *certain* information of those precise objects only, and that precise period of time which fell under its cognizance: But why this experience should be extended to future times and to other objects which, for aught we know, may be only in appearance similar, this is the main question on which I would insist. The bread which I formerly ate nourished me; that is, a body of such sensible qualities was, at that time, endued with such secret powers. But does it follow that other bread must also nourish me at another time, and that like sensible qualities must always be attended with like secret powers? The consequence seems nowise necessary. At least, it must be acknowledged that there is here a consequence drawn by the mind that there is a certain step taken, a process of thought, and an inference which wants to be explained. These two propositions are far from being the same: *I have found that such an object has always been attended with such an effect,* and *I foresee that other objects which are in appearance similar will be attended with similar effects.* I shall allow, if you please, that the one proposition may justly be inferred from the other: I know, in fact, that it always is inferred. But if you insist that the inference is made by a chain of reasoning, I desire you to produce that reasoning. The connection between these propositions is not intuitive. There is required a medium which may enable the mind to draw such an inference, if indeed it be drawn by reasoning and argument. What that medium is I must confess passes my comprehension; and it is incumbent on those to produce it who assert that it really exists and is the original of all our conclusions concerning matter of fact.

This negative argument must certainly, in process of time, become altogether convincing if many penetrating and able philosophers shall turn their inquiries this way, and no one be ever able to discover any connecting proposition or intermediate step which supports the understanding in this conclusion. But as the question is yet new, every reader may not trust so far to his own penetration as to conclude, because an argument escapes his inquiry, that therefore it does not really exist. For this reason it may be requisite to venture upon a more difficult task, and, enumerating all the branches of human knowledge, endeavor to show that none of them can afford such an argument.

All reasonings may be divided into two kinds, namely, demonstrative reasoning, or that concerning relations of ideas, and moral [2] reasoning, or that concerning matter of fact and existence. That there are no demonstrative arguments in the case seems evident, since it implies no contradiction that the course of nature may change and that an object, seemingly like those which we have experienced, may be attended with different or contrary effects. May I not clearly and distinctly conceive that a body, falling from the clouds and which in all other respects resembles snow, has yet the taste of salt or feeling of fire? Is there any more intelligible proposition than to affirm that all the trees will flourish in December and January, and will decay in May and June? Now, whatever is intelligible and can be distinctly conceived implies no contradiction and can never be proved false by any demonstrative argument or abstract reasoning *a priori.*

If we be, therefore, engaged by arguments to put trust in past experience and make it the standard of our future judgment, these arguments must be probable only, or such as regard matter of fact and real existence, according to the division above mentioned. But that there is no argument of this kind must appear if our explication of that species of reasoning be admitted as solid and satisfactory. We have said that all arguments concerning existence are founded on the relation of cause and effect, that our knowledge of that relation is derived entirely from experience, and that all our experimental conclusions proceed upon the supposition that the future will be conformable to the past. To endeavor,

[2] [Editions K and L: "moral or probable."]

therefore, the proof of this last supposition by probable arguments, or arguments regarding existence, must be evidently going in a circle and taking that for granted which is the very point in question.

In reality, all arguments from experience are founded on the similarity which we discover among natural objects, and by which we are induced to expect effects similar to those which we have found to follow from such objects. And though none but a fool or madman will ever pretend to dispute the authority of experience or to reject that great guide of human life, it may surely be allowed a philosopher to have so much curiosity at least as to examine the principle of human nature which gives this mighty authority to experience and makes us draw advantage from that similarity which nature has placed among different objects. From causes which appear similar, we expect similar effects. This is the sum of all our experimental conclusions. Now it seems evident that, if this conclusion were formed by reason, it would be as perfect at first, and upon one instance, as after ever so long a course of experience; but the case is far otherwise. Nothing so like as eggs, yet no one, on account of this appearing similarity, expects the same taste and relish in all of them. It is only after a long course of uniform experiments in any kind that we attain a firm reliance and security with regard to a particular event. Now, where is that process of reasoning which, from one instance, draws a conclusion so different from that which it infers from a hundred instances that are nowise different from that single one? This question I propose as much for the sake of information as with an intention of raising difficulties. I cannot find, I cannot imagine any such reasoning. But I keep my mind still open to instruction if anyone will vouchsafe to bestow it on me.

Should it be said that, from a number of uniform experiments, we *infer* a connection between the sensible qualities and the secret powers, this, I must confess, seems the same difficulty, couched in different terms. The question still occurs, On what process of argument is this *inference* founded? Where is the medium, the interposing ideas which join propositions so very wide of each other? It is confessed that the color, consistency, and other sensible qualities of bread appear not of themselves to have any connection with the secret powers of nourishment and support; for otherwise we could infer these secret powers from the first appearance of these sensible qualities without the aid of experience, contrary to the sentiment of all philosophers, and contrary to plain matter of fact. Here, then, is our natural state of ignorance with regard to the powers and influence of all objects. How is this remedied by experience? It only shows us a number of uniform effects resulting from certain objects, and teaches us that those particular objects, at that particular time, were endowed with such powers and forces. When a new object endowed with similar sensible qualities is produced, we expect similar powers and forces, and look for a like effect. From a body of like color and consistency with bread, we expect like nourishment and support. But this surely is a step or progress of the mind which wants to be explained. When a man says, *I have found, in all past instances, such sensible qualities, conjoined with such secret powers,* and when he says, *similar sensible qualities will always be conjoined with similar secret powers,* he is not guilty of a tautology, nor are these propositions in any respect the same. You say that the one proposition is an inference from the other; but you must confess that the inference is not intuitive, neither is it demonstrative. Of what nature is it then? To say it is experimental is begging the question. For all inferences from experience suppose, as their foundation, that the future will resemble the past and that similar powers will be conjoined with similar sensible qualities. If there be any suspicion that the course of nature may change, and that the past may be no rule for the future, all experience becomes useless and can give rise to no inference or conclusion. It is impossible, therefore, that any arguments from experience can prove this resemblance of the past to the future, since all these arguments are founded on the supposition of that resemblance. Let the course of things be allowed hitherto ever so regular, that alone, without some new argument or inference, proves not that for the future it will continue so. In vain do you pretend to have learned the nature of bodies from your past experience. Their secret nature, and consequently all their effects and influence, may change without any change in their sensible qualities. This happens sometimes, and with regard to some objects. Why may it not happen always, and with regard to all objects? What logic, what process of argument secures you against this supposition? My practice, you say, refutes my doubts. But you mistake the purport of my question. As an agent, I am quite satisfied in the point; but as a philosopher who has some share of curiosity, I will not say skepticism, I want to learn the foundation of this inference. No reading, no inquiry has yet been able to remove my difficulty or give me satisfaction in a matter of such importance. Can I do better than propose the difficulty to the public, even though, perhaps, I have small hopes of obtaining a solution? We shall at least, by this means, be sensible of our ignorance, if we do not augment our knowledge.

I must confess that a man is guilty of unpardonable arrogance who concludes, because an argument has escaped his own investigation, that therefore it does not really exist. I must also confess that, though all the learned, for several ages, should have employed themselves in fruitless search upon any subject, it may still, perhaps, be rash to conclude positively that the subject must therefore pass all human comprehension. Even though we examine all the sources of our knowledge and conclude them unfit for such a subject, there may still remain a suspicion that the enumeration is not complete or the examination not accurate. But with regard to the present subject, there are some considerations which seem to remove all this accusation of arrogance or suspicion of mistake.

It is certain that the most ignorant and stupid peasants, nay infants, nay even brute beasts, improve by experience and learn the qualities of natural objects by observing the effects which result from them. When a child has felt the sensation of pain from touching the flame of a candle, he will be careful not to put his hand near any candle, but will expect a similar effect from a cause which is similar in its sensible qualities and appearance. If you assert, therefore, that the understanding of the child is led into this conclusion by any process of argument or ratiocination, I may justly require you to produce that argument, nor have you any pretense to refuse so equitable a demand. You cannot say that the argument is abstruse and may possibly escape your inquiry, since you confess that it is obvious to the capacity of a mere infant. If you hesitate, therefore, a moment or if, after reflection, you produce an intricate or profound argument, you, in a manner, give up the question and confess that it is not reasoning which engages us to suppose the past resembling the future, and to expect similar effects from causes which are to appearance similar. This is the proposition which I intended to enforce in the present section. If I be right, I pretend not to have made any mighty discovery. And if I be wrong, I must acknowledge myself to be indeed a very backward scholar, since I cannot now discover an argument which, it seems, was perfectly familiar to me long before I was out of my cradle.

SECTION V

SKEPTICAL SOLUTION OF THESE DOUBTS

PART I

THE PASSION FOR PHILOSOPHY, like that for religion, seems liable to this inconvenience, that though it aims at the correction of our manners and extirpation of our vices, it may only serve, by imprudent management, to foster a predominant inclination and push the mind with more determined resolution toward that side which already *draws* too much by the bias and propensity of the natural temper. It is certain that, while we aspire to the magnanimous firmness of the philosophic sage and endeavor to confine our pleasures altogether within our own minds, we may, at last, render our philosophy, like that of Epictetus and other Stoics, only a more refined system of selfishness, and reason ourselves out of all virtue as well as social enjoyment. While we study with attention the vanity of human life and turn all our thoughts toward the empty and transitory nature of riches and honors, we are, perhaps, all the while flattering our natural indolence which, hating the bustle of the world and drudgery of business, seeks a pretense of reason to give itself a full and uncontrolled indulgence. There is, however, one species of philosophy which seems little liable to this inconvenience, and that because it strikes in with no disorderly passion of the human mind, nor can mingle itself with any natural affection or propensity; and that is the Academic or Skeptical philosophy.[1] The Academics always talk of doubt and suspense of

1 [Academic philosophy or skepticism refers to the form of philosophy in the later Academy from the 4th century B.C. on. Hume distinguished it from Pyrrhonian skepticism which was extreme and, in his eyes, a kind of negative dogmatism. A passage from Cicero's *Of the Nature of the Gods* is typical of the academic philosophy: "Thus reasons Carneades (the academic skeptic) not with any design to destroy the existence of the gods—

judgment, of danger in hasty determinations, of confining to very narrow bounds the inquiries of the understanding, and of renouncing all speculations which lie not within the limits of common life and practice. Nothing, therefore, can be more contrary than such a philosophy to the supine indolence of the mind, its rash arrogance, its lofty pretensions, and its superstitious credulity. Every passion is mortified by it, except the love of truth; and that passion never is nor can be carried to too high a degree. It is surprising, therefore, that this philosophy, which in almost every instance must be harmless and innocent, should be the subject of so much groundless reproach and obloquy. But, perhaps, the very circumstance which renders it so innocent is what chiefly exposes it to the public hatred and resentment. By flattering no irregular passion, it gains few partisans. By opposing so many vices and follies, it raises to itself abundance of enemies who stigmatize it as libertine, profane, and irreligious.

Nor need we fear that this philosophy, while it endeavors to limit our inquiries to common life, should ever undermine the reasonings of common life and carry its doubts so far as to destroy all action as well as speculation. Nature will always maintain her rights and prevail in the end over any abstract reasoning whatsoever. Though we should conclude, for instance, as in the foregoing section, that in all reasonings from experience there is a step taken by the mind which is not supported by any argument or process of the understanding, there is no danger that these reasonings, on which almost all knowledge depends, will ever be affected by such a discovery. If the mind be not engaged by argument to make this

---

for what would less become a philosopher?—but to convince us that, on that matter, the Stoics have said nothing plausible" (XVII). And though all rational arguments are shown defective and inconclusive, nevertheless man must in practical life decide and take a position. Cicero's philosophical writings were thoroughly imbued with this teaching and they figured considerably in the education of most of the modern philosophers, and notably of Locke, Berkeley, and Hume. Pragmatism derives in part from this "academic" tradition in modern empiricism.—Ed.]

step, it must be induced by some other principle of equal weight and authority; and that principle will preserve its influence as long as human nature remains the same. What that principle is may well be worth the pains of inquiry.

Suppose a person, though endowed with the strongest faculties of reason and reflection, to be brought on a sudden into this world; he would, indeed, immediately observe a continual succession of objects and one event following another, but he would not be able to discover anything further. He would not at first, by any reasoning, be able to reach the idea of cause and effect, since the particular powers by which all natural operations are performed never appear to the senses; nor is it reasonable to conclude, merely because one event in one instance precedes another, that therefore the one is the cause, the other the effect. The conjunction may be arbitrary and casual. There may be no reason to infer the existence of one from the appearance of the other: and, in a word, such a person without more experience could never employ his conjecture or reasoning concerning any matter of fact or be assured of anything beyond what was immediately present to his memory or senses.

Suppose again that he has acquired more experience and has lived so long in the world as to have observed similar objects or events to be constantly conjoined together—what is the consequence of this experience? He immediately infers the existence of one object from the appearance of the other, yet he has not, by all his experience, acquired any idea or knowledge of the secret power by which the one object produces the other, nor is it by any process of reasoning he is engaged to draw this inference; but still he finds himself determined to draw it, and though he should be convinced that his understanding has no part in the operation, he would nevertheless continue in the same course of thinking. There is some other principle which determines him to form such a conclusion.

This principle is *custom* or *habit*. For wherever the repetition of any particular act or operation produces a propensity to renew the same act or operation without being impelled by any reasoning or process of the understanding, we always say that this propensity is the effect of *custom*. By employing that word we pretend not to have given the ultimate reason of such a propensity. We only point out a principle of human nature which is universally acknowledged, and which is well known by its effects. Perhaps we can push our inquiries no further or pretend to give the cause of this cause, but must rest contented with it as the ultimate principle which we can assign of all our conclusions from experience. It is sufficient satisfaction that we can go so far without repining at the narrowness of our faculties, because they will carry us no further. And it is certain we here advance a very intelligible proposition at least, if not a true one, when we assert that after the constant conjunction of two objects, heat and flame, for instance, weight and solidity, we are determined by custom alone to expect the one from the appearance of the other. This hypothesis seems even the only one which explains the difficulty why we draw from a thousand instances an inference which we are not able to draw from one instance that is in no respect different from them. Reason is incapable of any such variation. The conclusions which it draws from considering one circle are the same which it would form upon surveying all the circles in the universe. But no man, having seen only one body move after being impelled by another, could infer that every other body will move after a like impulse. All inferences from experience, therefore, are effects of custom, not of reasoning.[2]

---

[2] Nothing is more usual than for writers, even on *moral, political,* or *physical* subjects, to distinguish between *reason* and *experience,* and to suppose that these species of argumentation are entirely different from each other. The former are taken for the mere result of our intellectual faculties, which, by considering *a priori* the nature of things, and examining the effects that must follow from their operation, establish particular principles of science and philosophy. The latter are supposed to be derived entirely from sense and observation, by which we learn what has actually resulted from the operation of particular objects, and are thence able to infer what will for the future result from them. Thus, for instance, the limitations and restraints of civil government and a

Custom, then, is the great guide of human life. It is that principle alone which renders our experience useful to us and makes us expect, for the future, a similar train of events with those which have appeared in the past. Without the influence of custom we should be entirely ignorant of every

---

legal constitution may be defended, either from *reason,* which, reflecting on the great frailty and corruption of human nature, teaches that no man can safely be trusted with unlimited authority; or from *experience* and history, which inform us of the enormous abuses that ambition in every age and country has been found to make of so imprudent a confidence.

The same distinction between reason and experience is maintained in all our deliberations concerning the conduct of life, while the experienced statesman, general physician, or merchant, is trusted and followed, and the unpracticed novice, with whatever natural talents endowed, neglected and despised. Though it be allowed that reason may form very plausible conjectures with regard to the consequences of such a particular conduct in such particular circumstances, it is still supposed imperfect without the assistance of experience, which is alone able to give stability and certainty to the maxim derived from study and reflection.

But notwithstanding that this distinction be thus universally received, both in the active and speculative scenes of life, I shall not scruple to pronounce that it is, at bottom, erroneous, or at least superficial.

If we examine those arguments which, in any of the sciences above mentioned, are supposed to be the mere effects of reasoning and reflection, they will be found to terminate at last in some general principle or conclusion for which we can assign no reason but observation and experience. The only difference between them and those maxims which are vulgarly esteemed the result of pure experience is that the former cannot be established without some process of thought, and some reflection on what we have observed, in order to distinguish its circumstances and trace its consequences—whereas, in the latter, the experienced event is exactly and fully similar to that which we infer as the result of any particular situation. The history of a Tiberius or a Nero makes us dread a like tyranny, were our monarchs freed from the restraints of laws and senates: but the observation of any fraud or cruelty in private life is sufficient, with the aid of a little thought, to give us the same apprehension, while it serves as an instance of the general corruption of human nature, and shows us the danger which we must incur by reposing an entire confidence in mankind. In both cases, it is experience which is ultimately the foundation of our inference and conclusion.

There is no man so young and inexperienced as not to have formed matter of fact beyond what is immediately present to the memory and senses. We should never know how to adjust means to ends or to employ our natural powers in the production of any effect. There would be an end at once of all action as well as of the chief part of speculation.

But here it may be proper to remark that though our conclusions from experience carry us beyond our memory and senses and assure us of matters of fact which happened in the most distant places and most remote ages, yet some fact must always be present to the senses or memory from which we may first proceed in drawing these conclusions. A man who should find in a desert country the remains of pompous buildings would conclude that the country had, in ancient times, been cultivated by civilized inhabitants; but did nothing of this nature occur to him, he could never form such an inference. We learn the events of former ages from history, but then we must peruse the volume in which this instruction is contained, and thence carry up our inferences from one testimony to another, till we arrive at the eyewitnesses and spectators of these distant events. In a word, if we proceed not upon some fact present to the memory or senses, our reasonings would be merely hypothetical; and however the particular links might be connected with each other, the whole chain of inferences would have nothing to support it, nor could we

---

from observation many general and just maxims concerning human affairs and the conduct of life; but it must be confessed that when a man comes to put these in practice he will be extremely liable to error, till time and further experience both enlarge these maxims, and teach him their proper use and application. In every situation or incident there are many particular and seemingly minute circumstances which the man of greatest talents is at first apt to overlook, though on them the justness of his conclusions, and consequently the prudence of his conduct, entirely depend. Not to mention that, to a young beginner, the general observations and maxims occur not always on the proper occasions, nor can be immediately applied with due calmness and distinction. The truth is, an inexperienced reasoner could be no reasoner at all were he absolutely inexperienced; and when we assign that character to anyone, we mean it only in a comparative sense, and suppose him possessed of experience in a smaller and more imperfect degree.

ever, by its means, arrive at the knowledge of any real existence. If I ask why you believe any particular matter of fact
which you relate, you must tell me some reason; and this reason will be some other fact connected with it. But as you cannot proceed after this manner *in infinitum,* you must at last
terminate in some fact which is present to your memory or
senses or must allow that your belief is entirely without
foundation.

What, then, is the conclusion of the whole matter? A simple
one, though, it must be confessed, pretty remote from the
common theories of philosophy. All belief of matter of fact or
real existence is derived merely from some object present to
the memory or senses and a customary conjunction between
that and some other object; or, in other words, having found,
in many instances, that any two kinds of objects, flame and
heat, snow and cold, have always been conjoined together: if
flame or snow be presented anew to the senses, the mind is
carried by custom to expect heat or cold, and to *believe* that
such a quality does exist and will discover itself upon a
nearer approach. This belief is the necessary result of placing
the mind in such circumstances. It is an operation of the soul,
when we are so situated, as unavoidable as to feel the passion
of love, when we receive benefits; or hatred, when we meet
with injuries. All these operations are a species of natural instincts, which no reasoning or process of the thought and understanding is able either to produce or to prevent. At this
point it would be very allowable for us to stop our philosophical researches. In most questions we can never make a
single step further; and in all questions we must terminate
here at last, after our most restless and curious inquiries. But
still our curiosity will be pardonable. perhaps commendable,
if it carry us on to still further researches and make us examine more accurately the nature of this *belief* and of the *customary conjunction* whence it is derived. By this means we
may meet with some explications and analogies that will give
satisfaction, at least to such as love the abstract sciences, and
can be entertained with speculations which, however accurate,

may still retain a degree of doubt and uncertainty. As to readers of a different taste, the remaining part of this Section is not calculated for them; and the following inquiries may well be understood, though it be neglected.

PART II

Nothing is more free than the imagination of man, and though it cannot exceed that original stock of ideas furnished by the internal and external senses, it has unlimited power of mixing, compounding, separating, and dividing these ideas in all the varieties of fiction and vision. It can feign a train of events with all the appearance of reality, ascribe to them a particular time and place, conceive them as existent, and paint them out to itself with every circumstance that belongs to any historical fact which it believes with the greatest certainty. Wherein, therefore, consists the difference between such a fiction and belief? It lies not merely in any peculiar idea which is annexed to such a conception as commands our assent, and which is wanting to every known fiction. For as the mind has authority over all its ideas, it could voluntarily annex this particular idea to any fiction, and consequently be able to believe whatever it pleases, contrary to what we find by daily experience. We can, in our conception, join the head of a man to the body of a horse, but it is not in our power to believe that such an animal has ever really existed.

It follows, therefore, that the difference between *fiction* and *belief* lies in some sentiment or feeling which is annexed to the latter, not to the former, and which depends not on the will, nor can be demanded at pleasure. It must be excited by nature like all other sentiments and must rise from the particular situation in which the mind is placed at any particular juncture. Whenever any object is presented to the memory or senses, it immediately, by the force of custom, carries the imagination to conceive that object which is usually conjoined to it; and this conception is attended with a feeling or sentiment different from the loose reveries of the fancy. In this consists the whole nature of belief. For as there is no matter of fact which we believe so firmly that we cannot conceive the contrary, there would be no difference between the conception assented to and that which is rejected were it not for some sentiment which distinguishes the one from the other. If I see a billiard ball moving toward another on a smooth table, I can easily conceive it to stop upon contact. This conception implies no contradiction, but still it feels very differently from that conception by which I represent to myself the impulse and the communication of motion from one ball to another.

Were we to attempt a *definition* of this sentiment, we should, perhaps, find it a very difficult, if not an impossible, task; in the same manner as if we should endeavor to define the feeling of cold, or passion of anger, to a creature who never had any experience of these sentiments. Belief is the true and proper name of this feeling, and no one is ever at a loss to know the meaning of that term, because every man is every moment conscious of the sentiment represented by it. It may not, however, be improper to attempt a *description* of this sentiment, in hopes we may by that means arrive at some analogies which may afford a more perfect explication of it. I say that belief is nothing but a more vivid, lively, forcible, firm, steady conception of an object than what the imagination alone is ever able to attain. This variety of terms, which may seem so unphilosophical, is intended only to express that act of the mind which renders realities, or what is taken for such, more present to us than fictions, causes them to weigh more in the thought, and gives them a superior influence on the passions and imagination. Provided we agree about the thing, it is needless to dispute about the terms. The imagination has the command over all its ideas and can join and mix and vary them in all the ways possible. It may conceive fictitious objects with all the circumstances of place and time. It may set them in a manner before our eyes, in their true colors, just as they might have existed. But as it is impossible that this faculty of imagination can ever, of itself, reach belief, it is evident that belief consists not in the peculiar nature or order of ideas, but in the *manner* of their conception and in their *feeling* to the mind. I confess that it is impossible perfectly to explain this feeling or manner of conception. We may make use of words which express something near it. But its true and proper name, as we observed before, is "belief," which is a term that everyone sufficiently understands in common life. And in philosophy we can go no further than assert that *belief* is something felt by the mind, which distinguishes the ideas of the judgment from the fictions of the imagination. It gives them more weight and influence, makes them appear of greater importance, enforces them in the mind, and renders them the governing principle of our actions. I hear at present, for instance, a person's voice with whom I am acquainted, and the sound comes as from the next room. This impression of my senses immediately conveys my thought to the person, together with all the surrounding objects. I paint them out to myself as existing at present, with the same qualities and relations of which I formerly knew them possessed. These ideas take faster hold of my mind than ideas of an enchanted castle. They are very different from the feeling and have a much greater influence of every kind, either to give pleasure or pain, joy or sorrow.

Let us, then, take in the whole compass of this doctrine and allow that the sentiment of belief is nothing but a conception more intense and steady than what attends the mere fictions of the imagination, and that this *manner* of conception arises from a customary conjunction of the object with something present to the memory or senses. I believe that it will not be difficult, upon these suppositions, to find other operations of the mind analogous to it and to trace up these phenomena to principles still more general.

We have already observed that nature has established connections among particular ideas, and that no sooner one idea occurs to our thoughts than it introduces its correlative and carries our attention toward it by a gentle and insensible movement. These principles of connection or association we have reduced to three, namely, "resemblance," "contiguity," and "causation," which are the only bonds that unite our thoughts together and beget that regular train of reflection or discourse which, in a greater or less degree, takes place among all mankind. Now here arises a question on which the solution of the present difficulty will depend. Does it happen in all these relations that when one of the objects is presented to the senses or memory, the mind is not only carried to the conception of the correlative, but reaches a steadier and stronger conception of it than what otherwise it would have been able to attain? This seems to be the case with that belief which arises from the relation of cause and effect. And if the case be the same with the other relations or principles of association, this may be established as a general law which takes place in all the operations of the mind.

We may, therefore, observe, as the first experiment to our present purpose, that upon the appearance of the picture of an absent friend our idea of him is evidently enlivened by the *resemblance*, and that every passion which that idea occasions, whether of joy or sorrow, acquires new force and vigor. In producing this effect there concur both a relation and a present impression. Where the picture bears him no resemblance, at least was not intended for him, it never so much as conveys our thought to him. And where it is absent, as well as the person, though the mind may pass from the thought of one to that of the other, it feels its idea to be rather weakened than enlivened by that transition. We take a pleasure in viewing the picture of a friend when it is set before us; but when it is removed, rather choose to consider him directly than by reflection on an image which is equally distant and obscure.

The ceremonies of the Roman Catholic religion may be considered as instances of the same nature. The devotees of that superstition usually plead, in excuse for the mummeries with which they are upbraided, that they feel the good effect of those external motions, and postures, and actions in enlivening their devotion and quickening their fervor, which otherwise would decay if directed entirely to distant and immaterial objects. We shadow out the objects of our faith, say they, in sensible types and images, and render them more present to us by the immediate presence of these types than it is possible for us to do merely by an intellectual view and contemplation. Sensible objects have always a greater influence on the fancy than any other, and this influence they readily convey to those ideas to which they are related and which they resemble. I shall only infer from these practices and this reasoning that the effect of resemblance in enlivening the ideas is very common; and as in every case a resemblance and a present impression must concur, we are abundantly supplied with experiments to prove the reality of the foregoing principle.

We may add force to these experiments by others of a different kind, in considering the effects of *contiguity* as well as of *resemblance*. It is certain that distance diminishes the force of every idea and that, upon our approach to any object, though it does not discover itself to our senses, it operates upon the mind with an influence which imitates an immediate impression. The thinking on any object readily transports the mind to what is contiguous; but it is only the actual presence of an object that transports it with a superior vivacity. When I am a few miles from home, whatever relates to it touches me more nearly than when I am two hundred leagues distant, though even at that distance the reflecting on anything in the neighborhood of my friends or family naturally produces an idea of them. But, as in this latter case, both the objects of the mind are ideas, notwithstanding there is an easy transition between them; that transition alone is not able to give a superior vivacity to any of the ideas, for want of some immediate impression.[1]

---

[1] "Naturane nobis, inquit, datum dicam, an errore quodam, ut, cum ea loca videamus, in quibus memoria dignos viros acceperimus multum esse versatos, magis moveamur, quam siquando eorum ipsorum aut facta audiamus aut scriptum aliquod legamus? Velut ego nunc moveor. Venit enim mihi Platonis in mentem, quem accepimus primum hic disputare solitum: Cujus etiam illi hortuli propinqui non memoriam solum mihi afferunt, sed ipsum videntur in conspectu meo hic ponere. Hic Speusippus,

No one can doubt but *causation* has the same influence as the other two relations of resemblance and contiguity. Superstitious people are fond of the relics of saints and holy men, for the same reason that they seek after types or images in order to enliven their devotion and give them a more intimate and strong conception of those exemplary lives which they desire to imitate. Now it is evident that one of the best relics which a devotee could procure would be the handiwork of a saint; and if his clothes and furniture are ever to be considered in this light, it is because they were once at his disposal and were moved and affected by him; in which respect they are to be considered as imperfect effects, and as connected with him by a shorter chain of consequences than any of those by which we learn the reality of his existence.

Suppose that the son of a friend who had been long dead or absent were presented to us; it is evident that this object would instantly revive its correlative idea and recall to our thoughts all past intimacies and familiarities in more lively

----

hic Xenocrates, hic ejus auditor Polemo; cujus ipsa illa sessio fuit, quam vidamus. Equidem etiam curiam nostram Hostiliam dico, non hanc novam, quae mihi minor esse videtur postquam est major, solebam intuens, Scipionem, Catonem, Lælium, nostrum vero in primis avum cogitare. Tanta vis admonitionis est in locis: ut non sine causa ex his memoriæ deducta sit disciplina." *Cicero de Finibus* v. 2. ["Should I say," he replied, "that it is nature or that it is some error that causes us to be more intensely moved when we see places where, as we have been told, men who deserve to be remembered spent a lot of time, than we are if, at some time or other, we hear about the things which they have done, or read something written by them? I, for example, feel moved at present. For Plato comes to my mind who, we have learned, was the first man to conduct regular discussions here: those very gardens close by not only evoke the memory of him in me, but seem to place him personally here for me to see. Speusippus is here, Xenocrates is here, and so is his disciple Polemo: it is the place where he used to sit that we see before us. Indeed, also when I looked at our senate house—I mean the one Hostilius built and not the new building which strikes me as lesser after it has been enlarged—I used to think of Scipio, Cato, and Laelius, but above all of my grandfather. So great a power of evoking recollections do places have: it is, therefore, not without good reason that the training of memory has been derived from them."—Ed.]

color than they would otherwise have appeared to us. This is another phenomenon which seems to prove the principle above mentioned.

We may observe that in these phenomena the belief of the correlative object is always presupposed, without which the relation could have no effect. The influence of the picture supposes that we *believe* our friend to have once existed. Contiguity to home can never excite our ideas of home unless we *believe* that it really exists. Now I assert that this belief, where it reaches beyond the memory or senses, is of a similar nature and arises from similar causes with the transition of thought and vivacity of conception here explained. When I throw a piece of dry wood into a fire, my mind is immediately carried to conceive that it augments, not extinguishes, the flame. This transition of thought from the cause to the effect proceeds not from reason. It derives its origin altogether from custom and experience. And, as it first begins from an object present to the senses, it renders the idea or conception of flame more strong or lively than any loose floating reverie of the imagination. That idea arises immediately. The thought moves instantly toward it and conveys to it all that force of conception which is derived from the impression present to the senses. When a sword is leveled at my breast, does not the idea of wound and pain strike me more strongly than when a glass of wine is presented to me, even though by accident this idea should occur after the appearance of the latter object? But what is there in this whole matter to cause such a strong conception except only a present object and a customary transition to the idea of another object which we have been accustomed to conjoin with the former? This is the whole operation of the mind in all our conclusions concerning matter of fact and existence; and it is a satisfaction to find some analogies by which it may be explained. The transition from a present object does in all cases give strength and solidity to the related idea.

Here, then, is a kind of pre-established harmony between the course of nature and the succession of our ideas; and though the powers and forces by which the former is governed be wholly unknown to us, yet our thoughts and conceptions have still, we find, gone on in the same train with the other works of nature. Custom is that principle by which this correspondence has been effected, so necessary to the subsistence of our species and the regulation of our conduct in every circumstance and occurrence of human life. Had not the presence of an object instantly excited the idea of those objects commonly conjoined with it, all our knowledge must have been limited to the narrow sphere of our memory and senses, and we should never have been able to adjust means to ends or employ our natural powers either to the producing of good or avoiding of evil. Those who delight in the discovery and contemplation of *final causes* have here ample subject to employ their wonder and admiration.

I shall add, for a further confirmation of the foregoing theory, that as this operation of the mind, by which we infer like effects from like causes, and *vice versa,* is so essential to the subsistence of all human creatures, it is not probable that it could be trusted to the fallacious deductions of our reason, which is slow in its operations, appears not, in any degree, during the first years of infancy, and, at best, is in every age and period of human life extremely liable to error and mistake. It is more conformable to the ordinary wisdom of nature to secure so necessary an act of the mind by some instinct or mechanical tendency which may be infallible in its operations, may discover itself at the first appearance of life and thought, and may be independent of all the labored deductions of the understanding. As nature has taught us the use of our limbs without giving us the knowledge of the muscles and nerves by which they are actuated, so has she implanted in us an instinct which carries forward the thought in a correspondent course to that which she has established among external objects, though we are ignorant of those powers and forces on which this regular course and succession of objects totally depends.

SECTION VI

OF PROBABILITY [1]

THOUGH THERE BE no such thing as *chance* in the world, our ignorance of the real cause of any event has the same influence on the understanding and begets a like species of belief or opinion.

There is certainly a probability which arises from a superiority of chances on any side; and, according as this superiority increases and surpasses the opposite chances, the probability receives a proportionable increase and begets still a higher degree of belief or assent to that side in which we discover the superiority. If a die were marked with one figure or number of spots on four sides, and with another figure or number of spots on the two remaining sides, it would be more probable that the former would turn up than the latter, though, if it had a thousand sides marked in the same manner, and only one side different, the probability would be much higher and our belief or expectation of the event more steady and secure. This process of the thought or reasoning may seem trivial and obvious; but to those who consider it more narrowly it may, perhaps, afford matter for curious speculation.

It seems evident that when the mind looks forward to discover the event which may result from the throw of such a die, it considers the turning up of each particular side as alike probable; and this is the very nature of chance, to render all the particular events comprehended in it entirely equal. But

[1] Mr. Locke divides all arguments into "demonstrative" and "probable." In this view, we must say that it is only probable all men must die, or that the sun will rise tomorrow. But to conform our language more to common use, we ought to divide arguments into *demonstrations*, *proofs*, and *probabilities;* by proofs, meaning such arguments from experience as leave no room for doubt or opposition.

finding a greater number of sides concur in the one event than in the other, the mind is carried more frequently to that event and meets it oftener in revolving the various possibilities or chances on which the ultimate result depends. This concurrence of several views in one particular event begets immediately, by an explicable contrivance of nature, the sentiment of belief and gives that event the advantage over its antagonist which is supported by a smaller number of views and recurs less frequently to the mind. If we allow that belief is nothing but a firmer and stronger conception of an object than what attends the mere fictions of the imagination, this operation may, perhaps, in some measure be accounted for. The concurrence of these several views or glimpses imprints the idea more strongly on the imagination, gives it superior force and vigor, renders its influence on the passions and affections more sensible, and, in a word, begets that reliance or security which constitutes the nature of belief and opinion.

The case is the same with the probability of causes as with that of chance. There are some cases which are entirely uniform and constant in producing a particular effect, and no instance has ever yet been found of any failure or irregularity in their operation. Fire has always burned, and water suffocated, every human creature. The production of motion by impulse and gravity is a universal law which has hitherto admitted of no exception. But there are other causes which have been found more irregular and uncertain, nor has rhubarb always proved a purge, or opium a soporific, to everyone who has taken these medicines. It is true, when any cause fails of producing its usual effect, philosophers ascribe not this to any irregularity in nature, but suppose that some secret causes in the particular structure of parts have prevented the operation. Our reasonings, however, and conclusions concerning the event are the same as if this principle had no place. Being determined by custom to transfer the past to the future in all our inferences, where the past has been entirely regular and uniform we expect the event with the greatest assurance and leave no room for any contrary supposition. But where different effects have been found to follow from causes which are to *appearance* exactly similar, all these various effects must occur to the mind in transferring the past to the future, and enter into our consideration when we determine the probability of the event. Though we give the preference to that which has been found most usual, and believe that this effect will exist, we must not overlook the other effects, but must assign to each of them a particular weight and authority in proportion as we have found it to be more or less frequent. It is more probable, in almost every country of Europe, that there will be frost sometime in January than that the weather will continue open throughout that whole month, though this probability varies according to the different climates, and approaches to a certainty in the more northern kingdoms. Here, then, it seems evident that when we transfer the past to the future in order to determine the effect which will result from any cause, we transfer all the different events in the same proportion as they have appeared in the past, and conceive one to have existed a hundred times, for instance, another ten times, and another once. As a great number of views do here concur in one event, they fortify and confirm it to the imagination, beget that sentiment which we call "belief," and give its object the preference above the contrary event which is not supported by an equal number of experiments and recurs not so frequently to the thought in transferring the past to the future. Let anyone try to account for this operation of the mind upon any of the received systems of philosophy, and he will be sensible of the difficulty. For my part, I shall think it sufficient if the present hints excite the curiosity of philosophers and make them sensible how defective all common theories are in treating of such curious and such sublime subjects.

SECTION VII

OF THE IDEA OF NECESSARY CONNECTION [1]

PART I

THE GREAT ADVANTAGE of the mathematical sciences above the moral consists in this, that the ideas of the former, being sensible, are always clear and determinate, the smallest distinction between them is immediately perceptible, and the same terms are still expressive of the same ideas without ambiguity or variation. An oval is never mistaken for a circle, nor a hyperbola for an ellipsis. The isosceles and scalenum are distinguished by boundaries more exact than vice and virtue, right and wrong. If any term be defined in geometry, the mind readily, of itself, substitutes on all occasions the definition for the term defined, or, even when no definition is employed, the object itself may be presented to the senses and by that means be steadily and clearly apprehended. But the finer sentiments of the mind, the operations of the understanding, the various agitations of the passions, though really in themselves distinct, easily escape us when surveyed by reflection, nor is it in our power to recall the original object as often as we have occasion to contemplate it. Ambiguity, by this means, is gradually introduced into our reasonings: similar objects are readily taken to be the same, and the conclusion becomes at last very wide of the premises.

One may safely, however, affirm that if we consider these sciences in a proper light, their advantages and disadvantages nearly compensate each other and reduce both of them to a state of equality. If the mind, with greater facility, retains the ideas of geometry clear and determinate, it must carry on a much longer and more intricate chain of reasoning and com-

1 [Entitled in Editions K and L: "Of the Idea of Power, or Necessary Connexion."]

pare ideas much wider of each other in order to reach the abstruser truths of that science. And if moral ideas are apt, without extreme care, to fall into obscurity and confusion, the inferences are always much shorter in these disquisitions, and the intermediate steps which lead to the conclusion much fewer than in the sciences which treat of quantity and number. In reality, there is scarcely a proposition in Euclid so simple as not to consist of more parts than are to be found in any moral reasoning which runs not into chimera and conceit. Where we trace the principles of the human mind through a few steps, we may be very well satisfied with our progress, considering how soon nature throws a bar to all our inquiries concerning causes and reduces us to an acknowledgment of our ignorance. The chief obstacle, therefore, to our improvement in the moral or metaphysical sciences is the obscurity of the ideas and ambiguity of the terms. The principal difficulty in the mathematics is the length of inferences and compass of thought requisite to the forming of any conclusion. And, perhaps, our progress in natural philosophy is chiefly retarded by the want of proper experiments and phenomena, which are often discovered by chance and cannot always be found when requisite, even by the most diligent and prudent inquiry. As moral philosophy seems hitherto to have received less improvement than either geometry or physics, we may conclude that if there be any difference in this respect among these sciences, the difficulties which obstruct the progress of the former require superior care and capacity to be surmounted.

There are no ideas which occur in metaphysics more obscure and uncertain than those of "power," "force," "energy," or "necessary connection," of which it is every moment necessary for us to treat in all our disquisitions. We shall, therefore, endeavor in this Section to fix, if possible, the precise meaning of these terms and thereby remove some part of that obscurity which is so much complained of in this species of philosophy.

It seems a proposition which will not admit of much dispute that all our ideas are nothing but copies of our impressions, or, in other words, that it is impossible for us to *think* of anything which we have not antecedently *felt,* either by our external or internal senses. I have endeavored [2] to explain and prove this proposition, and have expressed my hopes that by a proper application of it men may reach a greater clearness and precision in philosophical reasonings than what they have hitherto been able to attain. Complex ideas may, perhaps, be well known by definition, which is nothing but an enumeration of those parts or simple ideas that compose them. But when we have pushed up definitions to the most simple ideas and find still some ambiguity and obscurity, what resources are we then possessed of? By what invention can we throw light upon these ideas and render them altogether precise and determinate to our intellectual view? Produce the impressions or original sentiments from which the ideas are copied. These impressions are all strong and sensible. They admit not of ambiguity. They are not only placed in a full light themselves, but may throw light on their correspondent ideas, which lie in obscurity. And by this means we may perhaps obtain a new microscope or species of optics by which, in the moral sciences, the most minute and most simple ideas may be so enlarged as to fall readily under our apprehension and be equally known with the grossest and most sensible ideas that can be the object of our inquiry.

To be fully acquainted, therefore, with the idea of power or necessary connection, let us examine its impression and, in order to find the impression with greater certainty, let us search for it in all the sources from which it may possibly be derived.

When we look about us toward external objects and consider the operation of causes, we are never able, in a single instance, to discover any power or necessary connection, any quality which binds the effect to the cause and renders the one an infallible consequence of the other. We only find that the one does actually in fact follow the other. The impulse of

2 Section II.

one billiard ball is attended with motion in the second. This is the whole that appears to the *outward* senses. The mind feels no sentiment or *inward* impression from this succession of objects; consequently, there is not, in any single particular instance of cause and effect, anything which can suggest the idea of power or necessary connection.

From the first appearance of an object we never can conjecture what effect will result from it. But were the power or energy of any cause discoverable by the mind, we could foresee the effect, even without experience, and might, at first, pronounce with certainty concerning it by the mere dint of thought and reasoning.

In reality, there is no part of matter that does ever, by its sensible qualities, discover any power or energy, or give us ground to imagine that it could produce anything, or be followed by any other object, which we could denominate its effect. Solidity, extension, motion—these qualities are all complete in themselves and never point out any other event which may result from them. The scenes of the universe are continually shifting, and one object follows another in an uninterrupted succession; but the power or force which actuates the whole machine is entirely concealed from us and never discovers itself in any of the sensible qualities of body. We know that, in fact, heat is a constant attendant of flame; but what is the connection between them we have no room so much as to conjecture or imagine. It is impossible, therefore, that the idea of power can be derived from the contemplation of bodies in single instances of their operation, because no bodies ever discover any power which can be the original of this idea.[3]

Since, therefore, external objects as they appear to the senses give us no idea of power or necessary connection by

[3] Mr. Locke, in his chapter of Power, says that, finding from experience that there are several new productions in matter, and concluding that there must somewhere be a power capable of producing them, we arrive at last by this reasoning at the idea of power. But no reasoning can ever give us a new, original, simple idea, as this philosopher himself confesses. This, therefore, can never be the origin of that idea.

their operation in particular instances, let us see whether this idea be derived from reflection on the operations of our own minds and be copied from any internal impression. It may be said that we are every moment conscious of internal power while we feel that, by the simple command of our will, we can move the organs of our body or direct the faculties of our mind. An act of volition produces motion in our limbs or raises a new idea in our imagination. This influence of the will we know by consciousness. Hence we acquire the idea of power or energy, and are certain that we ourselves and all other intelligent beings are possessed of power.[4] This idea, then, is an idea of reflection since it arises from reflecting on the operations of our own mind and on the command which is exercised by will both over the organs of the body and faculties of the soul.[5]

We shall proceed to examine this pretension [6] and, first, with regard to the influence of volition over the organs of the body. This influence, we may observe, is a fact which, like all other natural events, can be known only by experience, and can never be foreseen from any apparent energy or power in the cause which connects it with the effect and renders the one an infallible consequence of the other. The motion of our body follows upon the command of our will. Of this we are every moment conscious. But the means by which this is effected, the energy by which the will performs so extraordinary an operation—of this we are so far from being immediately conscious that it must forever escape our most diligent inquiry.

For, *first,* is there any principle in all nature more mysterious than the union of soul with body, by which a supposed

---

4 [Editions K and L add: "The operations and mutual influence of bodies are perhaps sufficient to prove that they also are possessed of it."]

5 [Editions K to N: "of the mind."]

6 [Editions K and L read: "We shall proceed to examine this pretension, and shall endeavor to avoid, as far as we are able, all jargon and confusion in treating of such subtile and such profound subjects.

"I assert then, in the first place, that the influence of volition over the organs of the body is a fact, etc."]

spiritual substance acquires such an influence over a material one that the most refined thought is able to actuate the grossest matter? Were we empowered by a secret wish to remove mountains or control the planets in their orbit, this extensive authority would not be more extraordinary, nor more beyond our comprehension. But if, by consciousness, we perceived any power or energy in the will, we must know this power; we must know its connection with the effect; we must know the secret union of soul and body, and the nature of both these substances by which the one is able to operate in so many instances upon the other.

Secondly, we are not able to move all the organs of the body with a like authority, though we cannot assign any reason, besides experience, for so remarkable a difference between one and the other. Why has the will an influence over the tongue and fingers, not over the heart or liver? This question would never embarrass us were we conscious of a power in the former case, not in the latter. We should then perceive, independent of experience, why the authority of the will over the organs of the body is circumscribed within such particular limits. Being in that case fully acquainted with the power or force by which it operates, we should also know why its influence reaches precisely to such boundaries, and no further.

A man suddenly struck with a palsy in the leg or arm, or who had newly lost those members, frequently endeavors, at first, to move them and employ them in their usual offices. Here he is as much conscious of power to command such limbs as a man in perfect health is conscious of power to actuate any member which remains in its natural state and condition. But consciousness never deceives. Consequently, neither in the one case nor in the other are we ever conscious of any power. We learn the influence of our will from experience alone. And experience only teaches us how one event constantly follows another, without instructing us in the secret connection which binds them together and renders them inseparable.

Thirdly, we learn from anatomy that the immediate object of power in voluntary motion is not the member itself which is moved, but certain muscles and nerves and animal spirits, and, perhaps, something still more minute and more unknown, through which the motion is successively propagated ere it reach the member itself whose motion is the immediate object of volition. Can there be a more certain proof that the power by which this whole operation is performed, so far from being directly and fully known by an inward sentiment or consciousness, is to the last degree mysterious and unintelligible? Here the mind wills a certain event; immediately another event, unknown to ourselves and totally different from the one intended, is produced. This event produces another, equally unknown, till, at last, through a long succession the desired event is produced. But if the original power were felt, it must be known; were it known, its effect must also be known, since all power is relative to its effect. And, *vice versa,* if the effect be not known, the power cannot be known nor felt. How indeed can we be conscious of a power to move our limbs when we have no such power, but only that to move certain animal spirits which, though they produce at last the motion of our limbs, yet operate in such a manner as is wholly beyond our comprehension?

We may therefore conclude from the whole, I hope, without any temerity, though with assurance, that our idea of power is not copied from any sentiment or consciousness of power within ourselves when we give rise to animal motion or apply our limbs to their proper use and office. That their motion follows the command of the will is a matter of common experience, like other natural events; but the power or energy by which this is effected, like that in other natural events, is unknown and inconceivable.[7]

---

[7] It may be pretended, that the resistance which we meet with in bodies, obliging us frequently to exert our force and call up all our power, this gives us the idea of force and power. It is this *nisus* or strong endeavor of which we are conscious, that is the original impression from which this idea is copied. But, *first,* we attribute power to a vast number of objects where we never can suppose this resistance or exertion of force to take place: to the Supreme Being, who never meets with any

Shall we then assert that we are conscious of a power or energy in our own minds when, by an act or command of our will, we raise up a new idea, fix the mind to the contemplation of it, turn it on all sides, and at last dismiss it for some other idea when we think that we have surveyed it with sufficient accuracy? I believe the same arguments will prove that even this command of the will gives us no real idea of force or energy.

First, it must be allowed that when we know a power, we know that very circumstance in the cause by which it is enabled to produce the effect, for these are supposed to be synonymous. We must, therefore, know both the cause and effect and the relation between them. But do we pretend to be acquainted with the nature of the human soul and the nature of an idea, or the aptitude of the one to produce the other? This is a real creation, a production of something out of nothing, which implies a power so great that it may seem, at first sight, beyond the reach of any being less than infinite. At least it must be owned that such a power is not felt, nor known, nor even conceivable by the mind. We only feel the event, namely, the existence of an idea consequent to a command of the will; but the manner in which this operation is performed, the power by which it is produced, is entirely beyond our comprehension.

Secondly, the command of the mind over itself is limited, as well as its command over the body; and these limits are not known by reason or any acquaintance with the nature of cause and effect, but only by experience and observation, as in all other natural events and in the operation of external

---

resistance; to the mind in its command over its ideas and limbs, in common thinking and motion, where the effect follows immediately upon the will, without any exertion or summoning up of force; to inanimate matter, which is not capable of this sentiment. *Secondly*, this sentiment of an endeavor to overcome resistance has no known connection with any event: What follows it we know by experience, but could not know it *a priori*. It must, however, be confessed that the animal *nisus* which we experience, though it can afford no accurate precise idea of power, enters very much into that vulgar, inaccurate idea which is formed of it.*

* The last sentence is not in Editions K and L.

objects. Our authority over our sentiments and passions is much weaker than that over our ideas; and even the latter authority is circumscribed within very narrow boundaries. Will anyone pretend to assign the ultimate reason of these boundaries, or show why the power is deficient in one case, not in another?

Thirdly, this self-command is very different at different times. A man in health possesses more of it than one languishing with sickness. We are more master of our thoughts in the morning than in the evening; fasting, than after a full meal. Can we give any reason for these variations except experience? Where then is the power of which we pretend to be conscious? Is there not here, either in a spiritual or material substance, or both, some secret mechanism or structure of parts upon which the effect depends, and which, being entirely unknown to us, renders the power or energy of the will equally unknown and incomprehensible?

Volition is surely an act of the mind with which we are sufficiently acquainted. Reflect upon it. Consider it on all sides. Do you find anything in it like this creative power by which it raises from nothing a new idea and, with a kind of *fiat,* imitates the omnipotence of its Maker, if I may be allowed so to speak, who called forth into existence all the various scenes of nature? So far from being conscious of this energy in the will, it requires as certain experience as that of which we are possessed to convince us that such extraordinary effects do ever result from a simple act of volition.

The generality of mankind never find any difficulty in accounting for the more common and familiar operations of nature, such as the descent of heavy bodies, the growth of plants, the generation of animals, or the nourishment of bodies by food; but suppose that in all these cases they perceive the very force or energy of the cause by which it is connected with its effect, and is forever infallible in its operation. They acquire, by long habit, such a turn of mind that upon the appearance of the cause they immediately expect, with assurance, its usual attendant, and hardly conceive it possible that any other event could result from it. It is only on the discovery of extraordinary phenomena, such as earth-quakes, pestilence, and prodigies of any kind, that they find themselves at a loss to assign a proper cause and to explain the manner in which the effect is produced by it. It is usual for men, in such difficulties, to have recourse to some invisible intelligent principle [8] as the immediate cause of that event which surprises them, and which they think cannot be accounted for from the common powers of nature. But philosophers, who carry their scrutiny a little further, immediately perceive that, even in the most familiar events, the energy of the cause is as unintelligible as in the most unusual, and that we only learn by experience the frequent conjunction of objects, without being ever able to comprehend anything like connection between them. Here, then, many philosophers think themselves obliged by reason to have recourse, on all occasions, to the same principle which the vulgar never appeal to but in cases that appear miraculous and supernatural. They acknowledge mind and intelligence to be, not only the ultimate and original cause of all things, but the immediate and sole cause of every event which appears in nature. They pretend that those objects which are commonly denominated "causes" are in reality nothing but "occasions," and that the true and direct principle of every effect is not any power or force in nature, but a volition of the Supreme Being, who wills that such particular objects should forever be conjoined with each other. Instead of saying that one billiard ball moves another by a force which it has derived from the author of nature, it is the Deity himself, they say, who, by a particular volition, moves the second ball, being determined to this operation by the impulse of the first ball, in consequence of those general laws which he has laid down to himself in the government of the universe. But philosophers, advancing still in their inquiries, discover that as we are totally ignorant of the power on which depends the mutual operation of bodies, we are no less ignorant of that power on which depends the

---

[8] Θεὸς ἀπὸ μηχανῆς. [Edition K reads: "*Quasi deus ex machina*." Edition L adds the reference: "Cicero *de Natura deorum*."]

operation of mind on body, or of body on mind; nor are we able, either from our senses or consciousness, to assign the ultimate principle in the one case more than in the other. The same ignorance, therefore, reduces them to the same conclusion. They assert that the Deity is the immediate cause of the union between soul and body, and that they are not the organs of sense which, being agitated by external objects, produce sensations in the mind; but that it is a particular volition of our omnipotent Maker which excites such a sensation in consequence of such a motion in the organ. In like manner, it is not any energy in the will that produces local motion in our members: It is God himself, who is pleased to second our will, in itself impotent, and to command that motion which we erroneously attribute to our own power and efficacy. Nor do philosophers stop at this conclusion. They sometimes extend the same inference to the mind itself in its internal operations. Our mental vision or conception of ideas is nothing but a revelation made to us by our Maker. When we voluntarily turn our thoughts to any object and raise up its image in the fancy, it is not the will which creates that idea, it is the universal Creator who discovers it to the mind and renders it present to us.[9]

Thus, according to these philosophers, everything is full of God. Not content with the principle that nothing exists but by his will, that nothing possesses any power but by his concession, they rob nature and all created beings of every power in order to render their dependence on the Deity still more sensible and immediate. They consider not that by this theory they diminish, instead of magnifying, the grandeur of those attributes which they affect so much to celebrate. It argues, surely, more power in the Deity to delegate a certain degree of power to inferior creatures than to produce everything by his own immediate volition. It argues more wisdom to contrive at first the fabric of the world with such perfect foresight that of itself, and by its proper operation, it may

9 [Hume refers here to the French philosopher, Nicolas de Malebranche (1638-1715), and his major work, *De la Recherche de la vérité* (1674).—Ed.]

serve all the purposes of Providence than if the great Creator were obliged every moment to adjust its parts and animate by his breath all the wheels of that stupendous machine.

But if we would have a more philosophical confutation of this theory, perhaps the two following reflections may suffice:

First, it seems to me that this theory of the universal energy and operation of the Supreme Being is too bold ever to carry conviction with it to a man sufficiently apprised of the weakness of human reason and the narrow limits to which it is confined in all its operations. Though the chain of arguments which conduct to it were ever so logical, there must arise a strong suspicion, if not an absolute assurance, that it has carried us quite beyond the reach of our faculties when it leads to conclusions so extraordinary and so remote from common life and experience. We are got into fairyland long ere we have reached the last steps of our theory; and *there* we have no reason to trust our common methods of argument or to think that our usual analogies and probabilities have any authority. Our line is too short to fathom such immense abysses. And however we may flatter ourselves that we are guided, in every step which we take, by a kind of verisimilitude and experience, we may be assured that this fancied experience has no authority when we thus apply it to subjects that lie entirely out of the sphere of experience. But on this we shall have occasion to touch afterwards.[10]

Secondly, I cannot perceive any force in the arguments on which this theory is founded. We are ignorant, it is true, of the manner in which bodies operate on each other. Their force or energy is entirely incomprehensible. But are we not equally ignorant of the manner or force by which a mind, even the Supreme Mind, operates, either on itself or on body? Whence, I beseech you, do we acquire any idea of it? We have no sentiment or consciousness of this power in ourselves. We have no idea of the Supreme Being but what we learn from reflection on our own faculties. Were our ignorance, therefore, a good reason for rejecting anything, we should be

[10] Section XII.

led into that principle of denying all energy in the Supreme Being, as much as in the grossest matter. We surely comprehend as little the operations of the one as of the other. Is it more difficult to conceive that motion may arise from impulse than that it may arise from volition? All we know is our profound ignorance in both cases.[11]

PART II

But to hasten to a conclusion of this argument, which is already drawn out to too great a length: We have sought in vain for an idea of power or necessary connection in all the sources from which we would suppose it to be derived. It appears that in single instances of the operation of bodies we never can, by our utmost scrutiny, discover anything but one event following another, without being able to comprehend

---

[11] I need not examine at length the *vis inertiae* which is so much talked of in the new philosophy, and which is ascribed to matter. We find by experience that a body at rest or in motion continues forever in its present state, till put from it by some new cause; and that a body impelled takes as much motion from the impelling body as it acquires itself. These are facts. When we call this a *vis inertiae,* we only mark these facts, without pretending to have any idea of the inert power, in the same manner as, when we talk of gravity, we mean certain effects without comprehending that active power.* It was never the meaning of Sir Isaac Newton to rob second causes of all force or energy, though some of his followers have endeavored to establish that theory upon his authority. On the contrary, that great philosopher had recourse to an ethereal active fluid to explain his universal attraction, though he was so cautious and modest as to allow that it was a mere hypothesis not to be insisted on without more experiments. I must confess that there is something in the fate of opinions a little extraordinary. Descartes insinuated that doctrine of the universal and sole efficacy of the Deity, without insisting on it. Malebranche and other Cartesians made it the foundation of all their philosophy. It had, however, no authority in England. Locke, Clarke, and Cudworth never so much as take notice of it, but suppose all along that matter has a real, though subordinate and derived, power. By what means has it become so prevalent among our modern metaphysicians?

* Editions K and L: "matter."

any force or power by which the cause operates or any connection between it and its supposed effect. The same difficulty
occurs in contemplating the operations of mind on body,
where we observe the motion of the latter to follow upon the
volition of the former, but are not able to observe or conceive the tie which binds together the motion and volition, or
the energy, by which the mind produces this effect. The
authority of the will over its own faculties and ideas is not a
whit more comprehensible, so that, upon the whole, there
appears not, throughout all nature, any one instance of connection which is conceivable by us. All events seem entirely
loose and separate. One event follows another, but we never
can observe any tie between them. They seem *conjoined,* but
never *connected.* But as we can have no idea of anything
which never appeared to our outward sense or inward sentiment, the necessary conclusion *seems* to-be that we have no
idea of connection or power at all, and that these words are
absolutely without any meaning when employed either in
philosophical reasonings or common life.

But there still remains one method of avoiding this conclusion, and one source which we have not yet examined.
When any natural object or event is presented, it is impossible
for us, by any sagacity or penetration, to discover, or even
conjecture, without experience, what event will result from
it, or to carry our foresight beyond that object which is immediately present to the memory and senses. Even after one
instance or experiment where we have observed a particular
event to follow upon another, we are not entitled to form a
general rule or foretell what will happen in like cases, it being
justly esteemed an unpardonable temerity to judge of the
whole course of nature from one single experiment, however
accurate or certain. But when one particular species of events
has always, in all instances, been conjoined with another, we
make no longer any scruple of foretelling one upon the appearance of the other, and of employing that reasoning which
can alone assure us of any matter of fact or existence. We then
call the one object "cause," the other "effect." We suppose
that there is some connection between them, some power in

the one by which it infallibly produces the other and operates with the greatest certainty and strongest necessity.

It appears, then, that this idea of a necessary connection among events arises from a number of similar instances which occur, of the constant conjunction of these events; nor can that idea ever be suggested by any one of these instances surveyed in all possible lights and positions. But there is nothing in a number of instances, different from every single instance, which is supposed to be exactly similar, except only that after a repetition of similar instances the mind is carried by habit, upon the appearance of one event, to expect its usual attendant and to believe that it will exist. This connection, therefore, which we *feel* in the mind, this customary transition of the imagination from one object to its usual attendant, is the sentiment or impression from which we form the idea of power or necessary connection. Nothing further is in the case. Contemplate the subjects on all sides, you will never find any other origin of that idea. This is the sole difference between one instance, from which we can never receive the idea of connection, and a number of similar instances by which it is suggested. The first time a man saw the communication of motion by impulse, as by the shock of two billiard balls, he could not pronounce that the one event was *connected,* but only that it was *conjoined* with the other. After he has observed several instances of this nature, he then pronounces them to be *connected.* What alteration has happened to give rise to this new idea of *connection?* Nothing but that he now *feels* these events to be *connected* in his imagination, and can readily foretell the existence of one from the appearance of the other. When we say, therefore, that one object is connected with another, we mean only that they have acquired a connection in our thought and gave rise to this inference by which they become proofs of each other's existence—a conclusion which is somewhat extraordinary, but which seems founded on sufficient evidence. Nor will its evidence be weakened by any general diffidence of the understanding or skeptical suspicion concerning every conclusion which is new and extraordinary. No conclusions can be more agreeable to skepticism than such as make discoveries concerning the weakness and narrow limits of human reason and capacity.

And what stronger instance can be produced of the surprising ignorance and weakness of the understanding than the present? For surely, if there be any relation among objects which it imports us to know perfectly, it is that of cause and effect. On this are founded all our reasonings concerning matter of fact or existence. By means of it alone we attain any assurance concerning objects which are removed from the present testimony of our memory and senses. The only immediate utility of all sciences is to teach us how to control and regulate future events by their causes. Our thoughts and inquiries are, therefore, every moment employed about this relation; yet so imperfect are the ideas which we form concerning it that it is impossible to give any just definition of cause, except what is drawn from something extraneous and foreign to it. Similar objects are always conjoined with similar. Of this we have experience. Suitably to this experience, therefore, we may define a cause to be *an object followed by another, and where all the objects, similar to the first, are followed by objects similar to the second.* Or, in other words, *where, if the first object had not been, the second never had existed.* The appearance of a cause always conveys the mind, by a customary transition, to the idea of the effect. Of this also we have experience. We may, therefore, suitably to this experience, form another definition of cause and call it *an object followed by another, and whose appearance always conveys the thought to that other.* But though both these definitions be drawn from circumstances foreign to the cause, we cannot remedy this inconvenience or attain any more perfect definition which may point out that circumstance in the cause which gives it a connection with its effect. We have no idea of this connection, nor even any distinct notion what it is we desire to know when we endeavor at a conception of it. We say, for instance, that the vibration of this string is the cause of this particular sound. But what do we mean by that affirmation? We either mean *that this vibration is followed*

*by this sound, and that all similar vibrations have been
followed by similar sounds; or, that this vibration is followed
by this sound, and that, upon the appearance of one, the mind
anticipates the senses and forms immediately an idea of the
other.* We may consider the relation of cause and effect in
either of these two lights; but beyond these we have no idea
of it.[1]

To recapitulate, therefore, the reasonings of this Section:

[1] According to these explications and definitions, the idea of *power*
is relative as much as that of *cause*; and both have a reference to an effect, or some other event constantly conjoined with the former. When
we consider the *unknown* circumstance of an object by which the degree
or quantity of its effect is fixed and determined, we call that its power.
And accordingly, it is allowed by all philosophers that the effect is the
measure of the power. But if they had any idea of power as it is in itself, why could they not measure it in itself? The dispute, whether the
force of a body in motion be as its velocity, or the square of its velocity;
this dispute, I say, needed not be decided by comparing its effects in
equal or unequal times, but by a direct mensuration and comparison.*

As to the frequent use of the words "force," "power," "energy," etc.,
which everywhere occur in common conversation as well as in philosophy, that is no proof that we are acquainted, in any instance, with the
connecting principle between cause and effect, or can account ultimately
for the production of one thing by another. These words, as commonly
used, have very loose meanings annexed to them, and their ideas are very
uncertain and confused. No animal can put external bodies in motion
without the sentiment of a *nisus* or endeavor; and every animal has a
sentiment or feeling from the stroke or blow of an external object that is
in motion. These sensations, which are merely animal, and from which
we can *a priori* draw no inference, we are apt to transfer to inanimate
objects, and to suppose that they have some such feelings whenever they
transfer or receive motion. With regard to energies, which are exerted
without our annexing to them any idea of communicated motion, we
consider only the constant experienced conjunction of the events; and
as we *feel* a customary connection between the ideas, we transfer that
feeling to the objects, as nothing is more usual than to apply to external
bodies every internal sensation which they occasion.†

* This note was first introduced in Edition L.
† Instead of this concluding passage there stood in Edition L: "A
cause is different from a *sign*, as it implies precedence and contiguity in
time and place, as well as constant conjunction. A *sign* is nothing but
a correlative effect from the same cause."

Every idea is copied from some preceding impression or sentiment; and where we cannot find any impression, we may be certain that there is no idea. In all single instances of the operation of bodies or minds there is nothing that produces any impression, nor consequently can suggest any idea, of power or necessary connection. But when many uniform instances appear, and the same object is always followed by the same event, we then begin to entertain the notion of cause and connection. We then *feel* a new sentiment or impression, to wit, a customary connection in the thought or imagination between one object and its usual attendant; and this sentiment is the original of that idea which we seek for. For as this idea arises from a number of similar instances, and not from any single instance, it must arise from that circumstance in which the number of instances differ from every individual instance. But this customary connection or transition of the imagination is the only circumstance in which they differ. In every other particular they are alike. The first instance which we saw of motion, communicated by the shock of two billiard balls (to return to this obvious illustration), is exactly similar to any instance that may at present occur to us, except only that we could not at first *infer* one event from the other, which we are enabled to do at present, after so long a course of uniform experience. I know not whether the reader will readily apprehend this reasoning. I am afraid that, should I multiply words about it or throw it into a greater variety of lights, it would only become more obscure and intricate. In all abstract reasonings there is one point of view which, if we can happily hit, we shall go further toward illustrating the subject than by all the eloquence and copious expression in the world. This point of view we should endeavor to reach, and reserve the flowers of rhetoric for subjects which are more adapted to them.

SECTION VIII

OF LIBERTY AND NECESSITY

PART I

It might reasonably be expected, in questions which have been canvassed and disputed with great eagerness since the first origin of science and philosophy, that the meaning of all the terms, at least, should have been agreed upon among the disputants, and our inquiries, in the course of two thousand years, been able to pass from words to the true and real subject of the controversy. For how easy may it seem to give exact definitions of the terms employed in reasoning, and make these definitions, not the mere sound of words, the object of future scrutiny and examination? But if we consider the matter more narrowly, we shall be apt to draw a quite opposite conclusion. From this circumstance alone, that a controversy has been long kept on foot and remains still undecided, we may presume that there is some ambiguity in the expression, and that the disputants affix different ideas to the terms employed in the controversy. For as the faculties of the mind are supposed to be naturally alike in every individual—otherwise nothing could be more fruitless than to reason or dispute together—it were impossible, if men affix the same ideas to their terms, that they could so long form different opinions of the same subject, especially when they communicate their views and each party turn themselves on all sides in search of arguments which may give them the victory over their antagonists. It is true, if men attempt the discussion of questions which lie entirely beyond the reach of human capacity, such as those concerning the origin of worlds or the economy of the intellectual system or region of spirits, they may long beat the air in their fruitless contests and never arrive at any determinate conclusion. But if the question regard any subject of common life and experience, nothing, one would think, could preserve the dispute so long undecided, but some ambiguous expressions which keep the antagonists still at a distance and hinder them from grappling with each other.

This has been the case in the long-disputed question concerning liberty and necessity, and to so remarkable a degree that, if I be not much mistaken, we shall find that all mankind, both learned and ignorant, have always been of the same opinion with regard to this subject, and that a few intelligible definitions would immediately have put an end to the whole controversy. I own that this dispute has been so much canvassed on all hands, and has led philosophers into such a labyrinth of obscure sophistry, that it is no wonder if a sensible reader indulge his ease so far as to turn a deaf ear to the proposal of such a question from which he can expect neither instruction nor entertainment. But the state of the argument here proposed may, perhaps, serve to renew his attention, as it has more novelty, promises at least some decision of the controversy, and will not much disturb his ease by any intricate or obscure reasoning.

I hope, therefore, to make it appear that all men have ever agreed in the doctrine both of necessity and of liberty, according to any reasonable sense which can be put on these terms, and that the whole controversy has hitherto turned merely upon words. We shall begin with examining the doctrine of necessity.

It is universally allowed that matter, in all its operations, is actuated by a necessary force, and that every natural effect is so precisely determined by the energy of its cause that no other effect, in such particular circumstances, could possibly have resulted from it. The degree and direction of every motion is, by the laws of nature, prescribed with such exactness that a living creature may as soon arise from the shock of two bodies, as motion, in any other degree or direction than what is actually produced by it. Would we, therefore, form a just and precise idea of *necessity*, we must consider whence that idea arises when we apply it to the operation of bodies.

It seems evident that, if all the scenes of nature were continually shifted in such a manner that no two events bore any resemblance to each other, but every object was entirely new, without any similitude to whatever had been seen before, we should never, in that case, have attained the least idea of necessity or of a connection among these objects. We might say, upon such a supposition, that one object or event has followed another, not that one was produced by the other. The relation of cause and effect must be utterly unknown to mankind. Inference and reasoning concerning the operations of nature would, from that moment, be at an end; and the memory and senses remain the only canals by which the knowledge of any real existence could possibly have access to the mind. Our idea, therefore, of necessity and causation arises entirely from the uniformity observable in the operations of nature, where similar objects are constantly conjoined together, and the mind is determined by custom to infer the one from the appearance of the other. These two circumstances form the whole of that necessity which we ascribe to matter. Beyond the constant *conjunction* of similar objects and the consequent *inference* from one to the other, we have no notion of any necessity of connection.

If it appear, therefore, that all mankind have ever allowed, without any doubt or hesitation, that these two circumstances take place in the voluntary actions of men and in the operations of mind, it must follow that all mankind have ever agreed in the doctrine of necessity, and that they have hitherto disputed merely for not understanding each other.

As to the first circumstance, the constant and regular conjunction of similar events, we may possibly satisfy ourselves by the following considerations. It is universally acknowledged that there is a great uniformity among the actions of men, in all nations and ages, and that human nature remains still the same in its principles and operations. The same motives always produce the same actions; the same events follow from the same causes. Ambition, avarice, self-love, vanity, friendship, generosity, public spirit—these passions, mixed in various degrees and distributed through society, have been, from the beginning of the world, and still are, the source of all the actions and enterprises which have ever been observed among mankind. Would you know the sentiments, inclinations, and course of life of the Greeks and Romans? Study well the temper and actions of the French and English: you cannot be much mistaken in transferring to the former *most* of the observations which you have made with regard to the latter. Mankind are so much the same, in all times and places, that history informs us of nothing new or strange in this particular. Its chief use is only to discover the constant and universal principles of human nature by showing men in all varieties of circumstances and situations, and furnishing us with materials from which we may form our observations and become acquainted with the regular springs of human action and behavior. These records of wars, intrigues, factions, and revolutions are so many collections of experiments by which the politician or moral philosopher fixes the principles of his science, in the same manner as the physician or natural philosopher becomes acquainted with the nature of plants, minerals, and other external objects, by the experiments which he forms concerning them. Nor are the earth, water, and other elements examined by Aristotle and Hippocrates [1] more like to those which at present lie under our observation than the men described by Polybius [2] and Tacitus [3] are to those who now govern the world.

[1] [Hippocrates (460?-377 B.C.), the foremost Greek physician of antiquity, who systematized the medical knowledge of his time in more than eighty treatises. The authorship of these treatises, however, is now in doubt.—Ed.]

[2] [Polybius (201?-120 B.C.), a Greek historian who in his later years lived in Rome. He wrote a history of Rome from the beginning of the Hannibalic War to the battle of Pydna (168 B.C.).—Ed.]

[3] [Cornelius Tacitus (A.D. 55-128), a Roman historian whose works have become a major source of historical information. His chief works are the *Histories; Annals; Germania; Life of Agricola.—*Ed.]

Should a traveler, returning from a far country, bring us an account of men wholly different from any with whom we were ever acquainted, men who were entirely divested of avarice, ambition, or revenge, who knew no pleasure but friendship, generosity, and public spirit, we should immediately, from these circumstances, detect the falsehood and prove him a liar with the same certainty as if he had stuffed his narration with stories of centaurs and dragons, miracles and prodigies. And if we would explode any forgery in history, we cannot make use of a more convincing argument than to prove that the actions ascribed to any person are directly contrary to the course of nature, and that no human motives, in such circumstances, could ever induce him to such a conduct. The veracity of Quintus Curtius [4] is as much to be suspected when he describes the supernatural courage of Alexander by which he was hurried on singly to attack multitudes, as when he describes his supernatural force and activity by which he was able to resist them. So readily and universally do we acknowledge a uniformity in human motives and actions as well as in the operations of body.

Hence, likewise, the benefit of that experience acquired by long life and a variety of business and company, in order to instruct us in the principles of human nature and regulate our future conduct as well as speculation. By means of this guide we mount up to the knowledge of men's inclinations and motives from their actions, expressions, and even gestures, and again descend to the interpretation of their actions from our knowledge of their motives and inclinations. The general observations, treasured up by a course of experience, give us the clue of human nature and teach us to unravel all its intricacies. Pretexts and appearances no longer deceive us. Public declarations pass for the specious coloring of a cause. And though virtue and honor be allowed their proper weight and authority, that perfect disinterestedness, so often pretended to, is never expected in multitudes and parties, seldom in

4 [Quintus Curtius Rufus (1st century A.D.), Roman author of an uncritical biography of Alexander the Great.—Ed.]

their leaders, and scarcely even in individuals of any rank or station. But were there no uniformity in human actions, and were every experiment which we could form of this kind irregular and anomalous, it were impossible to collect any general observations concerning mankind, and no experience, however accurately digested by reflection, would ever serve to any purpose. Why is the aged husbandman more skillful in his calling than the young beginner, but because there is a certain uniformity in the operation of the sun, rain, and earth toward the production of vegetables, and experience teaches the old practitioner the rules by which this operation is governed and directed?

We must not, however, expect that this uniformity of human actions should be carried to such a length as that all men, in the same circumstances, will always act precisely in the same manner, without making any allowance for the diversity of characters, prejudices, and opinions. Such a uniformity, in every particular, is found in no part of nature. On the contrary, from observing the variety of conduct in different men we are enabled to form a greater variety of maxims which still suppose a degree of uniformity and regularity.

Are the manners of men different in different ages and countries? We learn thence the great force of custom and education, which mold the human mind from its infancy and form it into a fixed and established character. Is the behavior and conduct of the one sex very unlike that of the other? It is thence we become acquainted with the different characters which nature has impressed upon the sexes, and which she preserves with constancy and regularity. Are the actions of the same person much diversified in the different periods of his life from infancy to old age? This affords room for many general observations concerning the gradual change of our sentiments and inclinations, and the different maxims which prevail in the different ages of human creatures. Even the characters which are peculiar to each individual have a uniformity in their influence, otherwise our acquaintance with the persons, and our observations of their conduct, could never teach us their dispositions or serve to direct our behavior with regard to them.

I grant it possible to find some actions which seem to have no regular connection with any known motives and are exceptions to all the measures of conduct which have ever been established for the government of men. But if we could willingly know what judgment should be formed of such irregular and extraordinary actions, we may consider the sentiments commonly entertained with regard to those irregular events which appear in the course of nature and the operations of external objects. All causes are not conjoined to their usual effects with like uniformity. An artificer who handles only dead matter may be disappointed of his aim, as well as the politician who directs the conduct of sensible and intelligent agents.

The vulgar, who take things according to their first appearance, attribute the uncertainty of events to such an uncertainty in the causes as makes the latter often fail of their usual influence, though they meet with no impediment in their operation. But philosophers, observing that almost in every part of nature there is contained a vast variety of springs and principles which are hid by reason of their minuteness or remoteness, find that it is at least possible the contrariety of events may not proceed from any contingency in the cause but from the secret operation of contrary causes. This possibility is converted into certainty by further observation, when they remark that, upon an exact scrutiny, a contrariety of effects always betrays a contrariety of causes and proceeds from their mutual opposition. A peasant can give no better reason for the stopping of any clock or watch than to say that it does not commonly go right. But an artist easily perceives that the same force in the spring or pendulum has always the same influence on the wheels, but fails of its usual effect perhaps by reason of a grain of dust which puts a stop to the whole movement. From the observation of several parallel instances philosophers form a maxim that the connection between all causes and effects is equally necessary, and that its seeming uncertainty in some instances proceeds from the secret opposition of contrary causes.

Thus, for instance, in the human body, when the usual symptoms of health or sickness disappoint our expectation, when medicines operate not with their wonted powers, when irregular events follow from any particular cause, the philosopher and physician are not surprised at the matter, nor are ever tempted to deny, in general, the necessity and uniformity of those principles by which the animal economy is conducted. They know that a human body is a mighty complicated machine, that many secret powers lurk in it which are altogether beyond our comprehension, that to us it must often appear very uncertain in its operations, and that, therefore, the irregular events which outwardly discover themselves can be no proof that the laws of nature are not observed with the greatest regularity in its internal operations and government.

The philosopher, if he be consistent, must apply the same reasonings to the actions and volitions of intelligent agents. The most irregular and unexpected resolutions of men may frequently be accounted for by those who know every particular circumstance of their character and situation. A person of an obliging disposition gives a peevish answer; but he has the toothache, or has not dined. A stupid fellow discovers an uncommon alacrity in his carriage; but he has met with a sudden piece of good fortune. Or even when an action, as sometimes happens, cannot be particularly accounted for, either by the person himself or by others, we know, in general, that the characters of men are to a certain degree inconstant and irregular. This is, in a manner, the constant character of human nature, though it be applicable, in a more particular manner, to some persons who have no fixed rule for their conduct, but proceed in a continual course of caprice and inconstancy. The internal principles and motives may operate in a uniform manner, notwithstanding these seeming irregularities—in the same manner as the winds, rains, clouds, and other variations of the weather are supposed to be governed by steady principles, though not easily discoverable by human sagacity and inquiry.

Thus it appears not only that the conjunction between motives and voluntary actions is as regular and uniform as that between the cause and effect in any part of nature, but also that this regular conjunction has been universally acknowledged among mankind and has never been the subject of dispute either in philosophy or common life. Now, as it is from past experience that we draw all inferences concerning the future, and as we conclude that objects will always be conjoined together which we find to have always been conjoined, it may seem superfluous to prove that this experienced uniformity in human actions is a source whence we draw *inferences* concerning them.[5] But in order to throw the argument into a greater variety of lights, we shall also insist, though briefly, on this latter topic.

The mutual dependence of men is so great in all societies that scarce any human action is entirely complete in itself or is performed without some reference to the actions of others, which are requisite to make it answer fully the intention of the agent. The poorest artificer who labors alone expects at least the protection of the magistrate to insure him the enjoyment of the fruits of his labor. He also expects that when he carries his goods to market and offers them at a reasonable price, he shall find purchasers and shall be able, by the money he acquires, to engage others to supply him with those commodities which are requisite for his subsistence. In proportion as men extend their dealings and render their intercourse with others more complicated, they always comprehend in their schemes of life a greater variety of voluntary actions which they expect, from the proper motives, to co-operate with their own. In all these conclusions they take their measures from past experience, in the same manner as in their reasonings concerning external objects, and firmly believe that men, as well as all the elements, are to continue in their op-

[5] [Editions K to M read: ". . . the source of all *inferences* which we form concerning them."]

erations the same that they have ever found them. A manufacturer reckons upon the labor of his servants for the execution of any work as much as upon the tools which he employs, and would be equally surprised were his expectations disappointed. In short, this experimental inference and reasoning concerning the actions of others enters so much into human life that no man, while awake, is ever a moment without employing it. Have we not reason, therefore, to affirm that all mankind have always agreed in the doctrine of necessity, according to the foregoing definition and explication of it?

Nor have philosophers ever entertained a different opinion from the people in this particular. For, not to mention that almost every action of their life supposes that opinion, there are even few of the speculative parts of learning to which it is not essential. What would become of *history* had we not a dependence on the veracity of the historian according to the experience which we have had of mankind? How could *politics* be a science if laws and forms of government had not a uniform influence upon society? Where would be the foundation of *morals* if particular characters had no certain or determinate power to produce particular sentiments, and if these sentiments had no constant operation on actions? And with what pretense could we employ our *criticism* upon any poet or polite author if we could not pronounce the conduct and sentiments of his actors either natural or unnatural to such characters and in such circumstances? It seems almost impossible, therefore, to engage either in science or action of any kind without acknowledging the doctrine of necessity, and this *inference* from motives to voluntary action, from characters to conduct.

And, indeed, when we consider how aptly *natural* and *moral* evidence link together and form only one chain of argument, we shall make no scruple to allow that they are of the same nature and derived from the same principles. A prisoner who has neither money nor interest discovers the impossibility of his escape as well when he considers the obstinacy of the jailer as the walls and bars with which he is surrounded, and in all attempts for his freedom chooses rather to work upon the stone and iron of the one than upon the inflexible nature of the other. The same prisoner, when conducted to the scaffold, foresees his death as certainly from the constancy and fidelity of his guards as from the operation of the ax or wheel. His mind runs along a certain train of ideas: the refusal of the soldiers to consent to his escape; the action of the executioner; the separation of the head and body; bleeding, convulsive motions, and death. Here is a connected chain of natural causes and voluntary actions, but the mind feels no difference between them in passing from one link to another, nor is less certain of the future event than if it were connected with the objects present to the memory or senses by a train of causes cemented together by what we are pleased to call a "physical" necessity. The same experienced union has the same effect on the mind, whether the united objects be motives, volition, and actions, or figure and motion. We may change the names of things, but their nature and their operation on the understanding never change.

[Were a man whom I know to be honest and opulent, and with whom I lived in intimate friendship, to come into my house, where I am surrounded with my servants, I rest assured that he is not to stab me before he leaves it in order to rob me of my silver standish; and I no more suspect this event than the falling of the house itself, which is new and solidly built and founded.—*But he may have been seized with a sudden and unknown frenzy.*—So may a sudden earthquake arise, and shake and tumble my house about my ears. I shall, therefore, change the suppositions. I shall say that I know with certainty that he is not to put his hand into the fire and hold it there till it be consumed. And this event I think I can foretell with the same assurance as that, if he throw himself out of the window and meet with no obstruction, he will not remain a moment suspended in the air. No suspicion of an unknown frenzy can give the least possibility to the former event which is so contrary to all the known principles of human nature. A man who at noon leaves his purse full of gold on the pavement at Charing Cross may as well expect that it will fly away like a feather as that he will find it untouched an hour after. Above one-half of human reasonings contain inferences of a similar nature, attended with more or less degrees of certainty, proportioned to our experience of the usual conduct of mankind in such particular situations.] [6]

I have frequently considered what could possibly be the reason why all mankind, though they have ever, without hesitation, acknowledged the doctrine of necessity in their whole practice and reasoning, have yet discovered such a reluctance to acknowledge it in words, and have rather shown a propensity, in all ages, to profess the contrary opinion. The matter, I think, may be accounted for after the following manner. If we examine the operations of body and the production of effects from their causes, we shall find that all our faculties can never carry us further in our knowledge of this relation than barely to observe that particular objects are *constantly conjoined* together, and that the mind is carried, by a *customary transition,* from the appearance of the one to the belief of the other. But though this conclusion concerning human ignorance be the result of the strictest scrutiny of this subject, men still entertain a strong propensity to believe that they penetrate further into the powers of nature and perceive something like a necessary connection between the cause and the effect. When, again, they turn their reflections toward the operations of their own minds and *feel* no such connection of the motive and the action, they are thence apt to suppose that there is a difference between the effects which result from material force and those which arise from thought and intelligence. But being once convinced that we know nothing further of causation of any kind than merely the *constant conjunction* of objects and the consequent *inference* of the mind from one to another, and finding that these two circumstances are universally allowed to have place in voluntary actions, we may be more easily led to own the same necessity common

[6] [This paragraph occurs only in the last corrected Edition of 1777 (Edition O).]

to all causes. And though this reasoning may contradict the systems of many philosophers in ascribing necessity to the determinations of the will, we shall find, upon reflection, that they dissent from it in words only, not in their real sentiments. Necessity, according to the sense in which it is here taken, has never yet been rejected, nor can ever, I think, be rejected by any philosopher. It may only, perhaps, be pretended that the mind can perceive in the operations of matter some further connection between the cause and effect, and a connection that has not place in the voluntary actions of intelligent beings. Now, whether it be so or not can only appear upon examination, and it is incumbent on these philosophers to make good their assertion by defining or describing that necessity and pointing it out to us in the operations of material causes.

It would seem, indeed, that men begin at the wrong end of this question concerning liberty and necessity when they enter upon it by examining the faculties of the soul, the influence of the understanding, and the operations of the will. Let them first discuss a more simple question, namely, the question of body and brute unintelligent matter, and try whether they can there form any idea of causation and necessity, except that of a constant conjunction of objects and subsequent inference of the mind from one to another. If these circumstances form, in reality, the whole of that necessity which we conceive in matter, and if these circumstances be also universally acknowledged to take place in the operations of the mind, the dispute is at an end; at least, must be owned to be thenceforth merely verbal. But as long as we will rashly suppose that we have some further idea of necessity and causation in the operations of external objects, at the same time that we can find nothing further in the voluntary actions of the mind, there is no possibility of bringing the question to any determinate issue while we proceed upon so erroneous a supposition. The only method of undeceiving us is to mount up higher, to examine the narrow extent of science when applied to material causes, and to convince ourselves that all we know of them is the constant conjunction and inference above mentioned. We may, perhaps, find that it is with difficulty we are induced to fix such narrow limits to human understanding, but we can afterwards find no difficulty when we come to apply this doctrine to the actions of the will. For as it is evident that these have a regular conjunction with motives and circumstances and character, and as we always draw inferences from one to the other, we must be obliged to acknowledge in words that necessity which we have already avowed in every deliberation of our lives and in every step of our conduct and behavior.[7]

[7] The prevalence of the doctrine of liberty may be accounted for from another cause, viz., a false sensation, or seeming experience, which we have, or may have, of liberty or indifference in many of our actions. The necessity of any action, whether of matter or of mind, is not, properly speaking, a quality in the agent but in any thinking or intelligent being who may consider the action; and it consists chiefly in the determination of his thoughts to infer the existence of that action from some preceding objects; as liberty, when opposed to necessity, is nothing but the want of that determination, and a certain looseness or indifference which we feel in passing, or not passing, from the idea of one object to that of any succeeding one. Now we may observe that though, in *reflecting* on human actions, we seldom feel such a looseness or indifference, but are commonly able to infer them with considerable certainty from their motives, and from the disposition of the agent; yet it frequently happens that, in *performing* the actions themselves, we are sensible of something like it; and as all resembling objects are readily taken for each other, this has been employed as a demonstrative and even intuitive proof of human liberty. We feel that our actions are subject to our will on most occasions, and imagine we feel that the will itself is subject to nothing, because, when by a denial of it we are provoked to try, we feel that it moves easily every way, and produces an image of itself (or a "velleity," as it is called in the schools), even on that side on which it did not settle. This image, or faint motion, we persuade ourselves, could at that time have been completed into the thing itself, because, should that be denied, we find upon a second trial that at present it can. We consider not that the fantastical desire of showing liberty is here the motive of our actions. And it seems certain that however we may imagine we feel a liberty within ourselves, a spectator can commonly infer our actions from our motives and character; and even where he cannot, he concludes in general that he might, were he perfectly acquainted with

But to proceed in this reconciling project with regard to the question of liberty and necessity—the most contentious question of metaphysics, the most contentious science—it will not require many words to prove that all mankind have ever agreed in the doctrine of liberty as well as in that of necessity, and that the whole dispute, in this respect also, has been hitherto merely verbal. For what is meant by liberty when applied to voluntary actions? We cannot surely mean that actions have so little connection with motives, inclinations, and circumstances that one does not follow with a certain degree of uniformity from the other, and that one affords no inference by which we can conclude the existence of the other. For these are plain and acknowledged matters of fact. By liberty, then, we can only mean *a power of acting or not acting according to the determinations of the will;* that is, if we choose to remain at rest, we may; if we choose to move, we also may. Now this hypothetical liberty is universally allowed to belong to everyone who is not a prisoner and in chains. Here then is no subject of dispute.

Whatever definition we may give of liberty, we should be careful to observe two requisite circumstances: *first,* that it be consistent with plain matter of fact; *secondly,* that it be consistent with itself. If we observe these circumstances and render our definition intelligible, I am persuaded that all mankind will be found of one opinion with regard to it.

It is universally allowed that nothing exists without a cause of its existence, and that chance, when strictly examined, is a mere negative word and means not any real power which has anywhere a being in nature. But it is pretended that some causes are necessary, some not necessary. Here then is the advantage of definitions. Let anyone *define* a cause without comprehending, as a part of the definition, a *necessary connection* with its effect, and let him show distinctly the origin of the idea expressed by the definition, and I shall readily

---

every circumstance of our situation and temper, and the most secret springs of our complexion and disposition. Now this is the very essence of necessity, according to the foregoing doctrine.

give up the whole controversy. But if the foregoing explication of the matter be received, this must be absolutely impracticable. Had not objects a regular conjunction with each other, we should never have entertained any notion of cause and effect; and this regular conjunction produces that inference of the understanding which is the only connection that we can have any comprehension of. Whoever attempts a definition of cause exclusive of these circumstances will be obliged either to employ unintelligible terms or such as are synonymous to the term which he endeavors to define.[8] And if the definition above mentioned be admitted, liberty, when opposed to necessity, not to constraint, is the same thing with chance, which is universally allowed to have no existence.

PART II

There is no method of reasoning more common, and yet none more blamable, than in philosophical disputes to endeavor the refutation of any hypothesis by a pretense of its dangerous consequences to religion and morality. When any opinion leads to absurdity, it is certainly false; but it is not certain that an opinion is false because it is of dangerous consequence. Such topics, therefore, ought entirely to be forborne as serving nothing to the discovery of truth, but only to make the person of an antagonist odious. This I observe in general, without pretending to draw any advantage from it. I frankly submit to an examination of this kind, and shall venture to affirm that the doctrines both of necessity and lib-

---

[8] Thus, if a cause be defined, *that which produces anything*, it is easy to observe that *producing* is synonymous to *causing*. In like manner, if a cause be defined, *that by which anything exists*, this is liable to the same objection. For what is meant by these words, *"by which"*? Had it been said that a cause is *that* after which *anything constantly exists*, we should have understood the terms. For this is, indeed, all we know of the matter. And this constancy forms the very essence of necessity, nor have we any other idea of it.

erty, as above explained, are not only consistent with moral-ity,[1] but are absolutely essential to its support.

Necessity may be defined two ways, conformably to the two definitions of *cause* of which it makes an essential part. It consists either in the constant conjunction of like objects or in the inference of the understanding from one object to an-other. Now necessity, in both these senses (which, indeed, are at bottom the same), has universally, though tacitly, in the schools, in the pulpit, and in common life been allowed to belong to the will of man, and no one has ever pretended to deny that we can draw inferences concerning human actions, and that those inferences are founded on the experienced union of like actions, with like motives, inclinations, and cir-cumstances. The only particular in which anyone can differ is that either perhaps he will refuse to give the name of neces-sity to this property of human actions—but as long as the meaning is understood I hope the word can do no harm—or that he will maintain it possible to discover something fur-ther in the operations of matter. But this, it must be acknowl-edged, can be of no consequence to morality or religion, what-ever it may be to natural philosophy or metaphysics. We may here be mistaken in asserting that there is no idea of any other necessity or connection in the actions of the body, but surely we ascribe nothing to the actions of the mind but what everyone does and must readily allow of. We change no cir-cumstance in the received orthodox system with regard to the will, but only in that with regard to material objects and causes. Nothing, therefore, can be more innocent at least than this doctrine.

All laws being founded on rewards and punishments, it is supposed, as a fundamental principle, that these motives have a regular and uniform influence on the mind and both pro-duce the good and prevent the evil actions. We may give to this influence what name we please; but as it is usually con-joined with the action, it must be esteemed a *cause* and be

1 [Editions prior to O: "Consistent with morality *and religion*, but are absolutely essential to them."]

looked upon as an instance of that necessity which we would here establish.

The only proper object of hatred or vengeance is a person or creature endowed with thought and consciousness; and when any criminal or injurious actions excite that passion, it is only by their relation to the person, or connection with him. Actions are, by their very nature, temporary and perishing; and where they proceed not from some *cause* in the character and disposition of the person who performed them, they can neither redound to his honor if good, nor infamy if evil. The actions themselves may be blamable; they may be contrary to all the rules of morality and religion; but the person is not answerable for them and, as they proceeded from nothing in him that is durable and constant and leave nothing of that nature behind them, it is impossible he can, upon their account, become the object of punishment or vengeance. According to the principle, therefore, which denies necessity and, consequently, causes, a man is as pure and untainted, after having committed the most horrid crime, as at the first moment of his birth, nor is his character anywise concerned in his actions, since they are not derived from it; and the wickedness of the one can never be used as a proof of the depravity of the other.

Men are not blamed for such actions as they perform ignorantly and casually, whatever may be the consequences. Why? But because the principles of these actions are only momentary and terminate in them alone. Men are less blamed for such actions as they perform hastily and unpremeditately than for such as proceed from deliberation. For what reason? But because a hasty temper, though a constant cause or principle in the mind, operates only by intervals and infects not the whole character. Again, repentance wipes off every crime if attended with a reformation of life and manners. How is this to be accounted for? But by asserting that actions render a person criminal merely as they are proofs of criminal principles in the mind; and when, by an alteration of these principles, they cease to be just proofs, they likewise cease to be criminal. But, except upon the doctrine of necessity, they never were just proofs, and consequently never were criminal.

It will be equally easy to prove, and from the same arguments, that *liberty,* according to that definition above mentioned, in which all men agree, is also essential to morality, and that no human actions, where it is wanting, are susceptible of any moral qualities or can be the objects of approbation or dislike. For as actions are objects of our moral sentiment so far only as they are indications of the internal character, passions, and affections, it is impossible that they can give rise either to praise or blame where they proceed not from these principles, but are derived altogether from external violence.

I pretend not to have obviated or removed all objections to this theory with regard to necessity and liberty. I can foresee other objections derived from topics which have not here been treated of. It may be said, for instance, that if voluntary actions be subjected to the same laws of necessity with the operations of matter, there is a continued chain of necessary causes, preordained and predetermined, reaching from the Original Cause of all to every single volition of every human creature. No contingency anywhere in the universe, no indifference, no liberty. While we act, we are at the same time acted upon. The ultimate Author of all our volitions is the Creator of the world, who first bestowed motion on this immense machine and placed all beings in that particular position whence every subsequent event, by an inevitable necessity, must result. Human actions, therefore, either can have no moral turpitude at all, as proceeding from so good a cause, or if they have any turpitude, they must involve our Creator in the same guilt, while he is acknowledged to be their ultimate cause and Author. For as a man who fired a mine is answerable for all the consequences, whether the train he employed be long or short, so, wherever a continued chain of necessary causes is fixed, that Being, either finite or infinite, who produces the first is likewise the author of all the rest and must both bear the blame and acquire the praise which belong to them. Our clear and unalterable ideas of morality establish this rule upon unquestionable reasons when we examine the consequences of any human action; and these reasons must still have greater force when applied to the volitions and intentions of a Being infinitely wise and powerful. Ignorance or impotence may be pleaded for so limited a creature as man, but those imperfections have no place in our Creator. He foresaw, he ordained, he intended all those actions of men which we so rashly pronounce criminal. And we must, therefore, conclude either that they are not criminal or that the Deity, not man, is accountable for them. But as either of these positions is absurd and impious, it follows that the doctrine from which they are deduced cannot possibly be true, as being liable to all the same objections. An absurd consequence, if necessary, proves the original doctrine to be absurd in the same manner as criminal actions render criminal the original cause if the connection between them be necessary and inevitable.

This objection consists of two parts, which we shall examine separately:

First, that if human actions can be traced up, by a necessary chain, to the Deity, they can never be criminal, on account of the infinite perfection of that Being from whom they are derived, and who can intend nothing but what is altogether good and laudable. Or, *secondly,* if they be criminal, we must retract the attribute of perfection which we ascribe to the Deity and must acknowledge him to be the ultimate author of guilt and moral turpitude in all his creatures.

The answer to the first objection seems obvious and convincing. There are many philosophers who, after an exact scrutiny of the phenomena of nature, conclude that the WHOLE, considered as one system, is, in every period of its existence, ordered with perfect benevolence; and that the utmost possible happiness will, in the end, result to all created beings without any mixture of positive or absolute ill and misery. Every physical ill, say they, makes an essential part of this benevolent system, and could not possibly be removed, by even the Deity himself, considered as a wise agent, without giving entrance to greater ill or excluding greater good which will result from it. From this theory some philosophers, and the ancient Stoics among the rest, derived a topic of consolation under all afflictions, while they taught their pupils that those ills under which they labored were in reality goods to the universe, and that to an enlarged view which could comprehend the whole system of nature every event became an object of joy and exultation. But though this topic be specious and sublime, it was soon found in practice weak and ineffectual. You would surely more irritate than appease a man lying under the racking pains of the gout by preaching up to him the rectitude of those general laws which produced the malignant humors in his body and led them through the proper canals to the sinews and nerves, where they now excite such acute torments. These enlarged views may, for a moment, please the imagination of a speculative man who is placed in ease and security, but neither can they dwell with constancy on his mind, even though undisturbed by the emotions of pain or passion, much less can they maintain their ground when attacked by such powerful antagonists. The affections take a narrower and more natural survey of their object and, by an economy more suitable to the infirmity of human minds, regard alone the beings around us, and are actuated by such events as appear good or ill to the private system.

The case is the same with *moral* as with *physical* ill. It cannot reasonably be supposed that those remote considerations which are found of so little efficacy with regard to the one will have a more powerful influence with regard to the other. The mind of man is so formed by nature that, upon the appearance of certain characters, dispositions, and actions, it immediately feels the sentiment of approbation or blame; nor are there any emotions more essential to its frame and constitution. The characters which engage our approbation are chiefly such as contribute to the peace and security of human society, as the characters which excite blame are chiefly such as tend to public detriment and disturbance; whence it may reasonably be presumed that the moral sentiments arise, either mediately or immediately, from a reflection on these opposite interests. What though philosophical meditations establish a

onjecture that everything is right with
nd that the qualities which disturb so-
as beneficial, and are as suitable to the
nature, as those which more directly
and welfare? Are such remote and un-
ble to counterbalance the sentiments
atural and immediate view of the ob-
obbed of a considerable sum, does he
e loss anywise diminished by these sub-
, then, should his moral resentment
upposed incompatible with them? Or
nowledgment of a real distinction be-
be reconcilable to all speculative sys-
well as that of a real distinction be-
and deformity? Both these distinctions
ural sentiments of the human mind;
re not to be controlled or altered by
y or speculation whatsoever.

admits not of so easy and satisfactory
ossible to explain distinctly how the
diate cause of all the actions of men
without being the author of sin and moral turpitude. These
are mysteries which mere natural and unassisted reason is
very unfit to handle; and whatever system she embraces, she
must find herself involved in inextricable difficulties, and
even contradictions, at every step which she takes with regard
to such subjects. To reconcile the indifference and contingency of human actions with prescience or to defend absolute
decrees, and yet free the Deity from being the author of sin,
has been found hitherto to exceed all the power of philosophy. Happy, if she be thence sensible of her temerity, when
she pries into these sublime mysteries, and, leaving a scene so
full of obscurities and perplexities, return with suitable modesty to her true and proper province, the examination of common life, where she will find difficulties enough to employ
her inquiries without launching into so boundless an ocean
of doubt, uncertainty, and contradiction.

SECTION IX

OF THE REASON OF ANIMALS

ALL OUR REASONINGS concerning matter of fact are founded on a species of *analogy* which leads us to expect from any cause the same events which we have observed to result from similar causes. Where the causes are entirely similar, the analogy is perfect, and the inference drawn from it is regarded as certain and conclusive; nor does any man ever entertain a doubt, where he sees a piece of iron, that it will have weight and cohesion of parts as in all other instances which have ever fallen under his observation. But where the objects have not so exact a similarity, the analogy is less perfect and the inference is less conclusive, though still it has some force, in proportion to the degree of similarity and resemblance. The anatomical observations formed upon one animal are, by this species of reasoning, extended to all animals; and it is certain that, when the circulation of the blood, for instance, is clearly proved to have place in one creature, as a frog or fish, it forms a strong presumption that the same principle has place in all. These analogical observations may be carried further, even to this science of which we are now treating; and any theory by which we explain the operations of the understanding or the origin and connection of the passions in man will acquire additional authority if we find that the same theory is requisite to explain the same phenomena in all other animals. We shall make trial of this with regard to the hypothesis by which we have, in the foregoing discourse, endeavored to account for all experimental reasonings, and it is hoped that this new point of view will serve to confirm all our former observations.

First, it seems evident that animals, as well as men, learn many things from experience and infer that the same events will always follow from the same causes. By this principle they become acquainted with the more obvious properties of external objects and gradually, from their birth, treasure up a knowledge of the nature of fire, water, earth, stones, heights, depths, etc., and of the effects which result from their operation. The ignorance and inexperience of the young are here plainly distinguishable from the cunning and sagacity of the old, who have learned, by long observation, to avoid what hurt them and to pursue what gave ease or pleasure. A horse that has been accustomed to the field becomes acquainted with the proper height which he can leap, and will never attempt what exceeds his force and ability. An old greyhound will trust the more fatiguing part of the chase to the younger and will place himself so as to meet the hare in her doubles; nor are the conjectures which he forms on this occasion founded in anything but his observation and experience.

This is still more evident from the effects of discipline and education on animals, who by the proper application of rewards and punishments may be taught any course of action the most contrary to their natural instincts and propensities. Is it not experience which renders a dog apprehensive of pain when you menace him or lift up the whip to beat him? Is it not even experience which makes him answer to his name and infer, from such an arbitrary sound, that you mean him rather than any of his fellows, and intend to call him when you pronounce it in a certain manner and with a certain tone and accent?

In all these cases we may observe that the animal infers some fact beyond what immediately strikes his senses, and that this inference is altogether founded on past experience, while the creature expects from the present object the same consequences which it has always found in its observation to result from similar objects.

Secondly, it is impossible that this inference of the animal can be founded on any process of argument or reasoning by which he concludes that like events must follow like objects, and that the course of nature will always be regular in its operations. For if there be in reality any arguments of this nature, they surely lie too abstruse for the observation of such imperfect understandings, since it may well employ the utmost care and attention of a philosophic genius to discover and observe them. Animals, therefore, are not guided in these inferences by reasoning; neither are children; neither are the generality of mankind in their ordinary actions and conclusions; neither are philosophers themselves, who, in all the active parts of life, are in the main the same with the vulgar and are governed by the same maxims. Nature must have provided some other principle, of more ready and more general use and application, nor can an operation of such immense consequences in life as that of inferring effects from causes be trusted to the uncertain process of reasoning and argumentation. Were this doubtful with regard to men, it seems to admit of no question with regard to the brute creation; and the conclusion being once firmly established in the one, we have a strong presumption, from all the rules of analogy, that it ought to be universally admitted without any exception or reserve. It is custom alone which engages animals, from every object that strikes their senses, to infer its usual attendant, and carries their imagination from the appearance of the one to conceive the other in that particular manner which we denominate "belief." No other explication can be given of this operation, in all the higher as well as lower classes of sensitive beings which fall under our notice and observation.[1]

1 Since all reasonings concerning facts or causes is derived merely from custom, it may be asked how it happens that men so much surpass animals in reasoning, and one man so much surpasses another? Has not the same custom the same influence on all?

We shall here endeavor briefly to explain the great difference in human understanding, after which the reason of the difference between men and animals will easily be comprehended.

1. When we have lived any time and have been accustomed to the uniformity of nature, we acquire a general habit by which we always transfer the known to the unknown and conceive the latter to resemble the former. By means of this general habitual principle we regard even one experiment as the foundation of reasoning, and expect a similar event with some degree of certainty where the experiment has been made accurately and free from all foreign circumstances. It is there-

But though animals learn many parts of their knowledge from observation, there are also many parts of it which they derive from the original hand of nature, which much exceed the share of capacity they possess on ordinary occasions, and in which they improve little or nothing by the longest practice and experience. These we denominate "instincts," and are so apt to admire as something very extraordinary and inexplicable by all the disquisitions of human understanding. But our wonder will perhaps cease or diminish when we consider that the experimental reasoning itself, which we possess

---

fore considered as a matter of great importance to observe the consequences of things; and as one man may very much surpass another in attention, and memory, and observation, this will make a very great difference in their reasoning.

2. Where there is a complication of causes to produce any effect, one mind may be much larger than another, and better able to comprehend the whole system of objects and to infer justly their consequences.

3. One man is able to carry on a chain of consequences to a greater length than another.

4. Few men can think long without running into a confusion of ideas and mistaking one for another; and there are various degrees of this infirmity.

5. The circumstance on which the effect depends is frequently involved in other circumstances which are foreign and extrinsic. The separation of it often requires great attention, accuracy, and subtilty.

6. The forming of general maxims from particular observation is a very nice operation, and nothing is more usual, from haste or a narrowness of mind which sees not on all sides, than to commit mistakes in this particular.

7. When we reason from analogies, the man who has the greater experience or the greater promptitude of suggesting analogies will be the better reasoner.

8. Biases from prejudice, education, passion, party, etc., hang more upon one mind than another.

9. After we have acquired a confidence in human testimony, books and conversation enlarge much more the sphere of one man's experience and thought than those of another.

It would be easy to discover many other circumstances that make a difference in the understandings of men.*

* This note first appears in Edition L.

in common with beasts, and on which the whole conduct of life depends, is nothing but a species of instinct or mechanical power that acts in us unknown to ourselves, and in its chief operations is not directed by any such relations or comparison of ideas as are the proper objects of our intellectual faculties. Though the instinct be different, yet still it is an instinct which teaches a man to avoid the fire, as much as that which teaches a bird, with such exactness, the art of incubation and the whole economy and order of its nursery.

SECTION X

OF MIRACLES

PART I

THERE IS, in Dr. Tillotson's [1] writings, an argument against the *real presence* which is as concise and elegant and strong as any argument can possibly be supposed against a doctrine so little worthy of a serious refutation. It is acknowledged on all hands, says that learned prelate, that the authority either of the Scripture or of tradition is founded merely on the testimony of the Apostles, who were eyewitnesses to those miracles of our Saviour by which he proved his divine mission. Our evidence, then, for the truth of the *Christian* religion is less than the evidence for the truth of our senses, because, even in the first authors of our religion, it was no greater; and it is evident it must diminish in passing from them to their disciples, nor can anyone rest such confidence in their testimony as in the immediate object of his senses. But a weaker evidence can never destroy a stronger; and therefore, were the doctrine of the real presence ever so clearly revealed in Scripture, it were directly contrary to the rules of just reasoning to give our assent to it. It contradicts sense, though both the Scripture and tradition, on which it is supposed to be built, carry not such evidence with them as sense when they are considered merely as external evidences, and are not brought home to everyone's breast by the immediate operation of the Holy Spirit.

Nothing is so convenient as a decisive argument of this kind, which must at least *silence* the most arrogant bigotry and superstition and free us from their impertinent solicita-

---

1 [John Tillotson (1630-1694) was an influential Presbyterian theologian. He submitted to the Act of Uniformity (1662) and in 1691 became Archbishop of Canterbury. In later years, his sermons emphasized the practical side rather than the theological aspects of Christianity.—Ed.]

tions. I flatter myself that I have discovered an argument of a like nature which, if just, will, with the wise and learned, be an everlasting check to all kinds of superstitious delusion, and consequently will be useful as long as the world endures; for so long, I presume, will the accounts of miracles and prodigies be found in all history, sacred and profane.[2]

Though experience be our only guide in reasoning concerning matters of fact, it must be acknowledged that this guide is not altogether infallible, but in some cases is apt to lead us into errors. One who in our climate should expect better weather in any week of June than in one of December would reason justly and conformably to experience, but it is certain that he may happen, in the event, to find himself mistaken. However, we may observe that in such a case he would have no cause to complain of experience, because it commonly informs us beforehand of the uncertainty by that contrariety of events which we may learn from a diligent observation. All effects follow not with like certainty from their supposed causes. Some events are found, in all countries and all ages, to have been constantly conjoined together; others are found to have been more variable, and sometimes to disappoint our expectations, so that in our reasonings concerning matter of fact there are all imaginable degrees of assurance, from the highest certainty to the lowest species of moral evidence.

A wise man, therefore, proportions his belief to the evidence. In such conclusions as are founded on an infallible experience, he expects the event with the last degree of assurance and regards his past experience as a full *proof* of the future existence of that event. In other cases he proceeds with more caution: he weighs the opposite experiments; he considers which side is supported by the greater number of experiments—to that side he inclines with doubt and hesitation; and when at last he fixes his judgment, the evidence exceeds not what we properly call "probability." All probability, then,

----

2 [Editions K and L: "In all profane history."]

supposes an opposition of experiments and observations where the one side is found to overbalance the other and to produce a degree of evidence proportioned to the superiority. A hundred instances or experiments on one side, and fifty on another, afford a doubtful expectation of any event, though a hundred uniform experiments, with only one that is contradictory, reasonably beget a pretty strong degree of assurance. In all cases we must balance the opposite experiments where they are opposite, and deduct the smaller number from the greater in order to know the exact force of the superior evidence.

To apply these principles to a particular instance, we may observe that there is no species of reasoning more common, more useful, and even necessary to human life than that which is derived from the testimony of men and the reports of eyewitnesses and spectators. This species of reasoning, perhaps, one may deny to be founded on the relation of cause and effect. I shall not dispute about a word. It will be sufficient to observe that our assurance in any argument of this kind is derived from no other principle than our observation of the veracity of human testimony and of the usual conformity of facts to the report of witnesses. It being a general maxim that no objects have any discoverable connection together, and that all the inferences which we can draw from one to another are founded merely on our experience of their constant and regular conjunction, it is evident that we ought not to make an exception to this maxim in favor of human testimony whose connection with any event seems in itself as little necessary as any other.[3] Were not the memory tenacious to a certain degree, had not men commonly an inclination to truth and a principle of probity, were they not sensible to shame when detected in a falsehood—were not these, I say, discovered by *experience* to be qualities inherent in human nature, we should never repose the least confidence in human

[3] [Editions K to M read: "Did not men's imagination naturally follow their memory."]

testimony. A man delirious or noted for falsehood and villainy has no manner of authority with us.

And as the evidence derived from witnesses and human testimony is founded on past experience, so it varies with the experience and is regarded either as a *proof* or a *probability*, according as the conjunction between any particular kind of report and any kind of object has been found to be constant or variable. There are a number of circumstances to be taken into consideration in all judgments of this kind; and the ultimate standard by which we determine all disputes that may arise concerning them is always derived from experience and observation. Where this experience is not entirely uniform on any side, it is attended with an unavoidable contrariety in our judgments and with the same opposition and mutual destruction of argument as in every other kind of evidence. We frequently hesitate concerning the reports of others. We balance the opposite circumstances which cause any doubt or uncertainty; and when we discover a superiority on any side, we incline to it, but still with a diminution of assurance, in proportion to the force of its antagonist.

This contrariety of evidence, in the present case, may be derived from several different causes: from the opposition of contrary testimony, from the character or number of the witnesses, from the manner of their delivering their testimony, or from the union of all these circumstances. We entertain a suspicion concerning any matter of fact when the witnesses contradict each other, when they are but few or of a doubtful character, when they have an interest in what they affirm, when they deliver their testimony with hesitation or, on the contrary, with too violent asseverations. There are many other particulars of the same kind which may diminish or destroy the force of any argument derived from human testimony.

Suppose, for instance, that the fact which the testimony endeavors to establish partakes of the extraordinary and the marvelous—in that case the evidence resulting from the testimony admits of a diminution, greater or less in proportion as the fact is more or less unusual. The reason why we place any credit in witnesses and historians is not derived from any *connection* which we perceive *a priori* between testimony and reality, but because we are accustomed to find a conformity between them. But when the fact attested is such a one as has seldom fallen under our observation, here is a contest of two opposite experiences, of which the one destroys the other as far as its force goes, and the superior can only operate on the mind by the force which remains. The very same principle of experience which gives us a certain degree of assurance in the testimony of witnesses gives us also, in this case, another degree of assurance against the fact which they endeavor to establish; from which contradiction there necessarily arises a counterpoise and mutual destruction of belief and authority.

"I should not believe such a story were it told me by Cato" [4] was a proverbial saying in Rome, even during the lifetime of that philosophical patriot.[5] The incredibility of a fact, it was allowed, might invalidate so great an authority.

The Indian prince who refused to believe the first relations concerning the effects of frost reasoned justly, and it naturally required very strong testimony to engage his assent to facts that arose from a state of nature with which he was unacquainted, and which bore so little analogy to those events of which he had had constant and uniform experience. Though they were not contrary to his experience, they were not conformable to it.[6]

---

[4] [Reference is to Marcus Porcius Cato (234-149 B.C.), also known as Cato the Elder or the Censor. Of a stern character, he strongly favored Roman simplicity and opposed the influence of Hellenistic culture.—Ed.]

[5] Plutarch in *Vita Catonis*. [This paragraph and the reference to Plutarch were added in Edition M.]

[6] [This paragraph and the following note were added in Edition L.]

No Indian, it is evident, could have experience that water did not freeze in cold climates. This is placing nature in a situation quite unknown to him; and it is impossible for him to tell *a priori* what will result from it. It is making a new experiment, the consequence of which is always uncertain. One may sometimes conjecture from analogy what will follow, but still this is but conjecture. And it must be confessed that, in the present case of freezing, the event follows contrary to the rules of

But in order to increase the probability against the testimony of witnesses, let us suppose that the fact which they affirm, instead of being only marvelous, is really miraculous; and suppose also that the testimony, considered apart and in itself, amounts to an entire proof—in that case there is proof against proof, of which the strongest must prevail, but still with a diminution of its force, in proportion to that of its antagonist.

A miracle is a violation of the laws of nature; and as a firm and unalterable experience has established these laws, the proof against a miracle, from the very nature of the fact, is as entire as any argument from experience can possibly be imagined. Why is it more than probable that all men must die, that lead cannot of itself remain suspended in the air, that fire consumes wood and is extinguished by water, unless it be that these events are found agreeable to the laws of nature, and there is required a violation of these laws, or, in other words, a miracle to prevent them? Nothing is esteemed a miracle if it ever happen in the common course of nature. It is no miracle that a man, seemingly in good health, should die on a sudden, because such a kind of death, though more unusual than any other, has yet been frequently observed to happen. But it is a miracle that a dead man should come to life, because that has never been observed in any age or country. There must, therefore, be a uniform experience against every miraculous event, otherwise the event would not

___

analogy and is such as a rational Indian would not look for. The operations of cold upon water are not gradual, according to the degrees of cold; but whenever it comes to the freezing point, the water passes in a moment from the utmost liquidity to perfect hardness. Such an event, therefore, may be denominated "extraordinary" and requires a pretty strong testimony to render it credible to people in a warm climate; but still it is not *miraculous*, nor contrary to uniform experience of the course of nature in cases where all the circumstances are the same. The inhabitants of Sumatra have always seen water fluid in their own climate, and the freezing of their rivers ought to be deemed a prodigy, but they never saw water in Muscovy during the winter, and therefore they cannot reasonably be positive what would there be the consequence.

merit that appellation. And as a uniform experience amounts to a proof, there is here a direct and full *proof,* from the nature of the fact, against the existence of any miracle, nor can such a proof be destroyed or the miracle rendered credible but by an opposite proof which is superior.[7]

The plain consequence is (and it is a general maxim worthy of our attention) that no testimony is sufficient to establish a miracle unless the testimony be of such a kind that its falsehood would be more miraculous than the fact which it endeavors to establish. And even in that case there is a mutual destruction of arguments, and the superior only gives us an assurance suitable to that degree of force which remains after deducting the inferior. When anyone tells me that he saw a dead man restored to life, I immediately consider with myself whether it be more probable that this person should either deceive or be deceived, or that the fact which he relates should really have happened. I weigh the one miracle against the other, and according to the superiority which I discover I

[7] Sometimes an event may not, *in itself, seem* to be contrary to the laws of nature, and yet, if it were real, it might, by reason of some circumstances, be denominated a miracle; because, in *fact,* it is contrary to these laws. Thus if a person claiming a divine authority should command a sick person to be well, a healthful man to fall down dead, the clouds to pour rain, the winds to blow—in short, should order many natural events, which immediately follow upon his command—these might justly be esteemed miracles, because they are really, in this case, contrary to the laws of nature. For if any suspicion remain that the event and command concurred by accident, there is no miracle and no transgression of the laws of nature. If this suspicion be removed, there is evidently a miracle, and a transgression of these laws; because nothing can be more contrary to nature than that the voice or command of a man should have such an influence. A miracle may be accurately defined, *a trangression of a law of nature by a particular volition of the Deity, or by the interposition of some invisible agent.* A miracle may either be discovered by men or not. This alters not its nature and essence. The raising of a house or ship into the air is a visible miracle. The raising of a feather, when the wind wants ever so little of a force requisite for that purpose, is as real a miracle, though not so sensible with regard to us.

pronounce my decision, and always reject the greater miracle. If the falsehood of his testimony would be more miraculous than the event which he relates, then, and not till then, can he pretend to command my belief or opinion.

PART II

In the foregoing reasoning we have supposed that the testimony upon which a miracle is founded may possibly amount to entire proof, and that the falsehood of that testimony would be a real prodigy. But it is easy to show that we have been a great deal too liberal in our concession, and that there never was a miraculous event established [1] on so full an evidence.

For, *first*, there is not to be found, in all history, any miracle attested by a sufficient number of men of such unquestioned good sense, education, and learning as to secure us against all delusion in themselves; of such undoubted integrity as to place them beyond all suspicion of any design to deceive others; of such credit and reputation in the eyes of mankind as to have a great deal to lose in case of their being detected in any falsehood, and at the same time attesting facts performed in such a public manner and in so celebrated a part of the world as to render the detection unavoidable—all which circumstances are requisite to give us a full assurance in the testimony of men.

Secondly, we may observe in human nature a principle which, if strictly examined, will be found to diminish extremely the assurance which we might, from human testimony, have in any kind of prodigy. The maxim by which we commonly conduct ourselves in our reasonings is that the objects of which we have no experience resemble those of which we have; that what we have found to be most usual is always most probable; and that where there is an opposition of arguments, we ought to give the preference to such as are founded on the greatest number of past observations. But

---

[1] [Editions K and L: "in any history."]

though, in proceeding by this rule, we readily reject any fact which is unusual and incredible in an ordinary degree, yet in advancing further, the mind observes not always the same rule; but when anything is affirmed utterly absurd and miraculous, it rather the more readily admits of such a fact upon account of that very circumstance which ought to destroy all its authority. The passion of *surprise* and *wonder,* arising from miracles, being an agreeable emotion, gives a sensible tendency toward the belief of those events from which it is derived. And this goes so far that even those who cannot enjoy this pleasure immediately, nor can believe those miraculous events of which they are informed, yet love to partake the satisfaction at second hand, or by rebound, and place a pride and delight in exciting the admiration of others.

With what greediness are the miraculous accounts of travelers received, their descriptions of sea and land monsters, their relations of wonderful adventures, strange men and uncouth manners? But if the spirit of religion join itself to the love of wonder, there is an end of common sense, and human testimony in these circumstances loses all pretensions to authority. A religionist may be an enthusiast and imagine he sees what has no reality; he may know his narrative to be false, and yet persevere in it with the best intentions in the world, for the sake of promoting so holy a cause. Or even where this delusion has not place, vanity, excited by so strong a temptation, operates on him more powerfully than on the rest of mankind in any other circumstances; and self-interest, with equal force. His auditors may not have, and commonly have not, sufficient judgment to canvass his evidence; what judgment they have, they renounce by principle, in these sublime and mysterious subjects. Or if they were ever so willing to employ it, passion and a heated imagination disturb the regularity of its operations. Their credulity increases his impudence, and his impudence overpowers their credulity.

Eloquence, when at its highest pitch, leaves little room for reason or reflection, but addressing itself entirely to the fancy or the affections, captivates the willing hearers, and subdues their understanding. Happily, this pitch it seldom attains. But what a Tully [Cicero] or a Demosthenes could scarcely effect over a Roman or Athenian audience, every Capuchin, every itinerant or stationary teacher can perform over the generality of mankind, and in a higher degree, by touching such gross and vulgar passions.

The many instances of forged miracles and prophecies and supernatural events, which, in all ages, have either been detected by contrary evidence or which detect themselves by their absurdity, prove sufficiently the strong propensity of mankind to the extraordinary and marvelous, and ought reasonably to beget a suspicion against all relations of this kind. This is our natural way of thinking, even with regard to the most common and most credible events. For instance, there is no kind of report which arises so easily and spreads so quickly, especially in country places and provincial towns, as those concerning marriages, insomuch that two young persons of equal condition never see each other twice, but the whole neighborhood immediately join them together. The pleasure of telling a piece of news so interesting, of propagating it, and of being the first reporters of it spreads the intelligence; and this is so well known that no man of sense gives attention to these reports till he find them confirmed by some greater evidence. Do not the same passions, and others still stronger, incline the generality of mankind to believe and report with the greatest vehemence and assurance all religious miracles? [2]

Thirdly, it forms a strong presumption against all supernatural and miraculous relations that they are observed chiefly to abound among ignorant and barbarous nations; or if a civilized people has ever given admission to any of them, that people will be found to have received them from ignorant and barbarous ancestors, who transmitted them with that inviolable sanction and authority which always attend received opinions. When we peruse the first histories of all nations, we

[2] [This paragraph was published as a note in Editions K to N.]

are apt to imagine ourselves transported into some new world where the whole frame of nature is disjointed, and every element performs its operations in a different manner from what it does at present. Battles, revolutions, pestilence, famine, and death are never the effect of those natural causes which we experience. Prodigies, omens, oracles, judgments quite obscure the few natural events that are intermingled with them. But as the former grow thinner every page, in proportion as we advance nearer the enlightened ages, we soon learn that there is nothing mysterious or supernatural in the case, but that all proceeds from the usual propensity of mankind toward the marvelous, and that, though this inclination may at intervals receive a check from sense and learning, it can never be thoroughly extirpated from human nature.

"It is strange," a judicious reader is apt to say, upon the perusal of these wonderful historians, "that such prodigious events never happen in our days!" But it is nothing strange, I hope, that men should lie in all ages. You must surely have seen instances enough of that frailty. You have yourself heard many such marvelous relations started which, being treated with scorn by all the wise and judicious, have at last been abandoned even by the vulgar. Be assured that those renowned lies which have spread and flourished to such a monstrous height arose from like beginnings, but being sown in a more proper soil shot up at last into prodigies almost equal to those which they relate.

It was a wise policy in that false prophet [3] Alexander, who, though now forgotten, was once so famous, to lay the first scene of his impostures in Paphlagonia, where, as Lucian tells us, the people were extremely ignorant and stupid, and ready to swallow even the grossest delusion.[4] People at a distance,

[3] [Editions K to N: "cunning impostor."]

[4] [The story of Alexander, the false prophet, as related by Lucian, is, in short, the following: Alexander, who lived in the 2nd century A.D., was the leader of a cult. Being desirous of building up a lucrative oracle, he manufactured a miracle before the eyes of the people of Paphlagonia. He made god Asclepius appear in the form of a serpent with a human head.

who are weak enough to think the matter at all worthy inquiry, have no opportunity of receiving better information.
The stories come magnified to them by a hundred circumstances. Fools are industrious in propagating the imposture,
while the wise and learned are contented, in general, to deride
its absurdity, without informing themselves of the particular
facts by which it may be distinctly refuted. And thus the impostor above mentioned was enabled to proceed from his
ignorant Paphlagonians to the enlisting of votaries, even
among the Grecian philosophers and men of the most eminent
rank and distinction in Rome; nay, could engage the attention of that sage emperor Marcus Aurelius so far as to
make him trust the success of a military expedition to his
delusive prophecies.

The advantages are so great of starting an imposture among
an ignorant people that, even though the delusion should be
too gross to impose on the generality of them (*which, though
seldom, is sometimes the case*), it has a much better chance
for succeeding in remote countries than if the first scene had
been laid in a city renowned for arts and knowledge. The
most ignorant and barbarous of these barbarians carry the
report abroad. None of their countrymen have a large correspondence or sufficient credit and authority to contradict and
beat down the delusion. Men's inclination to the marvelous

To that end he hid a newborn snake in a blown goose egg on the temple
grounds, and kept a fully grown tame snake hidden in his room. On the
first day, he "discovered" the egg and had Asclepius born. A few days
later, he invited the townspeople to his house, where in a dimly lighted
room he displayed the full-grown snake, claiming this to be the snake
god which a few days earlier "appeared to the city." This in itself seemed
miraculous and gave credence to the major hoax, i.e., presenting the snake
with a head which appeared human. The snake's head was kept under
cover and was replaced by a head made of linen and painted to look
human: its mouth could be opened and closed by means of horsehairs.

Lucian tells us that the scheme was successful. The miracle was repeated
several times and seemed to have been generally accepted by the people
of Paphlagonia, and found credence in other parts of the Roman empire.
It should, however, be noted that Lucian is the sole source for this fan-
tastic story.—Ed.]

has full opportunity to display itself. And thus a story which is universally exploded in the place where it was first started shall pass for certain at a thousand miles distance. But had Alexander fixed his residence at Athens, the philosophers at that renowned mart of learning had immediately spread throughout the whole Roman empire their sense of the matter, which, being supported by so great authority and displayed by all the force of reason and eloquence, had entirely opened the eyes of mankind. It is true, Lucian, passing by chance through Paphlagonia, had an opportunity of performing this good office. But, though much to be wished, it does not always happen that every Alexander meets with a Lucian, ready to expose and detect his impostures.[5]

I may add, as a *fourth* reason which diminishes the authority of prodigies, that there is no testimony for any, even those which have not been expressly detected, that is not opposed by an infinite number of witnesses, so that not only the miracle destroys the credit of testimony, but the testimony destroys itself. To make this the better understood, let us consider that in matters of religion whatever is different is contrary, and that it is impossible the religions of ancient Rome, of Turkey, of Siam, and of China should all of them be established on any solid foundation. Every miracle, therefore, pretended to have been wrought in any of these religions (and all of them abound in miracles), as its direct scope is to establish the particular system to which it is attributed, so has it the same force, though more indirectly, to overthrow every other system. In destroying a rival system, it likewise

[5] It may perhaps be objected that I proceed rashly and form my notions of Alexander merely from the account given of him by Lucian, a professed enemy. It were indeed to be wished that some of the accounts published by his followers and accomplices had remained. The opposition and contrast betwixt the character and conduct of the same man as drawn by a friend or an enemy is as strong, even in common life, much more in these religious matters, as that betwixt any two men in the world; betwixt Alexander and St. Paul, for instance. See a Letter to Gilbert West, Esq., on the Conversion and Apostleship of St. Paul. [Note in the Editions prior to O.]

destroys the credit of those miracles on which that system was established, so that all the prodigies of different religions are to be regarded as contrary facts, and the evidences of these prodigies, whether weak or strong, as opposite to each other. According to this method of reasoning, when we believe any miracle of Mahomet or his successors, we have for our warrant the testimony of a few barbarous Arabians. And, on the other hand, we are to regard the authority of Titus Livius, Plutarch, Tacitus, and, in short, of all the authors and witnesses, Grecian, Chinese, and Roman Catholic, who have related any miracle in their particular religion—I say we are to regard their testimony in the same light as if they had mentioned the Mahometan miracle and had in express terms contradicted it with the same certainty as they have for the miracle they relate. This argument may appear oversubtile and refined, but is not in reality different from the reasoning of a judge who supposes that the credit of two witnesses maintaining a crime against anyone is destroyed by the testimony of two others who affirm him to have been two hundred leagues distant at the same instant when the crime is said to have been committed.

One of the best-attested miracles in all profane history is that which Tacitus reports of Vespasian, who cured a blind man in Alexandria by means of his spittle, and a lame man by the mere touch of his foot, in obedience to a vision of the god Serapis, who had enjoined them to have recourse to the emperor for these miraculous cures. The story may be seen in that fine historian,[6] where every circumstance seems to add weight to the testimony, and might be displayed at large with all the force of argument and eloquence, if anyone were now concerned to enforce the evidence of that exploded and idolatrous superstition: The gravity, solidity, age, and probity of so great an emperor, who, through the whole course of his life, conversed in a familiar manner with his friends and

---

[6] Hist. lib. v. cap. 8. Suetonius gives nearly the same account in *Vita Vesp.* [Added in Edition L.]

courtiers, and never affected those extraordinary airs of divinity assumed by Alexander and Demetrius; the historian, a contemporary writer noted for candor and veracity, and withal the greatest and most penetrating genius perhaps of all antiquity, and so free from any tendency to credulity that he even lies under the contrary imputation of atheism and profaneness; the persons from whose authority he related the miracle, of established character for judgment and veracity, as we may well presume; eyewitnesses of the fact, and confirming their testimony after the Flavian family was despoiled of the empire and could no longer give any reward as the price of a lie. *Utrumque, qui interfuere, nunc quoque memorant, postquam nullum mendacio pretium.*[7] To which, if we add the public nature of the facts, as related, it will appear that no evidence can well be supposed stronger for so gross and so palpable a falsehood.

There is also a memorable story related by Cardinal De Retz, which may well deserve our consideration. When that intriguing politician fled into Spain to avoid the persecution of his enemies, he passed through Saragossa, the capital of Aragon, where he was shown, in the cathedral, a man who had served seven[8] years as a doorkeeper and was well known to everybody in town that had ever paid his devotions at that church. He had been seen for so long a time wanting a leg, but recovered that limb by the rubbing of holy oil upon the stump; and the Cardinal assures us that he saw him with two legs. This miracle was vouched by all the canons of the church; and the whole company in town were appealed to for a confirmation of the fact, whom the Cardinal found, by their zealous devotion, to be thorough believers of the miracle. Here the relater was also contemporary to the supposed prodigy, of an incredulous and libertine character as well as of great genius; the miracle of so *singular* a nature as could

---

[7] ["Those who were present mention both incidents even now, when there is no longer any reward for telling a lie."—Ed.]

[8] [Editions prior to N read "twenty."]

scarcely admit of a counterfeit, and the witnesses very numerous, and all of them, in a manner, spectators of the fact to which they gave their testimony. And what adds mightily to the force of the evidence, and may double our surprise on this occasion, is that the Cardinal himself, who relates the story, seems not to give any credit to it and, consequently, cannot be suspected of any concurrence in the holy fraud. He considered justly that it was not requisite, in order to reject a fact of this nature, to be able accurately to disprove the testimony and to trace its falsehood through all the circumstances of knavery and credulity which produced it. He knew that, as this was commonly altogether impossible at any small distance of time and place, so was it extremely difficult, even where one was immediately present, by reason of the bigotry, ignorance, cunning, and roguery of a great part of mankind. He therefore concluded, like a just reasoner, that such an evidence carried falsehood upon the very face of it, and that a miracle, supported by any human testimony, was more properly a subject of derision than of argument.

There surely never was a greater number of miracles ascribed to one person than those which were lately said to have been wrought in France upon the tomb of Abbé Paris, the famous Jansenist, with whose sanctity the people were so long deluded. The curing of the sick, giving hearing to the deaf and sight to the blind, were everywhere talked of as the usual effects of that holy sepulcher. But what is more extraordinary, many of the miracles were immediately proved upon the spot, before judges of unquestioned integrity, attested by witnesses of credit and distinction, in a learned age, and on the most eminent theater that is now in the world. Nor is this all: a relation of them was published and dispersed everywhere, nor were the Jesuits, though a learned body supported by the civil magistrate, and determined enemies to those opinions in whose favor the miracles were said to have been wrought, ever able distinctly to refute or detect them.[9] Where

---

[9] This book was written by Mons. Montgeron, counselor or judge of the parliament of Paris, a man of figure and character who was also a

shall we find such a number of circumstances agreeing to the corroboration of one fact? And what have we to oppose to such a cloud of witnesses but the absolute impossibility or miraculous nature of the events which they relate? And this, surely, in the eyes of all reasonable people, will alone be regarded as a sufficient refutation.

---

martyr to the cause, and is now said to be somewhere in a dungeon on account of his book.

There is another book in three volumes (called *Recueil des Miracles de l'Abbé Paris*) giving an account of many of these miracles, and accompanied with prefatory discourses, which are very well written. There runs, however, through the whole of these a ridiculous comparison between the miracles of our Saviour and those of the Abbé, wherein it is asserted that the evidence for the latter is equal to that for the former, as if the testimony of men could ever be put in the balance with that of God himself, who conducted the pen of the inspired writers. If these writers indeed were to be considered merely as human testimony, the French author is very moderate in his comparison, since he might, with some appearance of reason, pretend that the Jansenist miracles much surpass the other in evidence and authority. The following circumstances are drawn from authentic papers, inserted in the above-mentioned book.

Many of the miracles of Abbé Paris were proved immediately by witnesses before the officiality, or bishop's court, at Paris, under the eye of Cardinal Noailles, whose character for integrity and capacity was never contested, even by his enemies.

His successor in the archbishopric was an enemy to the Jansenists, and for that reason promoted to the See by the Court. Yet twenty-two rectors or *curés* of Paris, with infinite earnestness, press him to examine those miracles which they assert to be known to the whole world, and indisputably certain. But he wisely forbore.

The Molinist party had tried to discredit these miracles in one instance, that of Mademoiselle la Franc. But besides that their proceedings were in many respects the most irregular in the world, particularly in citing only a few of the Jansenist witnesses whom they tampered with— besides this, I say, they soon found themselves overwhelmed by a cloud of new witnesses, one hundred and twenty in number, most of them persons of credit and substance in Paris, who gave oath for the miracle. This was accompanied with a solemn and earnest appeal to the parliament. But the parliament were forbidden, by authority, to meddle in the affair. It was at last observed that where men are heated by zeal and enthusiasm, there is no degree of human testimony so strong as may not be procured for the greatest absurdity. And those who will be so silly as to examine the affair by that medium and seek particular flaws in the testimony are

Is the consequence just because some human testimony has the utmost force and authority in some cases, when it relates the battles of Philippi or Pharsalia, for instance, that therefore all kinds of testimony must in all cases have equal force and authority? Suppose that the Caesarean or Pompeian

---

almost sure to be confounded. It must be a miserable imposture, indeed, that does not prevail in that contest.

All who have been in France about that time have heard of the reputation of Mons. Herault, the *Lieutenant de Police*, whose vigilance, penetration, activity, and extensive intelligence have been much talked of. This magistrate, who by the nature of his office is almost absolute, was invested with full powers on purpose to suppress or discredit these miracles, and he frequently seized immediately and examined the witnesses and subjects of them, but never could reach anything satisfactory against them.

In the case of Mademoiselle Thibaut, he sent the famous De Sylva to examine her, whose evidence is very curious. The physician declares that it was impossible she could have been so ill as was proved by witnesses, because it was impossible she could, in so short a time, have recovered so perfectly as he found her. He reasoned, like a man of sense, from natural causes, but the opposite party told him that the whole was a miracle, and that his evidence was the very best proof of it.

The Molinists were in a sad dilemma. They durst not assert the absolute insufficiency of human evidence to prove a miracle. They were obliged to say that these miracles were wrought by witchcraft and the devil. But they were told that this was the resource of the Jews of old.

No Jansenist was ever embarrassed to account for the cessation of the miracles when the churchyard was shut up by the king's edict. It was the touch of the tomb which produced these extraordinary effects; and when no one could approach the tomb, no effects could be expected. God, indeed, could have thrown down the walls in a moment, but he is master of his own graces and works, and it belongs not to us to account for them. He did not throw down the walls of every city, like those of Jericho, on the sounding of the rams' horns, nor break up the prison of every apostle, like that of St. Paul.

No less a man than the Duc de Chatillon, a duke and peer of France, of the highest rank and family, gives evidence of a miraculous cure, performed upon a servant of his who had lived several years in his house with a visible and palpable infirmity.

I shall conclude with observing that no clergy are more celebrated for strictness of life and manner than the secular clergy of France, particularly the rectors or curés of Paris who bear testimony to these impostures.

factions had, each of them, claimed the victory in these battles, and that the historians of each party had uniformly ascribed the advantage to their own side, how could mankind, at this distance, have been able to determine between them? The contrariety is equally strong between the miracles related by Herodotus or Plutarch, and those delivered by Mariana, Bede, or any monkish historian.

The wise lend a very academic faith to every report which favors the passion of the reported, whether it magnifies his country, his family, or. himself, or in any other way strikes in with his natural inclinations and propensities. But what

---

The learning, genius, and probity of the gentlemen, and the austerity of the nuns of Port Royal, have been much celebrated all over Europe. Yet they all give evidence for a miracle wrought on the niece of the famous Pascal, whose sanctity of life, as well as extraordinary capacity, is well known.* The famous Racine gives an account of this miracle in his famous history of Port Royal, and fortifies it with all the proofs which a multitude of nuns, priests, physicians, and men of the world, all of them of undoubted credit, could bestow upon it. Several men of letters, particularly the bishop of Tournay, thought this miracle so certain as to employ it in the refutation of atheists and freethinkers. The queen-regent of France, who was extremely prejudiced against the Port Royal, sent her own physician to examine the miracle, who returned an absolute convert. In short, the supernatural cure was so incontestable that it saved, for a time, that famous monastery from the ruin with which it was threatened by the Jesuits. Had it been a cheat, it had certainly been detected by such sagacious and powerful antagonists, and must have hastened the ruin of the contrivers. Our divines, who can build up a formidable castle upon such despicable materials—what a prodigious fabric could they have reared from these and many other circumstances which I have not mentioned! How often would the great names of Pascal, Racine, Arnaud, Nicole have resounded in our ears? But if they be wise, they had better adopt the miracle as being more worth a thousand times than all the rest of their collection. Besides, it may serve very much to their purpose. For that miracle was really performed by the touch of an authentic holy prickle of the holy thorn which composed the holy crown, which, etc. [*This note first occurs in Edition L, and the conclusion regarding the Port Royal miracle, beginning "The famous Racine," in Edition N.*]

* Edition L adds here: "Though he also was a believer in that and many other miracles which he had less opportunity of being informed of. See his Life."

greater temptation than to appear a missionary, a prophet, an ambassador from heaven? Who would not encounter many dangers and difficulties in order to attain so sublime a character? Or if, by the help of vanity and a heated imagination, a man has first made a convert of himself and entered seriously into the delusion, who ever scruples to make use of pious frauds in support of so holy and meritorious a cause?

The smallest spark may here kindle into the greatest flame, because the materials are always prepared for it. The *avidum genus auricularum,*[10] the gazing populace, receive greedily, without examination, whatever soothes superstition and promotes wonder.

How many stories of this nature have, in all ages, been detected and exploded in their infancy? How many more have been celebrated for a time, and have afterwards sunk into neglect and oblivion? Where such reports, therefore, fly about, the solution of the phenomenon is obvious, and we judge in conformity to regular experience and observation when we account for it by the known and natural principles of credulity and delusion. And shall we, rather than have recourse to so natural a solution, allow of a miraculous violation of the most established laws of nature?

I need not mention the difficulty of detecting a falsehood in any private or even public history at the place where it is said to happen, much more when the scene is removed to ever so small a distance. Even a court of judicature, with all the authority, accuracy, and judgment which they can employ, find themselves often at a loss to distinguish between truth and falsehood in the most recent actions. But the matter never comes to any issue if trusted to the common method of altercation and debate and flying rumors, especially when men's passions have taken part on either side.

In the infancy of new religions, the wise and learned commonly esteem the matter too inconsiderable to deserve their attention or regard. And when afterwards they would willingly detect the cheat, in order to undeceive the deluded

10 Lucretius. [IV. 594. This reference was added in Edition L.]

multitude, the season is now past and the records and witnesses which might clear up the matter have perished beyond recovery.

No means of detection remain but those which must be drawn from the very testimony itself of the reporters; and these, though always sufficient with the judicious and knowing, are commonly too fine to fall under the comprehension of the vulgar.

Upon the whole, then, it appears that no testimony for any kind of miracle has ever amounted [11] to a probability, much less to a proof; and that, even supposing it amounted to a proof, it would be opposed by another proof derived from the very nature of the fact which it would endeavor to establish. It is experience only which gives authority to human testimony, and it is the same experience which assures us of the laws of nature. When, therefore, these two kinds of experience are contrary, we have nothing to do but to subtract the one from the other and embrace an opinion either on one side or the other with that assurance which arises from the remainder. But according to the principle here explained, this subtraction with regard to all popular religions amounts to an entire annihilation; and therefore we may establish it as a maxim that no human testimony can have such force as to prove a miracle and make it a just foundation for any such system of religion.

I beg the limitations here made may be remarked, when I say that a miracle can never be proved so as to be the foundation of a system of religion. For I own that otherwise there may possibly be miracles or violations of the usual course of nature, of such a kind as to admit of proof from human testimony, though perhaps it will be impossible to find any such in all the records of history. Thus suppose all authors, in all languages, agree that from the first of January, 1600, there was a total darkness over the whole earth for eight days; suppose that the tradition of this extraordinary event is still strong and lively among the people; that all travelers who

---

[11] [Editions K and L: "can ever possibly amount."]

return from foreign countries bring us accounts of the same tradition without the least variation or contradiction—it is evident that our present philosophers, instead of doubting the fact, ought to receive it as certain and ought to search for the causes whence it might be derived. The decay, corruption, and dissolution of nature is an event rendered probable by so many analogies that any phenomenon which seems to have a tendency toward that catastrophe comes within the reach of human testimony if that testimony be very extensive and uniform.[12]

But suppose that all the historians who treat of England should agree that on the first of January, 1600, Queen Elizabeth died; that both before and after her death she was seen by her physicians and the whole court, as is usual with persons of her rank; that her successor was acknowledged and proclaimed by the Parliament; and that, after being interred for a month, she again appeared, resumed the throne, and governed England for three years—I must confess that I should be surprised at the concurrence of so many odd circumstances, but should not have the least inclination to believe so miraculous an event. I should not doubt of her pretended death and of those other public circumstances that followed it; I should only assert it to have been pretended, and that it neither was, nor possibly could be, real. You would in vain object to me the difficulty and almost impossibility of deceiving the world in an affair of such consequence; the wisdom [13] and solid judgment of that renowned Queen, with the little or no advantage which she could reap from so poor an artifice—all this might astonish me, but I would still reply that the knavery and folly of men are such common phenomena that I should rather believe the most extraordinary events to arise from their concurrence than admit of so signal a violation of the laws of nature.

But should this miracle be ascribed to any new system of

---

12 [This and the following paragraphs (to the passage quoted by Bacon) were printed as a note in Editions prior to N.]

13 [Editions prior to N had also: "and integrity."]

religion, men in all ages have been so much imposed on by ridiculous stories of that kind that this very circumstance would be a full proof of a cheat and sufficient, with all men of sense, not only to make them reject the fact but even reject it without further examination. Though the Being to whom the miracle is ascribed be in this case Almighty, it does not, upon that account, become a whit more probable, since it is impossible for us to know the attributes or actions of such a Being otherwise than from the experience which we have of his productions in the usual course of nature. This still reduces us to past observation and obliges us to compare the instances of the violation of truth in the testimony of men with those of the violation of the laws of nature by miracles, in order to judge which of them is most likely and probable. As the violations of truth are more common in the testimony concerning religious miracles than in that concerning any other matter of fact, this must diminish very much the authority of the former testimony and make us form a general resolution never to lend any attention to it, with whatever specious pretense it may be covered.

Lord Bacon seems to have embraced the same principles of reasoning.

> We ought [says he] to make a collection or particular history of all monsters and prodigious births or productions; and, in a word, of everything new, rare, and extraordinary in nature. But this must be done with the most severe scrutiny, lest we depart from truth. Above all, every relation must be considered as suspicious which depends in any degree upon religion, as the prodigies of Livy: And no less so everything that is to be found in the writers on natural magic or alchemy, or such authors who seem all of them to have an unconquerable appetite for falsehood and fable.[14]

I am the better pleased with the method of reasoning here delivered, as I think it may serve to confound those dangerous friends or disguised enemies to the *Christian religion* who have undertaken to defend it by the principles of human

[14] *Novum Organum* lib. ii. aph. 29.

reason. Our most holy religion is founded on *faith,* not on reason; and it is a sure method of exposing it to put it to such a trial as it is by no means fitted to endure. To make this more evident, let us examine those miracles related in Scripture, and, not to lose ourselves in too wide a field, let us confine ourselves to such as we find in the Pentateuch, which we shall examine according to the principles of these pretended Christians, not as the word or testimony of God himself, but as the production of a mere human writer and historian. Here, then, we are first to consider a book presented to us by a barbarous and ignorant people, written in an age when they were still more barbarous, and, in all probability, long after the facts which it relates, corroborated by no concurring testimony, and resembling those fabulous accounts which every nation gives of its origin. Upon reading this book we find it full of prodigies and miracles. It gives an account of a state of the world and of human nature entirely different from the present: Of our fall from that state; of the age of man extended to near a thousand years; of the destruction of the world by a deluge; of the arbitrary choice of one people as the favorites of heaven, and that people the countrymen of the author; of their deliverance from bondage by prodigies the most astonishing imaginable—I desire anyone to lay his hand upon his heart and, after a serious consideration, declare whether he thinks that the falsehood of such a book, supported by such a testimony, would be more extraordinary and miraculous than all the miracles it relates; which is, however, necessary to make it be received according to the measures of probability above established.

What we have said of miracles may be applied without any variation to prophecies; and, indeed, all prophecies are real miracles and as such only can be admitted as proofs of any revelation. If it did not exceed the capacity of human nature to foretell future events, it would be absurd to employ any prophecy as an argument for a divine mission or authority from heaven. So that, upon the whole, we may conclude that the Christian religion not only was at first attended with miracles, but even at this day cannot be believed by any reasonable person without one. Mere reason is insufficient to convince us of its veracity. And whoever is moved by *faith* to assent to it is conscious of a continued miracle in his own person which subverts all the principles of his understanding and gives him a determination to believe what is most contrary to custom and experience.

SECTION XI

OF A PARTICULAR PROVIDENCE AND OF A FUTURE STATE [1]

I WAS LATELY ENGAGED in conversation with a friend who loves skeptical paradoxes; where, though he advanced many principles of which I can by no means approve, yet, as they seem to be curious and to bear some relation to the chain of reasoning carried on throughout this inquiry, I shall here copy them from my memory as accurately as I can in order to submit them to the judgment of the reader.

Our conversation began with my admiring the singular good fortune of philosophy, which, as it requires entire liberty above all other privileges, and chiefly flourishes from the free opposition of sentiments and argumentation, received its first birth in an age and country of freedom and toleration, and was never cramped, even in its most extravagant principles, by any creeds, confessions, or penal statutes. For except the banishment of Protagoras and the death of Socrates, which last event proceeded partly from other motives, there are scarcely any instances to be met with, in ancient history, of this bigoted jealousy with which the present age is so much infested. Epicurus lived at Athens to an advanced age, in peace and tranquillity; Epicureans [2] were even admitted to receive the sacerdotal character and to officiate at the altar in the most sacred rites of the established religion. And the public encouragement [3] of pensions and salaries was afforded equally by the wisest of all the Roman emperors [4] to the professors of every sect of philosophy. How requisite such

---

1 [Edition K: "Of the Practical Consequences of Natural Religion."]

2 Luciani συμπ ἢ λαπίθαι 9.

3 Luciani εὐνοῦχος 3.

4 Id. and Dio. [Reference is to the emperor Marcus Aurelius.—Ed.]

kind of treatment was to philosophy, in her early youth, will easily be conceived if we reflect that even at present, when she may be supposed more hardy and robust, she bears with much difficulty the inclemency of the seasons and those harsh winds of calumny and persecution which blow upon her.

You admire, says my friend, as the singular good fortune of philosophy what seems to result from the natural course of things and to be unavoidable in every age and nation. This pertinacious bigotry, of which you complain as so fatal to philosophy, is really her offspring, who, after allying with superstition, separates himself entirely from the interest of his parent and becomes her most inveterate enemy and persecutor. Speculative dogmas of religion, the present occasions of such furious dispute, could not possibly be conceived or admitted in the early ages of the world, when mankind, being wholly illiterate, formed an idea of religion more suitable to their weak apprehension, and composed their secret tenets of such tales chiefly as were the objects of traditional belief more than of argument or disputation. After the first alarm, therefore, was over, which arose from the new paradoxes and principles of the philosophers, these teachers seem ever after, during the ages of antiquity, to have lived in great harmony with the established superstition and to have made a fair partition of mankind between them—the former claiming all the learned and wise, the latter possessing all the vulgar and illiterate.

It seems then, said I, that you leave politics entirely out of the question and never suppose that a wise magistrate can justly be jealous of certain tenets of philosophy, such as those of Epicurus, which, denying a divine existence and consequently a providence and a future state, seem to loosen in a great measure the ties of morality, and may be supposed, for that reason, pernicious to the peace of civil society.

I know, replied he, that in fact these persecutions never, in any age, proceeded from calm reason or from experience of the pernicious consequences of philosophy, but arose entirely from passion and prejudice. But what if I should advance further and assert that, if Epicurus had been accused before the people by any of the sycophants or informers of those days, he could easily have defended his cause and proved his principles of philosophy to be as salutary as those of his adversaries who endeavored with such zeal to expose him to the public hatred and jealousy.

I wish, said I, you would try your eloquence upon so extraordinary a topic and make a speech for Epicurus which might satisfy, not the mob of Athens, if you will allow that ancient and polite city to have contained any mob, but the more philosophical part of his audience, such as might be supposed capable of comprehending his arguments.

The matter would not be difficult upon such conditions, replied he; and if you please, I shall suppose myself Epicurus for a moment and make you stand for the Athenian people, and shall deliver you such a harangue as will fill all the urn with white beans and leave not a black one to gratify the malice of my adversaries.

Very well: Pray proceed upon these suppositions.

I come hither, O ye Athenians! to justify, in your assembly, what I maintained in my school, and I find myself impeached by furious antagonists, instead of reasoning with calm and dispassionate inquirers. Your deliberations, which of right should be directed to questions of public good and the interest of the commonwealth, are diverted to the disquisitions of speculative philosophy; and these magnificent but perhaps fruitless inquiries take place of your more familiar but more useful occupations. But so far as in me lies I will prevent this abuse. We shall not here dispute concerning the origin and government of worlds. We shall only inquire how far such questions concern the public interest. And if I can persuade you that they are entirely indifferent to the peace of society and security of government, I hope that you will presently send us back to our schools, there to examine at leisure the question, the most sublime, but, at the same time, the most speculative of all philosophy.

The religious philosophers, not satisfied with the tradition of your forefathers and doctrine of your priests (in which I willingly acquiesce), indulge a rash curiosity in trying how far they can establish religion upon the principles of reason; and they thereby excite, instead of satisfying, the doubts which naturally arise from a diligent and scrupulous inquiry. They paint in the most magnificent colors the order, beauty, and wise arrangement of the universe, and then ask if such a glorious display of intelligence could proceed from the fortuitous concourse of atoms, or if chance could produce what the greatest genius can never sufficiently admire. I shall not examine the justness of this argument. I shall allow it to be as solid as my antagonists and accusers can desire. It is sufficient if I can prove, from this very reasoning, that the question is entirely speculative, and that, when in my philosophical disquisitions I deny a providence and a future state, I undermine not the foundations of society but advance principles which they themselves, upon their own topics, if they argue consistently, must allow to be solid and satisfactory.

You, then, who are my accusers, have acknowledged that the chief or sole argument for a divine existence (which I never questioned) is derived from the order of nature, where there appear such marks of intelligence and design that you think it extravagant to assign for its cause either chance or the blind and unguided force of matter. You allow that this is an argument drawn from effects to causes. From the order of the work you infer that there must have been project and forethought in the workman. If you cannot make out this point, you allow that your conclusion fails, and you pretend not to establish the conclusion in a greater latitude than the phenomena of nature will justify. These are your concessions. I desire you to mark the consequences.

When we infer any particular cause from an effect, we must proportion the one to the other and can never be allowed to ascribe to the cause any qualities but what are exactly sufficient to produce the effect. A body of ten ounces raised in any scale may serve as a proof that the counterbalancing weight exceeds ten ounces, but can never afford a reason that it exceeds a hundred. If the cause assigned for any effect be not sufficient to produce it, we must either reject that cause or add to it such qualities as will give it a just proportion to the effect. But if we ascribe to it further qualities or affirm it capable of producing other effects, we can only indulge the license of conjecture and arbitrarily suppose the existence of qualities and energies without reason or authority.

The same rule holds whether the cause assigned be brute unconscious matter or a rational intelligent being. If the cause be known only by the effect, we never ought to ascribe to it any qualities beyond what are precisely requisite to produce the effect; nor can we, by any rules of just reasoning, return back from the cause and infer other effects from it, beyond those by which alone it is known to us. No one, merely from the sight of one of Zeuxis' pictures, could know that he was also a statuary or architect, and was an artist no less skillful in stone and marble than in colors. The talents and taste displayed in the particular work before us—these we may safely conclude the workman to be possessed of. The cause must be proportioned to the effect; and if we exactly and precisely proportion it, we shall never find in it any qualities that point further, or afford an inference concerning any other design or performance. Such qualities must be somewhat beyond what is merely requisite for producing the effect which we examine.

Allowing, therefore, the gods to be the authors of the existence or order of the universe, it follows that they possess that precise degree of power, intelligence, and benevolence which appears in their workmanship, but nothing further can ever be proved, except we call in the assistance of exaggeration and flattery to supply the defects of argument and reasoning. So far as the traces of any attributes at present appear, so far may we conclude these attributes to exist. The supposition of further attributes is mere hypothesis, much more the supposition that in distant regions of space or periods of time there has been, or will be, a more magnificent display of these attributes and a scheme of administration more suitable to such imaginary virtues. We can never be allowed to mount up from the universe, the effect, to Jupiter, the cause, and then descend downward to infer any new effect from that cause, as if the present effects alone were not entirely worthy of the glorious attributes which we ascribe to that deity. The knowledge of the cause being derived solely from the effect, they must be exactly adjusted to each other; and the one can never refer to anything further or be the foundation of any new inference and conclusion.

You find certain phenomena in nature. You seek a cause or author. You imagine that you have found him. You afterwards become so enamored of this offspring of your brain that you imagine it impossible but he must produce something greater and more perfect than the present scene of things, which is so full of ill and disorder. You forget that this superlative intelligence and benevolence are entirely imaginary, or, at least, without any foundation in reason, and that you have no ground to ascribe to him any qualities but what you see he has actually exerted and displayed in his productions. Let your gods, therefore, O philosophers! be suited to the present appearances of nature and presume not to alter these appearances by arbitrary suppositions in order to suit them to the attributes which you so fondly ascribe to your deities.

When priests and poets, supported by your authority, O Athenians! talk of a golden or silver age which preceded the present state of vice and misery, I hear them with attention and with reverence. But when philosophers who pretend to neglect authority and to cultivate reason hold the same discourse, I pay them not, I own, the same obsequious submission and pious deference. I ask, who carried them into the celestial regions, who admitted them into the councils of gods, who opened to them the book of fate, that they thus rashly affirm that their deities have executed, or will execute, any purpose beyond what has actually appeared? If they tell me that they have mounted on the steps,[5] or by the gradual ascent of reason, and by drawing inferences from effects or causes, I

5 [Edition K reads: "on the steps or scale of reason."]

still insist that they have aided the ascent [6] of reason by the wings of imagination, otherwise they could not thus change their manner of inference and argue from causes to effects, presuming that a more perfect production than the present world would be more suitable to such perfect beings as the gods, and forgetting that they have no reason to ascribe to these celestial beings any perfection or any attribute but what can be found in the present world.

Hence all the fruitless industry to account for the ill appearances of nature and save the honor of the gods, while we must acknowledge the reality of that evil and disorder with which the world so much abounds. The obstinate and intractable qualities of matter, we are told, or the observance of general laws, or some such reason, is the sole cause which controlled the power and benevolence of Jupiter and obliged him to create mankind and every sensible creature so imperfect and so unhappy. These attributes, then, are, it seems, beforehand taken for granted in their greatest latitude. And upon that supposition I own that such conjectures may, perhaps, be admitted as plausible solutions of the ill phenomena. But still I ask, why take these attributes for granted or why ascribe to the cause any qualities but what actually appear in the effect? Why torture your brain to justify the course of nature upon suppositions which, for aught you know, may be entirely imaginary, and of which there are to be found no traces in the course of nature?

The religious hypothesis, therefore, must be considered only as a particular method of accounting for the visible phenomena of the universe. But no just reasoner will ever presume to infer from it any single fact and alter or add to the phenomena in any single particular. If you think that the appearances of things prove such causes, it is allowable for you to draw an inference concerning the existence of these causes. In such complicated and sublime subjects, everyone should be indulged in the liberty of conjecture and argument. But here

6 [Edition K reads "scale" instead of "ascent."]

you ought to rest. If you come backward and, arguing from your inferred causes, conclude that any other fact has existed, or will exist, in the course of nature, which may serve as a fuller display of particular attributes, I must admonish you that you have departed from the method of reasoning attached to the present subject and have certainly added something to the attributes of the cause beyond what appears in the effect; otherwise you could never, with tolerable sense or propriety, add anything to the effect in order to render it more worthy of the cause.

Where, then, is the odiousness of that doctrine which I teach in my school, or rather, which I examine in my gardens? Or what do you find in this whole question wherein the security of good morals or the peace and order of society is in the least concerned?

I deny a providence, you say, and supreme governor of the world who guides the course of events, and punishes the vicious with infamy and disappointment, and rewards the virtuous with honor and success in all their undertakings. But surely I deny not the course itself of events, which lies open to everyone's inquiry and examination. I acknowledge that in the present order of things virtue is attended with more peace of mind than vice, and meets with a more favorable reception from the world. I am sensible that, according to the past experience of mankind, friendship is the chief joy of human life, and moderation the only source of tranquillity and happiness. I never balance between the virtuous and the vicious course of life, but am sensible that, to a well-disposed mind, every advantage is on the side of the former. And what can you say more, allowing all your suppositions and reasonings? You tell me, indeed, that this disposition of things proceeds from intelligence and design. But whatever it proceeds from, the disposition itself, on which depends our happiness or misery, and consequently our conduct and deportment in life, is still the same. It is still open for me, as well as you, to regulate my behavior by my experience of past events. And if you affirm that, while a divine providence is allowed, and a supreme distributive justice in the universe, I ought to expect some more particular reward of the good, and punishment of the bad, beyond the ordinary course of events, I here find the same fallacy which I have before endeavored to detect. You persist in imagining that if we grant that divine existence for which you so earnestly contend, you may safely infer consequences from it and add something to the experienced order of nature by arguing from the attributes which you ascribe to your gods. You seem not to remember that all your reasonings on this subject can only be drawn from effects to causes, and that every argument deduced from causes to effects must of necessity be a gross sophism, since it is impossible for you to know anything of the cause but what you have antecedently not inferred, but discovered to the full in the effect.

But what must a philosopher think of those vain reasoners who, instead of regarding the present scene of things as the sole object of their contemplation, so far reverse the whole course of nature as to render this life merely a passage to something further—a porch which leads to a greater and vastly different building, a prologue which serves only to introduce the piece and give it more grace and propriety? Whence, do you think, can such philosophers derive their idea of the gods? From their own conceit and imagination surely. For if they derive it from the present phenomena, it would never point to anything further, but must be exactly adjusted to them. That the divinity may *possibly* be endowed with attributes which we have never seen exerted, may be governed by principles of action which we cannot discover to be satisfied—all this will freely be allowed. But still this is mere *possibility* and hypothesis. We never can have reason to *infer* any attributes or any principles of action in him, but so far as we know them to have been exerted and satisfied.

Are there any marks of a distributive justice in the world? If you answer in the affirmative, I conclude that, since justice here exerts itself, it is satisfied. If you reply in the negative, I conclude that you have then no reason to ascribe justice, in our sense of it, to the gods. If you hold a medium between affirmation and negation, by saying that the justice of the gods at present exerts itself in part, but not in its full extent, I answer that you have no reason to give it any particular extent, but only so far as you see it, *at present*, exert itself.

Thus I bring the dispute, O Athenians! to a short issue with my antagonists. The course of nature lies open to my contemplation as well as to theirs. The experienced train of events is the great standard by which we all regulate our conduct. Nothing else can be appealed to in the field or in the senate. Nothing else ought ever to be heard of in the school or in the closet. In vain would our limited understanding break through those boundaries which are too narrow for our fond imagination. While we argue from the course of nature and infer a particular intelligent cause which first bestowed and still preserves order in the universe, we embrace a principle which is both uncertain and useless. It is uncertain because the subject lies entirely beyond the reach of human experience. It is useless because our knowledge of this cause being derived entirely from the course of nature, we can never, according to the rules of just reasoning, return back from the cause with any new inference or, making additions to the common and experienced course of nature, establish any principles of conduct and behavior.

I observe (said I, finding he had finished his harangue) that you neglect not the artifice of the demagogues of old, and as you were pleased to make me stand for the people, you insinuate yourself into my favor by embracing those principles to which, you know, I have always expressed a particular attachment. But allowing you to make experience (as indeed I think you ought) the only standard of our judgment concerning this and all other questions of fact, I doubt not but, from the very same experience to which you appeal, it may be possible to refute this reasoning which you have put into the mouth of Epicurus. If you saw, for instance, a half-finished building, surrounded with heaps of brick and stone and mortar, and all the instruments of masonry, could you not *infer* from the effect that it was a work of design and contrivance?

And could you not return again, from this inferred cause, to infer new additions to the effect and conclude that the building would soon be finished and receive all the further improvements which art could bestow upon it? If you saw upon the seashore the print of one human foot, you would conclude that a man had passed that way, and that he had also left the traces of the other foot, though effaced by the rolling of the sands or inundation of the waters. Why, then, do you refuse to admit the same method of reasoning with regard to the order of nature? Consider the world and the present life only as an imperfect building from which you can infer a superior intelligence; and arguing from that superior intelligence, which can leave nothing imperfect, why may you not infer a more finished scheme or plan which will receive its completion in some distant point of space or time? Are not these methods of reasoning exactly similar? And under what pretense can you embrace the one while you reject the other?

The infinite difference of the subjects, replied he, is a sufficient foundation for this difference in my conclusions. In works of *human* art and contrivance, it is allowable to advance from the effect to the cause, and, returning back from the cause, to form new inferences concerning the effect, and examine the alterations which it has probably undergone or may still undergo. But what is the foundation of this method of reasoning? Plainly this: that man is a being whom we know by experience, whose motives and designs we are acquainted with, and whose projects and inclinations have a certain connection and coherence according to the laws which nature has established for the government of such a creature. When, therefore, we find that any work has proceeded from the skill and industry of man, as we are otherwise acquainted with the nature of the animal, we can draw a hundred inferences concerning what may be expected from him; and these inferences will all be founded in experience and observation. But did we know man only from the single work or production which we examine, it were impossible for us to argue in this manner, because our knowledge of all the qualities which we ascribe to him, being in that case derived from the production, it is impossible they could point to anything further or be the foundation of any new inference. The print of a foot in the sand can only prove, when considered alone, that there was some figure adapted to it by which it was produced. But the print of a human foot proves likewise, from our other experience, that there was probably another foot which also left its impression, though effaced by time or other accidents. Here we mount from the effect to the cause, and, descending again from the cause, infer alterations in the effect; but this is not a continuation of the same simple chain of reasoning. We comprehend in this case a hundred other experiences and observations concerning the *usual* figure and members of that species of animal, without which this method of argument must be considered as fallacious and sophistical.

The case is not the same with our reasonings from the works of nature. The Deity is known to us only by his productions, and is a single being in the universe, not comprehended under any species or genus, from whose experienced attributes or qualities we can, by analogy, infer any attribute or quality in him. As the universe shows wisdom and goodness, we infer wisdom and goodness. As it shows a particular degree of these perfections, we infer a particular degree of them, precisely adapted to the effect which we examine. But further attributes, or further degrees of the same attributes, we can never be authorized to infer or suppose by any rules of just reasoning. Now, without some such license of supposition, it is impossible for us to argue from the cause or infer any alteration in the effect beyond what has immediately fallen under our observation. Greater good produced by this Being must still prove a greater degree of goodness. A more impartial distribution of rewards and punishments must proceed from a greater regard to justice and equity. Every supposed addition to the works of nature makes an addition to the attributes of the Author of nature; and, consequently, being entirely unsupported by any reason or argument, can never be admitted but as mere conjecture and hypothesis.[7]

The great source of our mistake on this subject and of the unbounded license of conjecture which we indulge is that we tacitly consider ourselves as in the place of the Supreme Being and conclude that he will, on every occasion, observe the same conduct which we ourselves, in his situation, would have embraced as reasonable and eligible. But besides that the ordinary course of nature may convince us that almost everything is regulated by principles and maxims very different from ours—besides this, I say, it must evidently appear contrary to all rule of analogy to reason from the projects and intentions of men to those of a Being so different and so much superior. In human nature there is a certain experienced coherence of designs and inclinations, so that, when from any fact we have discovered one intention of any man, it may often be reasonable, from experience, to infer another

---

[7] In general, it may, I think, be established as a maxim that where any cause is known only by its particular effects, it must be impossible to infer any new effects from that cause, since the qualities which are requisite to produce these new effects along with the former must either be different, or superior, or of more extensive operation than those which simply produced the effect, whence alone the cause is supposed to be known to us. We can never, therefore, have any reason to suppose the existence of these qualities.* To say that the new effects proceed only from a continuation of the same energy, which is already known from the first effects, will not remove the difficulty. For even granting this to be the case (which can seldom be supposed), the very continuation and exertion of a like energy (for it is impossible it can be absolutely the same), I say, this exertion of a like energy in a different period of space and time is a very arbitrary supposition, and what there cannot posibly be any traces of in the effects, from which all our knowledge of the cause is originally derived. Let the *inferred* cause be exactly proportioned (as it should be) to the known effect; and it is impossible that it can possess any qualities from which new or different effects can be *inferred*.

* In Editions K and L this note, as far as "these qualities," was printed in the text and the rest as a note.

and draw a long chain of conclusions concerning his past or future conduct. But this method of reasoning can never have place with regard to a being so remote and incomprehensible, who bears much less analogy to any other being in the universe than the sun to a waxen taper, and who discovers himself only by some faint traces or outlines beyond which we have no authority to ascribe to him any attribute or perfection. What we imagine to be a superior perfection may really be a defect. Or were it ever so much a perfection, the ascribing of it to the Supreme Being, where it appears not to have been really exerted to the full in his works, savors more of flattery and panegyric than of just reasoning and sound philosophy. All the philosophy, therefore, in the world, and all the religion, which is nothing but a species of philosophy, will never be able to carry us beyond the usual cause of experience or give us measures of conduct and behavior different from those which are furnished by reflections on common life. No new fact can ever be inferred from the religious hypothesis, no event foreseen or foretold, no reward or punishment expected or dreaded, beyond what is already known by practice and observation. So that my apology for Epicurus will still appear solid and satisfactory, nor have the political interests of society any connection with the philosophical disputes concerning metaphysics and religion.

There is still one circumstance, replied I, which you seem to have overlooked. Though I should allow your premises, I must deny your conclusion. You conclude that religious doctrines and reasonings *can* have no influence on life because they *ought* to have no influence, never considering that men reason not in the same manner you do, but draw many consequences from the belief of a divine existence and suppose that the Deity will inflict punishments on vice and bestow rewards on virtue beyond what appear in the ordinary course of nature. Whether this reasoning of theirs be just or not is no matter. Its influence on their life and conduct must still be the same. And those who attempt to disabuse them of such prejudices may, for aught I know, be good reasoners, but I cannot allow them to be good citizens and politicians, since they free men from one restraint upon their passions and make the infringement of the laws of society in one respect more easy and secure.

After all, I may perhaps agree to your general conclusion in favor of liberty, though upon different premises from those on which you endeavor to found it. I think that the state ought to tolerate every principle of philosophy, nor is there an instance that any government has suffered in its political interests by such indulgence. There is no enthusiasm among philosophers; their doctrines are not very alluring to the people, and no restraint can be put upon their reasonings but what must be of dangerous consequence to the sciences, and even to the state, by paving the way for persecution and oppression in points where the generality of mankind are more deeply interested and concerned.

But there occurs to me (continued I) with regard to your main topic a difficulty which I shall just propose to you, without insisting on it, lest it lead into reasonings of too nice and delicate a nature. In a word, I much doubt whether it be possible for a cause to be known only by its effect (as you have all along supposed) or to be of so singular and particular a nature as to have no parallel and no similarity with any other cause or object that has ever fallen under our observation. It is only when two *species* of objects are found to be constantly conjoined that we can infer the one from the other; and were an effect presented which was entirely singular and could not be comprehended under any known *species,* I do not see that we could form any conjecture or inference at all concerning its cause. If experience and observation, and analogy, be indeed the only guides which we can reasonably follow in inferences of this nature, both the effect and cause must bear a similarity and resemblance to other effects and causes which we know, and which we have found in many instances to be conjoined with each other. I leave it to your own reflection to pursue the consequences of this principle. I shall just observe that as the antagonists of Epicurus always suppose the universe, an effect quite singular and unparalleled, to be the proof of a Deity, a cause no less singular and unparalleled, your reasonings upon that supposition seem at least to merit our attention. There is, I own, some difficulty how we can ever return from the cause to the effect and, reasoning from our ideas of the former, infer any alteration on the latter or any addition to it.

OF THE ACADEMICAL OR SKEPTICAL PHILOSOPHY

PART I

THERE IS NOT a greater number of philosophical reasonings displayed upon any subject than those which prove the existence of a Deity and refute the fallacies of *atheists;* and yet the most religious philosophers still dispute whether any man can be so blinded as to be a speculative atheist. How shall we reconcile these contradictions? The knights-errant who wandered about to clear the world of dragons and of giants never entertained the least doubt with regard to the existence of these monsters.

The *skeptic* is another enemy of religion, who naturally provokes the indignation of all divines and graver philosophers, though it is certain that no man ever met with any such absurd creature or conversed with a man who had no opinion or principle concerning any subject, either of action or speculation. This begets a very natural question. What is meant by a skeptic? And how far is it possible to push these philosophical principles of doubt and uncertainty?

There is a species of skepticism, *antecedent* to all study and philosophy, which is much inculcated by Descartes and others as a sovereign preservative against error and precipitate judgment. It recommends a universal doubt, not only of all our former opinions and principles, but also of our very faculties, of whose veracity, say they, we must assure ourselves by a chain of reasoning deduced from some original principle which cannot possibly be fallacious or deceitful. But neither is there any such original principle which has a prerogative above others that are self-evident and convincing. Or if there were, could we advance a step beyond it but by the use of those very faculties of which we are supposed to be already diffident? The Cartesian doubt, therefore, were it ever possible to be attained by any human creature (as it plainly is not), would be entirely incurable, and no reasoning could ever bring us to a state of assurance and conviction upon any subject.

It must, however, be confessed that this species of skepticism, when more moderate, may be understood in a very reasonable sense, and is a necessary preparative to the study of philosophy by preserving a proper impartiality in our judgments and weaning our mind from all those prejudices which we may have imbibed from education or rash opinion. To begin with clear and self-evident principles, to advance by timorous and sure steps, to review frequently our conclusions and examine accurately all their consequences—though by these means we shall make both a slow and a short progress in our systems—are the only methods by which we can ever hope to reach truth and attain a proper stability and certainty in our determinations.

There is another species of skepticism, *consequent* to science and inquiry, when men are supposed to have discovered either the absolute fallaciousness of their mental faculties or their unfitness to reach any fixed determination in all those curious subjects of speculation about which they are commonly employed. Even our very senses are brought into dispute by a certain species of philosophers, and the maxims of common life are subjected to the same doubt as the most profound principles or conclusions of metaphysics and theology. As these paradoxical tenets (if they may be called "tenets") are to be met with in some philosophers, and the refutation of them in several, they naturally excite our curiosity and make us inquire into the arguments on which they may be founded.

I need not insist upon the more trite topics employed by the skeptics in all ages against the evidence of *sense*—such as those which are derived from the imperfection and fallaciousness of our organs on numberless occasions: the crooked appearance of an oar in water; the various aspects of objects according to their different distances; the double images which arise from the pressing one eye; with many other appearances of a like nature.[1] These skeptical topics, indeed, are only sufficient to prove that the senses alone are not implicitly to be depended on, but that we must correct their evidence by reason and by considerations derived from the nature of the medium, the distance of the object, and the disposition of the organ, in order to render them, within their sphere, the proper criteria of truth and falsehood. There are other more profound arguments against the senses which admit not of so easy a solution.

It seems evident that men are carried by a natural instinct or prepossession to repose faith in their senses, and that without any reasoning, or even almost before the use of reason, we always suppose an external universe which depends not on our perception but would exist though we and every sensible creature were absent or annihilated. Even the animal creation are governed by a like opinion and preserve this belief of external objects in all their thoughts, designs, and actions.

It seems also evident that when men follow this blind and powerful instinct of nature, they always suppose the very images presented by the senses to be the external objects, and never entertain any suspicion that the one are nothing but representations of the other. This very table which we see white, and which we feel hard, is believed to exist independent of our perception and to be something external to our mind which perceives it. Our presence bestows not being on it; our absence does not annihilate it. It preserves its existence uniform and entire, independent of the situation of intelligent beings who perceive or contemplate it.

But this universal and primary opinion of all men is soon destroyed by the slightest philosophy which teaches us that nothing can ever be present to the mind but an image or perception, and that the senses are only the inlets through which these images are conveyed, without being able to pro-

---

[1] [This is a reference to arguments discussed by George Berkeley in his *Principles* and *Three Dialogues.*—Ed.]

duce any immediate intercourse between the mind and the object. The table which we see seems to diminish as we remove further from it; but the real table, which exists independent of us, suffers no alteration. It was, therefore, nothing but its image which was present to the mind. These are the obvious dictates of reason; and no man who reflects ever doubted that the existences which we consider when we say *this house* and *that tree* are nothing but perceptions in the mind and fleeting copies or representations of other existences which remain uniform and independent.

So far, then, are we necessitated by reasoning to contradict or depart from the primary instincts of nature and to embrace a new system with regard to the evidence of our senses. But here philosophy finds herself extremely embarrassed when she would justify this new system and obviate the cavils and objections of the skeptics. She can no longer plead the infallible and irresistible instinct of nature; for that led us to a quite different system which is acknowledged fallible and even erroneous. And to justify this pretended philosophical system by a chain of clear and convincing argument, or even any appearance of argument, exceeds the power of all human capacity.

By what argument can it be proved that the perceptions of the mind must be caused by external objects, entirely different from them though resembling them (if that be possible), and could not arise either from the energy of the mind itself or from the suggestion of some invisible and unknown spirit or from some other cause still more unknown to us? It is acknowledged that in fact many of these perceptions arise not from anything external, as in dreams, madness, and other diseases. And nothing can be more inexplicable than the manner in which body should so operate upon mind as ever to convey an image of itself to a substance supposed of so different and even contrary a nature.

It is a question of fact whether the perceptions of the senses be produced by external objects resembling them. How shall this question be determined? By experience, surely, as all other questions of a like nature. But here experience is and must be entirely silent. The mind has never anything present to it but the perceptions, and cannot possibly reach any experience of their connection with objects. The supposition of such a connection is, therefore, without any foundation in reasoning.

To have recourse to the veracity of the Supreme Being in order to prove the veracity of our senses is surely making a very unexpected circuit. If his veracity were at all concerned in this matter, our senses would be entirely infallible, because it is not possible that he can ever deceive. Not to mention that, if the external world be once called in question, we shall be at a loss to find arguments by which we may prove the existence of that Being or any of his attributes.

This is a topic, therefore, in which the profounder and more philosophical skeptics will always triumph when they endeavor to introduce a universal doubt into all subjects of human knowledge and inquiry. Do you follow the instincts and propensities of nature, may they say, in assenting to the veracity of sense? But these lead you to believe that the very perception or sensible image is the external object. Do you disclaim this principle in order to embrace a more rational opinion that the perceptions are only representations of something external? You here depart from your natural propensities and more obvious sentiments, and yet are not able to satisfy your reason, which can never find any convincing argument from experience to prove that the perceptions are connected with any external objects.

There is another skeptical topic of a like nature, derived from the most profound philosophy, which might merit our attention were it requisite to dive so deep in order to discover arguments and reasonings which can serve so little any serious purpose. It is universally allowed by modern inquirers that all the sensible qualities of objects, such as hard, soft, hot, cold, white, black, etc., are merely secondary and exist not in the objects themselves, but are perceptions of the mind without any external archetype or model which they represent. If this be allowed with regard to secondary qualities, it must also follow with regard to the supposed primary qualities of extension and solidity, nor can the latter be any more entitled to that denomination than the former. The idea of extension is entirely acquired from the senses of sight and feeling; and if all the qualities perceived by the senses be in the mind, not in the object, the same conclusion must reach the idea of extension which is wholly dependent on the sensible ideas or the ideas of secondary qualities. Nothing can save us from this conclusion but the asserting that the ideas of those primary qualities are attained by *abstraction*—an opinion which, if we examine it accurately, we shall find to be unintelligible and even absurd. An extension that is neither tangible nor visible cannot possibly be conceived; and a tangible or visible extension which is neither hard nor soft, black nor white, is equally beyond the reach of human conception. Let any man try to conceive a triangle in general which is neither isosceles nor scalenum, nor has any particular length or proportion of sides, and he will soon perceive the absurdity of all the scholastic notions with regard to abstraction and general ideas.[2]

Thus the first philosophical objection to the evidence of sense, or to the opinion of external existence, consists in this, that such an opinion, if rested on natural instinct, is contrary to reason and, if referred to reason, is contrary to natural instinct, and at the same time carries no rational evidence with it to convince an impartial inquirer. The second objection goes further and represents this opinion as contrary to reason,

---

[2] This argument is drawn from Dr. Berkeley; and indeed most of the writings of that ingenious author form the best lessons of skepticism which are to be found either among the ancient or modern philosophers, Bayle not excepted. He professes, however, in his title page (and undoubtedly with great truth) to have composed his book against the skeptics as well as against the atheists and freethinkers. But that all his arguments, though otherwise intended, are in reality merely skeptical appears from this, *that they admit of no answer and produce no conviction.* Their only effect is to cause that momentary amazement and irresolution and confusion which is the result of skepticism.

at least, if it be a principle of reason that all sensible qualities are in the mind, not in the object. Bereave matter of all its intelligible qualities, both primary and secondary, you in a manner annihilate it and leave only a certain unknown, inexplicable *something* as the cause of our perceptions—a notion so imperfect that no skeptic will think it worth while to contend against it.[3]

PART II

It may seem a very extravagant attempt of the skeptics to destroy reason by argument and ratiocination, yet this is the grand scope of all their inquiries and disputes. They endeavor to find objections both to our abstract reasonings and to those which regard matter of fact and existence.

The chief objection against all *abstract* reasonings is derived from the ideas of space and time—ideas which in common life and to a careless view are very clear and intelligible, but when they pass through the scrutiny of the profound sciences (and they are the chief object of these sciences) afford principles which seem full of absurdity and contradiction. No priestly *dogmas* invented on purpose to tame and subdue the rebellious reason of mankind ever shocked common sense more than the doctrine of the infinite divisibility of extension, with its consequences, as they are pompously displayed by all geometricians and metaphysicians with a kind of triumph and exultation. A real quantity, infinitely less than any finite quantity, containing qualities infinitely less than itself, and so on *in infinitum*—this is an edifice so bold and prodigious that it is too weighty for any pretended demonstration to support because it shocks the clearest and most natural principles of human reason.[1] But what renders the matter

---

[3] [The last sentence of this paragraph was added in Edition O.]
[1] Whatever disputes there may be about mathematical points, we must allow that there are physical points, that is, parts of extension, which

more extraordinary is that these seemingly absurd opinions are supported by a chain of reasoning the clearest and most natural, nor is it possible for us to allow the premises without admitting the consequences. Nothing can be more convincing and satisfactory than all the conclusions concerning the properties of circles and triangles, and yet when these are once received, how can we deny that the angle of contact between a circle and its tangent is infinitely less than any rectilineal angle; that as you may increase the diameter of the circle *in infinitum,* this angle of contact becomes still less, even *in infinitum,* and that the angle of contact between other curves and their tangents may be infinitely less than those between any circle and its tangent, and so on, *in infinitum?* The demonstration of these principles seems as unexceptionable as that which proves the three angles of a triangle to be equal to two right ones, though the latter opinion be natural and easy, and the former big with contradiction and absurdity. Reason here seems to be thrown into a kind of amazement and suspense which, without the suggestions of any skeptic, gives her a diffidence of herself and of the ground on which she treads. She sees a full light which illuminates certain places, but that light borders upon the most profound darkness. And between these she is so dazzled and confounded that she scarcely can pronounce with certainty and assurance concerning any one object.

The absurdity of these bold determinations of the abstract sciences seems to become, if possible, still more palpable with regard to time than extension. An infinite number of real parts of time, passing in succession and exhausted one after another, appears so evident a contradiction that no man, one

---

cannot be divided or lessened either by the eye or imagination. These images, then, which are present to the fancy or senses are absolutely indivisible, and consequently must be allowed by mathematicians to be infinitely less than any real part of extension; and yet nothing appears more certain to reason than that an infinite number of them composes an infinite extension. How much more an infinite number of those infinitely small parts of extension which are still supposed infinitely divisible?

should think, whose judgment is not corrupted, instead of being improved, by the sciences, would ever be able to admit it.

Yet still reason must remain restless and unquiet, even with regard to that skepticism to which she is driven by these seeming absurdities and contradictions. How any clear, distinct idea can contain circumstances contradictory to itself, or to any other clear, distinct idea, is absolutely incomprehensible and is, perhaps, as absurd as any proposition which can be formed. So that nothing can be more skeptical or more full of doubt and hesitation than this skepticism itself which arises from some of the paradoxical conclusions of geometry or the science of quantity.[2]

The skeptical objections to *moral* evidence or to the reason-

---

[2] It seems to me not impossible to avoid these absurdities and contradictions if it be admitted that there is no such thing as abstract or general ideas, properly speaking, but that all general ideas are in reality particular ones attached to a general term which recalls, upon occasion, other particular ones that resemble in certain circumstances the idea present to the mind. Thus, when the term "horse" is pronounced, we immediately figure to ourselves the idea of a black or a white animal of a particular size or figure. But as that term is also usually applied to animals of other colors, figures, and sizes, these ideas, though not actually present to the imagination, are easily recalled, and our reasoning and conclusion proceed in the same way as if they were actually present. If this be admitted (as seems reasonable), it follows that all the ideas of quantity, upon which mathematicians reason, are nothing but particular, and such as are suggested by the senses and imagination, and consequently cannot be infinitely divisible.* It is sufficient to have dropped this hint at present, without prosecuting it any further. It certainly concerns all lovers of science not to expose themselves to the ridicule and contempt of the ignorant by their conclusions, and this seems the readiest solution of these difficulties.

* In general, we may pronounce that the ideas of "greater," "less," or "equal," which are the chief objects of geometry, are far from being so exact or determinate as to be the foundation of such extraordinary inferences. Ask a mathematician what he means when he pronounces two quantities to be equal, and he must say that the idea of "equality" is one of those which cannot be defined, and that it is sufficient to place two equal quantities before anyone, in order to suggest it. Now this is an appeal to the general appearances of objects to the imagination or senses, and consequently can never afford conclusions so directly contrary to these faculties. [Editions K and L.]

ings concerning matter of fact are either *popular* or *philosophical*. The popular objections are derived from the natural weakness of human understanding: the contradictory opinions which have been entertained in different ages and nations; the variations of our judgment in sickness and health, youth and old age, prosperity and adversity; the perpetual contradiction of each particular man's opinions and sentiments, with many other topics of that kind. It is needless to insist further on this head. These objections are but weak. For as, in common life, we reason every moment concerning fact and existence and cannot possibly subsist without continually employing this species of argument, any popular objections derived from thence must be insufficient to destroy that evidence. The great subverter of Pyrrhonism, or the excessive principles of skepticism, is action, and employment, and the occupations of common life. These principles may flourish and triumph in the schools, where it is indeed difficult, if not impossible, to refute them. But as soon as they leave the shade, and by the presence of the real objects which actuate our passions and sentiments are put in opposition to the more powerful principles of our nature, they vanish like smoke and leave the most determined skeptic in the same condition as other mortals.

The skeptic, therefore, had better keep within his proper sphere and display those *philosophical* objections which arise from more profound researches. Here he seems to have ample matter of triumph, while he justly insists that all our evidence for any matter of fact which lies beyond the testimony of sense or memory is derived entirely from the relation of cause and effect; that we have no other idea of this relation than that of two objects which have been frequently *conjoined* together; that we have no argument to convince us that objects which have, in our experience, been frequently conjoined will likewise in other instances be conjoined in the same manner; and that nothing leads us to this inference but custom or a certain instinct of our nature, which it is indeed difficult to resist, but which, like other instincts, may be fallacious and deceitful. While the skeptic insists upon these topics, he shows his force or rather, indeed, his own and our weakness, and seems, for the time at least, to destroy all assurance and conviction. These arguments might be displayed at greater length if any durable good or benefit to society could ever be expected to result from them.

For here is the chief and most confounding objection to *excessive* skepticism, that no durable good can ever result from it while it remains in its full force and vigor. We need only ask such a skeptic, *What his meaning is? And what he proposes by all these curious researches?* He is immediately at a loss and knows not what to answer. A *Copernican* or *Ptolemaic* who supports each his different system of astronomy may hope to produce a conviction which will remain constant and durable with his audience. A *Stoic* or *Epicurean* displays principles which may not only be durable, but which have an effect on conduct and behavior. But a *Pyrrhonian* cannot expect that his philosophy will have any constant influence on the mind or, if it had, that its influence would be beneficial to society. On the contrary, he must acknowledge, if he will acknowledge anything, that all human life must perish were his principles universally and steadily to prevail. All discourse, all action would immediately cease, and men remain in a total lethargy till the necessities of nature, unsatisfied, put an end to their miserable existence. It is true, so fatal an event is very little to be dreaded. Nature is always too strong for principle. And though a *Pyrrhonian* may throw himself or others into a momentary amazement and confusion by his profound reasonings, the first and most trivial event in life will put to flight all his doubts and scruples, and leave him the same, in every point of action and speculation, with the philosophers of every other sect or with those who never concerned themselves in any philosophical researches. When he awakes from his dream, he will be the first to join in the laugh against himself and to confess that all his objections are mere amusement, and can have no other tendency than to show the whimsical condition of mankind, who must act and reason and believe, though they are not able, by their most diligent inquiry, to satisfy themselves concerning the foundation of these operations or to remove the objections which may be raised against them.

PART III

There is, indeed, a more *mitigated* skepticism or *academical* philosophy which may be both durable and useful, and which may, in part, be the result of this Pyrrhonism or *excessive* skepticism when its undistinguished doubts are, in some measure, corrected by common sense and reflection. The greater part of mankind are naturally apt to be affirmative and dogmatical in their opinions, and while they see objects only on one side and have no idea of any counterpoising argument, they throw themselves precipitately into the principles to which they are inclined, nor have they any indulgence for those who entertain opposite sentiments. To hesitate or balance perplexes their understanding, checks their passion, and suspends their action. They are, therefore, impatient till they escape from a state which to them is so uneasy, and they think that they can never remove themselves far enough from it by the violence of their affirmations and obstinacy of their belief. But could such dogmatical reasoners become sensible of the strange infirmities of human understanding, even in its most perfect state and when most accurate and cautious in its determinations—such a reflection would naturally inspire them with more modesty and reserve, and diminish their fond opinion of themselves and their prejudice against antagonists. The illiterate may reflect on the disposition of the learned, who, amidst all the advantages of study and reflection, are commonly still diffident in their determinations. And if any of the learned be inclined, from their natural temper, to haughtiness and obstinacy, a small tincture of Pyrrhonism might abate their pride by showing them that the few advantages which they may have attained over their fellows are but inconsiderable if compared with the universal perplexity and confusion which is inherent in human nature. In general, there is a degree of doubt and caution and modesty which, in all kinds of scrutiny and decision, ought forever to accompany a just reasoner.

Another species of *mitigated* skepticism which may be of advantage to mankind, and which may be the natural result of the Pyrrhonian doubts and scruples, is the limitation of our inquiries to such subjects as are best adapted to the narrow capacity of human understanding. The *imagination* of man is naturally sublime, delighted with whatever is remote and extraordinary, and running, without control, into the most distant parts of space and time in order to avoid the objects which custom has rendered too familiar to it. A correct *judgment* observes a contrary method and, avoiding all distant and high inquiries, confines itself to common life and to such subjects as fall under daily practice and experience, leaving the more sublime topics to the embellishment of poets and orators or to the arts of priests and politicians. To bring us to so salutary a determination, nothing can be more serviceable than to be once thoroughly convinced of the force of the Pyrrhonian doubt and of the impossibility that anything but the strong power of natural instinct could free us from it. Those who have a propensity to philosophy will still continue their researches, because they reflect that, besides the immediate pleasure attending such an occupation, philosophical decisions are nothing but the reflections of common life, methodized and corrected. But they will never be tempted to go beyond common life so long as they consider the imperfection of those faculties which they employ, their narrow reach, and their inaccurate operations. While we cannot give a satisfactory reason why we believe, after a thousand experiments, that a stone will fall or fire burn, can we ever satisfy ourselves concerning any determination which we may form with regard to the origin of worlds and the situation of nature from and to eternity?

This narrow limitation, indeed, of our inquiries is in every respect so reasonable that it suffices to make the slightest examination into the natural powers of the human mind, and to compare them with their objects, in order to recommend it to us. We shall then find what are the proper subjects of science and inquiry.

It seems to me that the only objects of the abstract sciences, or of demonstration, are quantity and number, and that all attempts to extend this more perfect species of knowledge beyond these bounds are mere sophistry and illusion. As the component parts of quantity and number are entirely similar, their relations become intricate and involved, and nothing can be more curious, as well as useful, than to trace, by a variety of mediums, their equality or inequality through their different appearances. But as all other ideas are clearly distinct and different from each other, we can never advance further, by our utmost scrutiny, than to observe this diversity and, by an obvious reflection, pronounce one thing not to be another. Or if there be any difficulty in these decisions, it proceeds entirely from the undeterminate meaning of words, which is corrected by juster definitions. That *the square of the hypotenuse is equal to the squares of the other two sides* cannot be known, let the terms be ever so exactly defined, without a train of reasoning and inquiry. But to convince us of this proposition, *that where there is no property there can be no injustice,* it is only necessary to define the terms and explain injustice to be a violation of property. This proposition is, indeed, nothing but a more imperfect definition. It is the same case with all those pretended syllogistical reasonings which may be found in every other branch of learning except the sciences of quantity and number; and these may safely, I think, be pronounced the only proper objects of knowledge and demonstration.

All other inquiries of men regard only matter of fact and existence, and these are evidently incapable of demonstration. Whatever *is* may *not be.* No negation of a fact can involve a contradiction. The nonexistence of any being, without exception, is as clear and distinct an idea as its existence. The proposition which affirms it not to be, however false, is no less conceivable and intelligible than that which affirms it to be. The case is different with the sciences, properly so called. Every proposition which is not true is there confused and unintelligible. That the cube root of 64 is equal to the half of 10 is a false proposition and can never be distinctly conceived. But that Caesar, or the angel Gabriel, or any being never existed may be a false proposition, but still is perfectly conceivable and implies no contradiction.

The existence, therefore, of any being can only be proved by arguments from its cause or its effect, and these arguments are founded entirely on experience. If we reason *a priori*, anything may appear able to produce anything. The falling of a pebble may, for aught we know, extinguish the sun, or the wish of a man control the planets in their orbits. It is only experience which teaches us the nature and bounds of cause and effect and enables us to infer the existence of one object from that of another.[1] Such is the foundation of moral reasoning, which forms the greater part of human knowledge and is the source of all human action and behavior.

Moral reasonings are either concerning particular or general facts. All deliberations in life regard the former; as also all disquisitions in history, chronology, geography, and astronomy.

The sciences which treat of general facts are politics, natural philosophy, physics, chemistry, etc., where the qualities, causes, and effects of a whole species of objects are inquired into.

Divinity or theology, as it proves the existence of a deity and the immortality of souls, is composed partly of reasonings concerning particular, partly concerning general facts.

---

1 That impious maxim of the ancient philosophy, *Ex nihilo, nihil fit,** by which the creation of matter was excluded, ceases to be a maxim, according to this philosophy. Not only the will of the Supreme Being may create matter, but, for aught we know *a priori*, the will of any other being might create it, or any other cause that the most whimsical imagination can assign.

* "From nothing, nothing comes."—Ed.

It has a foundation in *reason* so far as it is supported by experience. But its best and most solid foundation is *faith* and divine revelation.

Morals and criticism are not so properly objects of the understanding as of taste and sentiment. Beauty, whether moral or natural, is felt more properly than perceived. Or if we reason concerning it and endeavor to fix the standard, we regard a new fact, to wit, the general taste of mankind, or some such fact which may be the object of reasoning and inquiry.

When we run over libraries, persuaded of these principles, what havoc must we make? If we take in our hand any volume —of divinity or school metaphysics, for instance—let us ask, *Does it contain any abstract reasoning concerning quantity or number?* No. *Does it contain any experimental reasoning concerning matter of fact and existence?* No. Commit it then to the flames, for it can contain nothing but sophistry and illusion.

APPENDIX

I

WHY A CAUSE IS ALWAYS NECESSARY
[From the *Treatise*, Bk. I, Pt. III, Sect. III.]

II

AN ABSTRACT OF
A TREATISE OF HUMAN NATURE

WHY A CAUSE IS ALWAYS NECESSARY [1]

To BEGIN WITH the first question concerning the necessity of a cause: 'Tis a general maxim in philosophy, that *whatever begins to exist must have a cause of existence.* This is commonly taken for granted in all reasonings, without any proof given or demanded. 'Tis supposed to be founded on intuition, and to be one of those maxims which, though they may be denied with the lips, 'tis impossible for men in their hearts really to doubt of. But if we examine this maxim by the idea of knowledge above explained, we shall discover in it no mark of any such intuitive certainty, but on the contrary shall find that 'tis of a nature quite foreign to that species of conviction.

All certainty arises from the comparison of ideas, and from the discovery of such relations as are unalterable so long as the ideas continue the same. These relations are *resemblance, proportions in quantity and number, degrees of any quality, and contrariety;* none of which are implied in this proposition, *Whatever has a beginning has also a cause of existence.* That proposition, therefore, is not intuitively certain. At least anyone who would assert it to be intuitively certain must deny these to be the only infallible relations, and must find some other relation of that kind to be implied in it; which it will then be time enough to examine.

But here is an argument which proves at once that the foregoing proposition is neither intuitively nor demonstrably certain. We can never demonstrate the necessity of a cause to every new existence, or new modification of existence, without showing at the same time the impossibility there is that anything can ever begin to exist without some productive principle; and where the latter proposition cannot be proved, we must despair of ever being able to prove the former. Now

---

[1] [Part III, Section III of the *Treatise of Human Nature.*]

that the latter proposition is utterly incapable of a demonstrative proof, we may satisfy ourselves by considering that as all distinct ideas are separable from each other, and as the ideas of cause and effect are evidently distinct, 'twill be easy for us to conceive any object to be nonexistent this moment, and existent the next, without conjoining to it the distinct idea of a cause or productive principle. The separation, therefore, of the idea of a cause from that of a beginning of existence is plainly possible for the imagination; and, consequently, the actual separation of these objects is so far possible that it implies no contradiction nor absurdity, and is therefore incapable of being refuted by any reasoning from mere ideas, without which 'tis impossible to demonstrate the necessity of a cause.

Accordingly, we shall find upon examination that every demonstration which has been produced for the necessity of a cause is fallacious and sophistical. All the points of time and place, say some philosophers,[2] in which we can suppose any object to begin to exist are in themselves equal; and unless there be some cause which is peculiar to one time and to one place, and which by that means determines and fixes the existence, it must remain in eternal suspense, and the object can never begin to be, for want of something to fix its beginning. But I ask, is there any more difficulty in supposing the time and place to be fixed without a cause than to suppose the existence to be determined in that manner! The first question that occurs on this subject is always, *whether* the object shall exist or not; the next, *when* and *where* it shall begin to exist. If the removal of a cause be intuitively absurd in the one case, it must be so in the other; and if that absurdity be not clear without a proof in the one case, it will equally require one in the other. The absurdity, then, of the one supposition can never be a proof of that of the other, since they are both upon the same footing and must stand or fall by the same reasoning.

[2] [Mr. Hobbes.]

The second argument [3] which I find used on this head labors under an equal difficulty. Every thing, 'tis said, must have a cause, for if any thing wanted a cause, *it* would produce *itself*, that is, exist before it existed, which is impossible. But this reasoning is plainly inconclusive because it supposes that in our denial of a cause we still grant what we expressly deny, viz., that there must be a cause, which therefore is taken to be the object itself; and *that*, no doubt, is an evident contradiction. But to say that any thing is produced or, to express myself more properly, comes into existence without a cause, is not to affirm that 'tis itself its own cause, but, on the contrary, in excluding all external causes excludes *a fortiori* the thing itself which is created. An object that exists absolutely without any cause certainly is not its own cause; and when you assert that the one follows from the other you suppose the very point in question and take it for granted that 'tis utterly impossible any thing can ever begin to exist without a cause, but that, upon the exclusion of one productive principle, we must still have recourse to another.

'Tis exactly the same case with the third argument,[4] which has been employed to demonstrate the necessity of a cause. Whatever is produced without any cause is produced by *nothing* or, in other words, has nothing for its cause. But nothing can never be a cause, no more than it can be something, or equal to two right angles. By the same intuition that we perceive nothing not to be equal to two right angles, or not to be something, we perceive that it can never be a cause, and consequently must perceive that every object has a real cause of its existence.

I believe it will not be necessary to employ many words in showing the weakness of this argument, after what I have said of the foregoing. They are all of them founded on the same fallacy and are derived from the same turn of thought. 'Tis

3 [Dr. Clarke and others.]
4 [Mr. Locke.]

sufficient only to observe that when we exclude all causes we really do exclude them, and neither suppose nothing nor the object itself to be the causes of the existence, and consequently can draw no argument from the absurdity of these suppositions to prove the absurdity of that exclusion. If every thing must have a cause it follows that, upon the exclusion of other causes, we must accept of the object itself or of nothing as causes. But 'tis the very point in question, whether every thing must have a cause or not, and therefore, according to all just reasoning, it ought never to be taken for granted.

They are still more frivolous who say that every effect must have a cause because 'tis implied in the very idea of effect. Every effect necessarily presupposes a cause; effect being a relative term of which cause is the correlative. But this does not prove that every being must be preceded by a cause, no more than it follows, because every husband must have a wife, that therefore every man must be married. The true state of the question is whether every object which begins to exist must owe its existence to a cause, and this I assert neither to be intuitively nor demonstratively certain, and hope to have proved it sufficiently by the foregoing arguments.

Since it is not from knowledge or any scientific reasoning that we derive the opinion of the necessity of a cause to every new production, that opinion must necessarily arise from observation and experience. The next question, then, should naturally be, *how experience gives rise to such a principle?* But as I find it will be more convenient to sink this question in the following, *why we conclude that such particular causes must necessarily have such particular effects, and why we form an inference from one to another?* we shall make that the subject of our future inquiry. 'Twill, perhaps, be found in the end that the same answer will serve for both questions.

An Abstract of
A Treatise of Human Nature

PREFACE

My expectations in this small performance may seem somewhat extraordinary when I declare that my intentions are to
render a larger work more intelligible to ordinary capacities
by abridging it. It is, however, certain that those who are not
accustomed to abstract reasoning are apt to lose the thread of
argument where it is drawn out to a great length, and each
part fortified with all the arguments, guarded against all the
objections, and illustrated with all the views which occur to a
writer in the diligent survey of his subject. Such readers will
more readily apprehend a chain of reasoning that is more
single and concise where the chief propositions only are linked
on to each other, illustrated by some simple examples, and
confirmed by a few of the more forcible arguments. The parts
lying nearer together can better be compared, and the connection be more easily traced from the first principles to the
last conclusion.

The work of which I here present the reader with an abstract has been complained of as obscure and difficult to be
comprehended, and I am apt to think that this proceeded as
much from the length as from the abstractedness of the argument. If I have remedied this inconvenience in any degree I
have attained my end. The book seemed to me to have such
an air of singularity and novelty as claimed the attention of
the public, especially if it be found—as the author seems to
insinuate—that were his philosophy received we must alter

from the foundation the greatest part of the sciences. Such bold attempts are always advantageous in the republic of letters because they shake off the yoke of authority, accustom men to think for themselves, give new hints which men of genius may carry further and, by the very opposition, illustrate points wherein no one before suspected any difficulty.

The author must be contented to wait with patience for some time before the learned world can agree in their sentiments of his performance. It is his misfortune that he cannot make an *appeal to the people,* who in all matters of common reason and eloquence are found so infallible a tribunal. He must be judged by the *few,* whose verdict is more apt to be corrupted by partiality and prejudice, especially as no one is a proper judge in these subjects who has not often thought of them, and *such* are apt to form to themselves systems of their own which they resolve not to relinquish. I hope the author will excuse me for intermeddling in this affair, since my aim is only to increase his auditory by removing some difficulties which have kept many from apprehending his meaning.

I have chosen one simple argument which I have carefully traced from the beginning to the end. This is the only point I have taken care to finish. The rest is only hints of particular passages which seemed to me curious and remarkable.

AN ABSTRACT OF
A TREATISE OF HUMAN NATURE

This book seems to be written upon the same plan with several other works that have had a great vogue of late years in England. The philosophical spirit, which has been so much improved all over Europe within these last fourscore years, has been carried to as great a length in this kingdom as in any other. Our writers seem even to have started a new kind of philosophy which promises more both to the entertainment and advantage of mankind than any other with which the world has been yet acquainted. Most of the philosophers of antiquity who treated of human nature have shown more of a delicacy of sentiment, a just sense of morals, or a greatness of soul, than a depth of reasoning and reflection. They content themselves with representing the common sense of mankind in the strongest lights, and with the best turn of thought and expression, without following out steadily a chain of propositions, or forming the several truths into a regular science. But it is at least worth while to try if the science of *man* will not admit of the same accuracy which several parts of natural philosophy are found susceptible of. There seems to be all the reason in the world to imagine that it may be carried to the greatest degree of exactness. If in examining several phenomena we find that they resolve themselves into one common principle, and can trace this principle into another, we shall at last arrive at those few simple principles on which all the rest depend. And though we can never arrive at the ultimate principles, it is a satisfaction to go as far as our faculties will allow us.

This seems to have been the aim of our late philosophers and, among the rest, of this author. He proposes to anatomize human nature in a regular manner, and promises to draw no conclusions but where he is authorized by experience. He talks with contempt of hypotheses and insinuates that such of our countrymen as have banished them from moral philosophy have done a more signal service to the world than my Lord Bacon, whom he considers as the father of experimental physics. He mentions, on this occasion, Mr. Locke, my Lord Shaftsbury, Dr. Mandeville, Mr. Hutchison, Dr. Butler, who, though they differ in many points among themselves, seem all to agree in founding their accurate disquisitions of human nature entirely upon experience.

Besides the satisfaction of being acquainted with what most nearly concerns us, it may be safely affirmed that almost all the sciences are comprehended in the science of human nature, and are dependent on it. *The sole end of* logic *is to explain the principles and operations of our reasoning faculty, and the nature of our ideas;* morals and criticism *regard our tastes and sentiments; and* politics *consider men as united in society and dependent on each other.* This treatise, therefore, of human nature seems intended for a system of the sciences. The author has finished what regards logic, and has laid the foundation of the other parts in his account of the passions.

The celebrated Monsieur Leibniz has observed it to be a defect in the common systems of logic that they are very copious when they explain the operations of the understanding in the forming of demonstrations, but are too concise when they treat of probabilities and those other measures of evidence on which life and action entirely depend, and which are our guides even in most of our philosophical speculations. In this censure, he comprehends the *Essay on Human Understanding*,[1] *Le* (sic) *Recherche de la verité*,[2] and *L'art de penser*.[3] The author of the *Treatise of Human Nature* seems to have been sensible of this defect in these philosophers and has endeavored, as much as he can, to supply it. As his book contains a great number of speculations very new and remarkable, it will be impossible to give the reader a just notion of the whole.

---

[1] [By John Locke.]   [2] [By Nicolas de Malebranche.]

[3] [Antoine Arnauld and others: *La Logique ou l'art de penser* (Port-Royal Logic), 1662.]

We shall, therefore, chiefly confine ourselves to his explication of our reasonings from cause and effect. If we can make this intelligible to the reader, it may serve as a specimen of the whole.

Our author begins with some definitions. He calls a "perception" whatever can be present to the mind, whether we employ our senses or are actuated with passion, or exercise our thought and reflection. He divides our perceptions into two kinds, viz., "impressions" and "ideas." When we feel a passion or emotion of any kind, or have the images of external objects conveyed by our senses, the perception of the mind is what he calls an "impression"—which is a word that he employs in a new sense. When we reflect on a passion or an object which is not present, this perception is an "idea." "Impressions," therefore, are our lively and strong perceptions; "ideas" are the fainter and weaker. This distinction is evident —as evident as that betwixt feeling and thinking.

The first proposition he advances is that all our ideas, or weak perceptions, are derived from our impressions or strong perceptions, and that we can never think of anything which we have not seen without us or felt in our own minds. This proposition seems to be equivalent to that which Mr. Locke has taken such pains to establish, viz., "that no ideas are innate." Only it may be observed, as an inaccuracy of that famous philosopher, that he comprehends all our perceptions under the term of "idea," in which sense it is false that we have no innate ideas. For it is evident our stronger perceptions or impressions are innate, and that natural affection, love of virtue, resentment, and all the other passions arise immediately from nature. I am persuaded whoever would take the question in this light would be easily able to reconcile all parties. Father Malebranche would find himself at a loss to point out any thought of the mind which did not represent something antecedently felt by it, either internally or by means of the external senses, and must allow that however we may compound and mix and augment and diminish our ideas, that they are all derived from these sources. Mr. Locke,

on the other hand, would readily acknowledge that all our
passions are a kind of natural instincts, derived from nothing
but the original constitution of the human mind.

Our author thinks—

> that no discovery could have been made more happily for
> deciding all controversies concerning ideas than this, that
> impressions always take the precedence of them, and that
> every idea with which the imagination is furnished first
> makes its appearance in a correspondent impression. These
> latter perceptions are all so clear and evident that they
> admit of no controversy, though many of our ideas are so
> obscure that 'tis almost impossible even for the mind which
> forms them to tell exactly their nature and composition.

Accordingly, wherever any idea is ambiguous he has always
recourse to the impression which must render it clear and
precise. And when he suspects that any philosophical term
has no idea annexed to it (as is too common), he always asks
"from what impression that idea is derived?" And if no impression can be produced, he concludes that the term is altogether insignificant. It is after this manner he examines our
idea of *substance* and *essence;* and it were to be wished that
this rigorous method were more practiced in all philosophical
debates.

It is evident that all reasonings concerning *matter of fact*
are founded on the relation of cause and effect, and that we
can never infer the existence of one object from another unless they be connected together, either mediately or immediately. In order, therefore, to understand these reasonings we
must be perfectly acquainted with the idea of a cause; and in
order to that, must look about us to find something that is the
cause of another.

Here is a billiard ball lying on the table, and another ball
moving toward it with rapidity. They strike; and the ball
which was formerly at rest now acquires a motion. This is as
perfect an instance of the relation of cause and effect as any
which we know either by sensation or reflection. Let us therefore examine it. It is evident that the two balls touched one

another before the motion was communicated, and that there was no interval betwixt the shock and the motion. *Contiguity* in time and place is therefore a requisite circumstance to the operation of all causes. It is evident, likewise, that the motion which was the cause is prior to the motion which was the effect. *Priority* in time is, therefore, another requisite circumstance in every cause. But this is not all. Let us try any other balls of the same kind in a like situation, and we shall always find that the impulse of the one produces motion in the other. Here, therefore, is a *third* circumstance, viz., that of a *constant conjunction* betwixt the cause and effect. Every object like the cause produces always some object like the effect. Beyond these three circumstances of contiguity, priority, and constant conjunction I can discover nothing in this cause. The first ball is in motion, touches the second, immediately the second is in motion—and when I try the experiment with the same or like balls, in the same or like circumstances, I find that upon the motion and touch of the one ball motion always follows in the other. In whatever shape I turn this matter, and however I examine it, I can find nothing further.

This is the case when both the cause and effect are present to the senses. Let us now see upon what our inference is founded when we conclude from the one that the other has existed or will exist. Suppose I see a ball moving in a straight line toward another—I immediately conclude that they will shock, and that the second will be in motion. This is the inference from cause to effect, and of this nature are all our reasonings in the conduct of life; on this is founded all our belief in history, and from hence is derived all philosophy excepting only geometry and arithmetic. If we can explain the inference from the shock of the two balls we shall be able to account for this operation of the mind in all instances.

Were a man such as Adam created in the full vigor of understanding, without experience, he would never be able to infer motion in the second ball from the motion and impulse of the first. It is not anything that reason sees in the cause which makes us *infer* the effect. Such an inference, were it possible, would amount to a demonstration, as being founded merely on the comparison of ideas. But no inference from cause to effect amounts to a demonstration. Of which there is this evident proof. The mind can always *conceive* any effect to follow from any cause, and indeed any event to follow upon another; whatever we *conceive* is possible, at least in a metaphysical sense; but wherever a demonstration takes place the contrary is impossible and implies a contradiction. There is no demonstration, therefore, for any conjunction of cause and effect. And this is a principle which is generally allowed by philosophers.

It would have been necessary, therefore, for Adam (if he was not inspired) to have had *experience* of the effect which followed upon the impulse of these two balls. He must have seen in several instances that when the one ball struck upon the other, the second always acquired motion. If he had seen a sufficient number of instances of this kind, whenever he saw the one ball moving toward the other, he would always conclude without hesitation that the second would acquire motion. His understanding would anticipate his sight and form a conclusion suitable to his past experience.

It follows, then, that all reasonings concerning cause and effect are founded on experience, and that all reasonings from experience are founded on the supposition that the course of nature will continue uniformly the same. We conclude that like causes, in like circumstances, will always produce like effects. It may now be worth while to consider what determines us to form a conclusion of such infinite consequence.

It is evident that Adam, with all his science, would never have been able to *demonstrate* that the course of nature must continue uniformly the same, and that the future must be conformable to the past. What is possible can never be demonstrated to be false; and it is possible the course of nature may change, since we can conceive such a change. Nay, I will go further and assert that he could not so much as prove by any *probable* arguments that the future must be conformable to the past. All probable arguments are built on the supposition that there is this conformity betwixt the future and the past, and therefore [he] can never prove it. This conformity is a *matter of fact*, and if it must be proved will admit of no proof but from experience. But our experience in the past can be a proof of nothing for the future but upon a supposition that there is a resemblance betwixt them. This, therefore, is a point which can admit of no proof at all, and which we take for granted without any proof.

We are determined by *custom* alone to suppose the future conformable to the past. When I see a billiard ball moving toward another, my mind is immediately carried by habit to the usual effect, and anticipates my sight by conceiving the second ball in motion. There is nothing in these objects—abstractly considered, and independent of experience—which leads me to form any such conclusion: and even after I have had experience of many repeated effects of this kind, there is no argument which determines me to suppose that the effect will be conformable to past experience. The powers by which bodies operate are entirely unknown. We perceive only their sensible qualities—and what *reason* have we to think that the same powers will always be conjoined with the same sensible qualities?

It is not, therefore, reason which is the guide of life, but custom. That alone determines the mind in all instances to suppose the future conformable to the past. However easy this step may seem, reason would never, to all eternity, be able to make it.

This is a very curious discovery, but leads us to others that are still more curious. *When I see a billiard ball moving toward another, my mind is immediately carried by habit to the usual effect, and anticipates my sight by conceiving the second ball in motion.* But is this all? Do I nothing but *conceive* the motion of the second ball? No, surely. I also *believe* that it will move. What then is this "belief"? And how does it differ from the simple conception of anything? Here is a new question unthought of by philosophers.

When a demonstration convinces me of any proposition, it

not only makes me conceive the proposition, but also makes me sensible that it is impossible to conceive anything contrary. What is demonstratively false implies a contradiction, and what implies a contradiction cannot be conceived. But with regard to any matter of fact, however strong the proof may be from experience, I can always conceive the contrary though I cannot always believe it. The belief, therefore, makes some difference betwixt the conception to which we assent and that to which we do not assent.

To account for this there are only two hypotheses. It may be said that belief joins some new idea to those which we may conceive without assenting to them. But this hypothesis is false. For, *first,* no such idea can be produced. When we simply conceive an object, we conceive it in all its parts. We conceive it as it might exist, though we do not believe it to exist. Our belief of it would discover no new qualities. We may paint out the entire object in imagination without believing it. We may set it, in a manner, before our eyes, with every circumstance of time and place. It is the very object conceived as it might exist; and when we believe it, we can do no more.

Secondly, the mind has a faculty of joining all ideas together which involve not a contradiction, and therefore, if belief consisted in some idea which we add to the simple conception, it would be in a man's power, by adding this idea to it, to believe anything which he can conceive.

Since, therefore, belief implies a conception and yet is something more, and since it adds no new idea to the conception, it follows that it is a different *manner* of conceiving an object—*something* that is distinguishable to the feeling and depends not upon our will, as all our ideas do. My mind runs by habit from the visible object of one ball moving toward another to the usual effect of motion in the second ball. It not only conceives that motion but *feels* something different in the conception of it from a mere reverie of the imagination. The presence of this visible object, and the constant conjunction of that particular effect, render the idea different to the *feeling* from those loose ideas which come into the mind without any introduction. This conclusion seems a little surprising, but we are led into it by a chain of propositions which admit of no doubt. To ease the reader's memory I shall briefly resume them: No matter of fact can be proved but from its cause or effect. Nothing can be known to be the cause of another but by experience. We can give no reason for extending to the future our experience in the past, but are entirely determined by custom when we conceive an effect to follow from its usual cause. But we also believe an effect to follow, as well as conceive it. This belief joins no new idea to the conception. It only varies the manner of conceiving and makes a difference to the feeling or sentiment. Belief, therefore, in all matters of fact arises only from custom and is an idea conceived in a peculiar *manner*.

Our author proceeds to explain the manner or feeling which renders belief different from a loose conception. He seems sensible that it is impossible by words to describe this feeling which everyone must be conscious of in his own breast. He calls it sometimes a *stronger* conception, sometimes a more *lively*, a more *vivid*, a *firmer*, or a more *intense* conception. And indeed, whatever name we may give to this feeling which constitutes belief, our author thinks it evident that it has a more forcible effect on the mind than fiction and mere conception. This he proves by its influence on the passions and on the imagination, which are only moved by truth or what is taken for such. Poetry with all its art can never cause a passion like one in real life. It fails in the original conception of its objects which never *feel* in the same manner as those which command our belief and opinion.

Our author, presuming that he had sufficiently proved that the ideas we assent to are different to the feeling from the other ideas, and that this feeling is more firm and lively than our common conception, endeavors in the next place to explain the cause of this lively feeling by an analogy with other acts of the mind. His reasoning seems to be curious, but could scarce be rendered intelligible, or at least probable, to the reader without a long detail which would exceed the compass I have prescribed to myself.

I have likewise omitted many arguments which he adduces to prove that belief consists merely in a peculiar feeling or sentiment. I shall only mention one: our past experience is not always uniform. Sometimes one effect follows from a cause, sometimes another, in which case we always believe that that will exist which is most common. I see a billiard ball moving toward another. I cannot distinguish whether it moves upon its axis or was struck so as to skim along the table. In the first case I know it will not stop after the shock. In the second it may stop. The first is most common, and therefore I lay my account with that effect. But I also conceive the other effect, and conceive it as possible and as connected with the cause. Were not the one conception different in the feeling or sentiment from the other there would be no difference betwixt them.

We have confined ourselves in this whole reasoning to the relation of cause and effect, as discovered in the motions and operations of matter. But the same reasoning extends to the operations of the mind. Whether we consider the influence of the will in moving our body or in governing our thought, it may safely be affirmed that we could never foretell the effect merely from the consideration of the cause, without experience. And even after we have experience of these effects, it is custom alone, not reason, which determines us to make it the standard of our future judgments. When the cause is presented, the mind, from habit, immediately passes to the conception and belief of the usual effect. This belief is something different from the conception. It does not, however, join any new idea to it. It only makes it be felt differently, and renders it stronger and more lively.

Having dispatched this material point concerning the nature of the inference from cause and effect, our author returns upon his footsteps and examines anew the idea of that relation. In the considering of motion communicated from one ball to another we could find nothing but contiguity, priority in the cause, and constant conjunction. But, besides these circumstances, it is commonly supposed that there is a necessary connection betwixt the cause and effect, and that the cause possesses something which we call a "power," or "force," or "energy." The question is, what idea is annexed to these terms? If all our ideas or thoughts be derived from our impressions, this power must either discover itself to our senses or to our internal feeling. But so little does any *power* discover itself to the senses in the operations of matter that the Cartesians have made no scruple to assert that matter is utterly deprived of energy, and that all its operations are performed merely by the energy of the Supreme Being. But the question still recurs, *What idea have we of energy or power even in the Supreme Being?* All our idea of a deity (according to those who deny innate ideas) is nothing but a composition of those ideas which we acquire from reflecting on the operations of our own minds. Now our own minds afford us no more notion of energy than matter does. When we consider our will or volition *a priori,* abstracting from experience, we should never be able to infer any effect from it. And when we take the assistance of experience it only shows us objects contiguous, successive, and constantly conjoined. Upon the whole, then, either we have no idea at all of force and energy, and these words are altogether insignificant, or they can mean nothing but that determination of the thought, acquired by habit, to pass from the cause to its usual effect. But whoever would thoroughly understand this must consult the author himself. It is sufficient if I can make the learned world apprehend that there is some difficulty in the case, and that whoever solves the difficulty must say something very new and extraordinary —as new as the difficulty itself.

By all that has been said the reader will easily perceive that the philosophy contained in this book is very skeptical and tends to give us a notion of the imperfections and narrow limits of human understanding. Almost all reasoning is there reduced to experience, and the belief which attends experience is explained to be nothing but a peculiar sentiment or lively conception produced by habit. Nor is this all; when we believe anything of *external* existence or suppose an object to exist a moment after it is no longer perceived, this belief is nothing but a sentiment of the same kind. Our author insists upon several other skeptical topics; and upon the whole concludes that we assent to our faculties and employ our reason only because we cannot help it. Philosophy would render us entirely Pyrrhonian, were not nature too strong for it.

I shall conclude the logics of this author with an account of two opinions which seem to be peculiar to himself, as indeed are most of his opinions. He asserts that the soul, as far as we can conceive it, is nothing but a system or train of different perceptions—those of heat and cold, love and anger, thoughts and sensations—all united together but without any perfect simplicity or identity. Descartes maintained that thought was the essence of the mind—not this thought or that thought, but thought in general. This seems to be absolutely unintelligible, since everything that exists is particular; and therefore it must be our several particular perceptions that compose the mind. I say *compose* the mind, not *belong* to it. The mind is not a substance in which the perceptions inhere. That notion is as unintelligible as the Cartesian, that thought or perception in general is the essence of the mind. We have no idea of substance of any kind since we have no idea but what is derived from some impression, and we have no impression of any substance either material or spiritual. We know nothing but particular qualities and perceptions. As our idea of any body, a peach, for instance, is only that of a particular taste, color, figure, size, consistency, etc., so our idea of any mind is only that of particular perceptions without the notion of anything we call substance, either simple or compound.

The second principle which I proposed to take notice of is with regard to geometry. Having denied the infinite divisibility of extension, our author finds himself obliged to refute those mathematical arguments which have been adduced for it—and these, indeed, are the only ones of any weight. This he does by denying geometry to be a science exact enough to admit of conclusions so subtile as those which regard infinite divisibility. His arguments may be thus explained: All geometry is founded on the notions of equality and inequality, and therefore, according as we have or have not an exact standard of that relation, the science itself will or will not admit of great exactness. Now there is an exact standard of equality, if we suppose that quantity is composed of indivisible points. Two lines are equal when the numbers of the points that compose them are equal, and when there is a point in one corresponding to a point in the other. But though this standard be exact, it is useless, since we can never compute the number of points in any line. It is, besides, founded on the supposition of finite divisibility, and therefore can never afford any conclusion against it. If we reject this standard of equality we have none that has any pretensions to exactness. I find two that are commonly made use of. Two lines above a yard, for instance, are said to be equal when they contain any inferior quantity, as an inch, an equal number of times. But this runs in a circle. For the quantity we call an inch in the one is supposed to be *equal* to what we call an inch in the other: and the question still is, by what standard we proceed when we judge them to be equal or, in other words, what we mean when we say they are equal. If we take still inferior quantities, we go on *in infinitum*. This, therefore, is no standard of equality. The greatest part of philosophers, when asked what they mean by "equality," say that the word admits of no definition, and that it is sufficient to place before us two equal bodies, such as two diameters of a circle, to make us understand that term. Now this is taking the *general appearance* of the objects for the standard of that proportion, and renders our imagination and senses the ultimate judges of it. But such a standard admits of no exactness, and can never afford any conclusion contrary to the imagination and senses. Whether this question be just or not must be left to the learned world to judge. It were certainly to be wished that some expedient were fallen upon to reconcile philosophy and common sense, which with regard to the question of infinite divisibility have waged most cruel wars with each other.

We must now proceed to give some account of the second volume of this work, which treats of the *Passions*. It is of more easy comprehension than the first, but contains opinions that are altogether as new and extraordinary. The author begins with *pride* and *humility*. He observes that the objects which excite these passions are very numerous and seemingly very different from each other. Pride or self-esteem may arise from the qualities of the mind—wit, good sense, learning, courage, integrity; from those of the body—beauty, strength, agility, good mein, address in dancing, riding, fencing; from external advantages—country, family, children, relations, riches, houses, gardens, horses, dogs, clothes. He afterward proceeds to find out that common circumstance in which all these objects agree, and which causes them to operate on the passions. His theory likewise extends to love and hatred and other affections. As these questions, though curious, could not be rendered intelligible without a long discourse, we shall here omit them.

It may perhaps be more acceptable to the reader to be informed of what our author says concerning *free will*. He has laid the foundation of his doctrine in what he said concerning cause and effect, as above explained.—

It is universally acknowledged that the operations of external bodies are necessary, and that in the communication of their motion, in their attraction and mutual cohesion, there are not the least traces of indifference or liberty. . . . Whatever, therefore, is in this respect on the same footing with matter must be acknowledged to be necessary. That we may know whether this be the case with the actions of the mind, we may examine matter and consider on what the idea of a necessity in its operations are founded, and why we conclude one body or action to be the infallible cause of another.

It has been observed already that in no single instance

the ultimate connection of any object is discoverable either by our senses or reason, and that we can never penetrate so far into the essence and construction of bodies as to perceive the principle on which their mutual influence is founded. It is their constant union alone with which we are acquainted; and it is from the constant union the necessity arises, when the mind is determined to pass from one object to its usual attendant and infer the existence of one from that of the other. Here, then, are two particulars which we are to regard as essential to *necessity,* viz., the constant *union* and the *inference* of the mind, and wherever we discover these we must acknowledge a necessity.

Now nothing is more evident than the constant union of particular actions with particular motives. If all actions be not constantly united with their proper motives, this uncertainty is no more than what may be observed every day in the actions of matter, where by reason of the mixture and uncertainty of causes the effect is often variable and uncertain. Thirty grains of opium will kill any man that is not accustomed to it, though thirty grains of rhubarb will not always purge him. In like manner the fear of death will always make a man go twenty paces out of his road, though it will not always make him do a bad action.

And as there is often a constant conjunction of the actions of the will with their motives, so the inference from the one to the other is often as certain as any reasoning concerning bodies; and there is always an inference proportioned to the constancy of the conjunction. On this is founded our belief in witnesses, our credit in history, and indeed all kinds of moral evidence, and almost the whole conduct of life.

Our author pretends that this reasoning puts the whole controversy in a new light by giving a new definition of necessity. And, indeed, the most zealous advocates for free will must allow this union and inference with regard to human actions. They will only deny that this makes the whole of necessity. But then they must show that we have an idea of something else in the actions of matter, which according to the foregoing reasoning is impossible.

Through this whole book there are great pretensions to new discoveries in philosophy; but if anything can entitle the author to so glorious a name as that of an "inventor," it is the use he makes of the principle of the association of ideas, which enters into most of his philosophy. Our imagination has a great authority over our ideas, and there are no ideas that are different from each other which it cannot separate and join and compose into all the varieties of fiction. But notwithstanding the empire of the imagination, there is a secret tie or union among particular ideas which causes the mind to conjoin them more frequently together and makes the one, upon its appearance, introduce the other. Hence arises what we call the *apropos* of discourse; hence the connection of writing; and hence that thread or chain of thought which a man naturally supports even in the loosest *reverie*. These principles of association are reduced to three, viz., "resemblance"—a picture naturally makes us think of the man it was drawn for; "contiguity"—when St. Dennis is mentioned, the idea of Paris naturally occurs; "causation"—when we think of the son we are apt to carry our attention to the father. It will be easy to conceive of what vast consequence these principles must be in the science of human nature if we consider that so far as regards the mind these are the only links that bind the parts of the universe together or connect us with any person or object exterior to ourselves. For as it is by means of thought only that anything operates upon our passions, and as these are the only ties of our thoughts, they are really *to us* the cement of the universe, and all the operations of the mind must, in a great measure, depend on them.

FINIS

The Library of Liberal Arts

Below is a representative selection from The Library of Liberal Arts. This partial listing—taken from the more than 200 scholarly editions of the world's finest literature and philosophy—indicates the scope, nature, and concept of this distinguished series.

AQUINAS, ST. T., The Principles of Nature, On Being and Essence, On Free Choice, *and* On the Virtues in General

ARISTOTLE, Nicomachean Ethics
   On Poetry and Music
   On Poetry and Style

BAYLE, P., Historical and Critical Dictionary (Selections)

BERGSON, H., Duration and Simultaneity
   Introduction to Metaphysics

BERKELEY, G., Principles, Dialogues, *and* Philosophical Correspondence
   Principles of Human Knowledge
   Three Dialogues
   Works on Vision

BOILEAU, N., Selected Criticism

BOLINGBROKE, H., The Idea of a Patriot King

BONAVENTURA, ST., The Mind's Road to God

BURKE, E., Reflections on the Revolution in France

BURKE, K., Permanence and Change

CALVIN, J., On God and Political Duty
   On the Christian Faith

CROCE, B., Guide to Aesthetics

CICERO, On the Commonwealth

DESCARTES, R., Discourse on Method
   Discourse on Method *and* Meditations
   Discourse on Method, Optics, Geometry, *and* Meteorology
   Meditations
   Philosophical Essays
   Rules for the Direction of the Mind

DIDEROT, D., Encyclopedia (Selections)
   Rameau's Nephew and Other Works

DOSTOEVSKI, F., The Grand Inquisitor

DRYDEN, J., An Essay of Dramatic Poesy and Other Essays

EPICTETUS, The Enchiridion

GOETHE, J., Faust I and II (verse)
   Faust I (prose)
   Faust II (prose)

HEGEL, G., Reason in History

HESIOD, Theogony